Studies in Evangelicalism

Edited by Donald W. Dayton, Northern Baptist Theological Seminary, and Kenneth E. Rowe, Drew University Theological School

PROPHETIC PENTECOSTALISM IN CHILE

A Case Study on Religion and Development Policy

Frans H. Kamsteeg

Studies in Evangelicalism, No. 15

The Scarecrow Press, Inc.
Lanham, Maryland & London
1998

SCARECROW PRESS, INC.

Published in the United States of America
by Scarecrow Press, Inc.
4720 Boston Way
Lanham, Maryland 20706

4 Pleydell Gardens, Folkestone
Kent CT20 2DN, England

British Library Cataloguing in Publication Information Available

Library of Congress Cataloging-in-Publication Data

Kamsteeg, Frans.
    Prophetic Pentecostalism in Chile : a case study on religion and
development policy / Frans H. Kamsteeg.
        p.   cm. — (Studies in envangelicalism ; no. 15)
    Includes bibliographical references and index.
    ISBN 0-8108-3440-5 (cloth : alk. paper)
    1. Pentecostal churches—Chile—La Victoria.   2. La Victoria
(Chile)—Church history.   3. Chile—Church history—Case studies.
I. Title.   II. Series.
    BX8762.Z7L395   1998
    289.9′4′0983315—DC21   97-43226
                                                                        CIP

∞ ™ The paper used in this publication meets the minimum requirements
of American National Standard for Information Sciences—Permanence of
Paper for Printed Library Materials, ANSI Z39.48-1984. Manufactured in
the United States of America.

Contents

Preface

Works are not finished . . . they are abandoned.
—Valéry, quoted in Geertz 1993 (1983): 6

I have been studying Latin American Pentecostalism for about nine years. My interest in born-again Protestantism dates from personal experience in the 1970s, but my research started in Peru in 1986. There I learned to be patient during Pentecostal services, and I became increasingly affected by the infectious enthusiasm believers often display, although their missionary drive toward me was not always pleasant. I continued my research doing anthropological fieldwork in Chile during the post-Pinochet years 1991 and 1992. The present book is based entirely upon these Chilean experiences, and it is also the provisional end of a research period.

Two of the major actors in this book have also taken a considerable part in the design of the research project. The Dutch development agency ICCO has always shown a major interest in the study of the Pentecostal world. I want to thank all staff involved for their cooperation, which was unhindered by the fact that ICCO's donor role was to be included as a major topic in the final book. Similarly, I want to express my gratitude to the SEPADE staff in Chile. They collaborated with my project that included a detailed study of the policies and practices of the nongovernmental organization they ran. Here I want to single out Samuel Palma and Juan Sepúlveda, who were strongly supportive during the research and highly critical of the results. Because I know that their view of the events described in this book differs from mine, I want to stress that I take full responsibility for the presentation of events. I also realize that this work is only one of many case studies. Moreover, the story I tell in this book did not end when I finished my text. I hope that, despite this unavoidable shortcoming, reading the book will provide expanded insight into the puzzling phenomenon of Latin American Pentecostalism.

Special thanks go to all those Chileans who made my stay in their country such a pleasant experience. Of the numerous Pentecostal churches I visited in Santiago, I want to mention especially the La Victoria congregation and its pastor, Erasmo Farfán. The people I met there are not just the materials for the present book; my stay with them also constituted one of the most meaningful periods of my life. I finally want to express my gratitude to the editors of this series for their positive reception of this case study.

1

Introduction

Formerly, we used to do street preaching, but at a given moment we realized that it was pure competition. Thus, we decided to stop doing it and instead visit the houses one by one. Yet soon our enthusiasm cooled down and that was it—Patricio, April 28, 1992

Our MIP church has developed in other evangelization aspects, such as social service and educational programs. Nevertheless, some of our congregations continue with the street preaching method, though with hardly tangible results—Pastor Erasmo Farfán, March 3, 1992

We had more important things to do in the street than preaching. Besides, street preaching was perhaps meaningful thirty years ago, but now it has become a mere ritual, to which nobody is still listening. It leads to a shallow kind of church—Pedro, March 12, 1992

Street preaching? That is really a waste of time. In the days of the protests, we were all on the streets, doing whatever we felt necessary, like raising barricades—Maria, July 21, 1992[1]

The above quotations hardly reflect the public image of Pentecostalism. They refer to the uselessness of street preaching, which is the most common proselytizing technique Pentecostals use. The youngsters mention their participation in violent street protests against General Pinochet's former military regime in Chile, instead of street preaching. The pastor admits that in his church conversion zeal has given way to carefully designed community service.

All four speakers identify themselves as Pentecostals. They belong to the Misión Iglesia Pentecostal (MIP, Pentecostal Mission Church) congregation in La Victoria, a working-class neighborhood

1

in Chile's capital, Santiago, which occupies a central place in this book. It is true that most La Victoria church members did not take part in the street fighting that is touched upon by one of the four speakers. In fact, they had strong reservations about these street protests, as did the rest of the members of the MIP. Yet, this MIP was not like the average Pentecostal church; social awareness and even active commitment were not anathema there. This colors the general cliché of Pentecostals as fanatical spiritualists who are not of this world. The genesis and vicissitudes of this nonstereotypical Pentecostalism are the general themes of the present study.

Moreover, the book is a study on religion and development (policy). Religion provides many people with what they perceive of as being the clearest directions for meaningful behavior. For this reason, religion provides a way to detect people's feelings about development and a suitable means of assessing the impact of development work (Quarles van Ufford and Schoffeleers 1988, 1). This is particularly so on the Latin American continent, where Catholicism in its various forms, and nowadays also Protestantism, is part and parcel of the people's daily life. In Latin America, religion is often the principal source for measuring events, including those related to development policies. In this study, I do not discuss the concept of development specifically, instead I focus on the impact of a particular set of Dutch development policies toward Chile, which were channeled through the Pentecostal Mission Church. The fact that these Pentecostals are engaged in development is exceptional; the vast majority of Pentecostal churches distance themselves completely from anything associated with overt development activities. A classic study on Chilean Pentecostalism emphatically maintains that turning Pentecostal in effect means going on a social strike (Lalive d'Epinay 1969). In this respect too, the small MIP church I studied was different, because it even made social development one of its major concerns. Therefore, this case is most interesting for comparative purposes.

Before we turn to the specific whereabouts of what I call prophetic Pentecostalism, we need to have a general idea of what Pentecostalism is. I will discuss the main theological and sociological traits of Pentecostalism in the next section. Pentecostalism is clearly a flexible religion, with many different faces. One of these faces is the prophetic variant discussed in this book, which I will reflect on later in this chapter. I will end the chapter by providing the reader with an overview of the book.

Pentecostalism: A Multifaceted Phenomenon

The Chilean Pentecostal world is a heterogeneous one. In addition to a few hundred officially registered churches, multiple groups, chapels, and house churches, which have no legal base, exist. To the naive observer, then, this mass of Pentecostal churches is an impenetrable world of schism, division, and competition. This competitiveness is even more puzzling to the outsider, who most of the time is unable to see much difference between the ways these various groups think and behave. Pentecostals themselves contribute to this confusion by addressing each other with the familiar "brother" (*hermano*) and "sister" (*hermana*), thus suggesting a sort of (ritual) kinship. Yet, among all those who call themselves Pentecostal, profound controversies exist regarding organizational matters and the contents of their religious convictions. The simple notion "Pentecostal" hides a huge variety of meanings and practices. Therefore, a discussion of the concept "Pentecostalism" cannot be omitted from a book that attempts to shed light on one of its specific tendencies.

In a recent article, Walter Hollenweger, author of a ten-volume handbook on the Pentecostal movement, pointed to the manifold roots of Pentecostalism: the black oral tradition in the United States, basic values of Catholicism, U.S. postmillennialist evangelicalism, the critical tradition of, for example, North American and South African blacks, Latin American Pentecostals and faith healers, and finally a sort of basic ecumenism (1992, 12–33). In such an all-compassing vision, the emphasis is clearly on the multifaced appearances of Pentecostalism. An attempt to discover Pentecostalism's core characteristics is therefore a complicated endeavor. A wide range of theological and ecclesiastical characteristics could be identified, producing an inevitably incomplete list. Moreover, it is useful to take note of the fact that there are huge differences among believers in acceptance and even awareness of the various elements I am about to discuss. I think, nevertheless, that it is necessary, if only for the sake of clarity (whom are we really talking about?), to discuss some elements of Pentecostalism that are accepted by most adherents.

The experience of conversion is commonly taken as the start of a new, Pentecostal, life. It is often formulated as the result of a personal encounter with Jesus, followed by a radical change in lifestyle. The promise of eternal life becomes a certainty at the moment the gospel is really accepted. This element of salvation is the first of the specific fourfold pattern of Pentecostalism that Donald Dayton advances in his *Theological Roots of Pentecostalism* (1987, 21).[2] Personal salvation of the believer is a recurrent theme in the conversion stories—testimonies[3]—, and it is directly related to the second element of Dayton's typology, the "baptism of the Holy Spirit." The so-called gifts of the Holy Spirit resulting from this baptism are listed by the apostle Paul in the New Testament, book of I Corinthians 12, but the narrative force of Acts 2, in which the Holy Spirit is said to have descended on Jesus' disciples, is probably stronger, because it is a story of *people being endowed with power*, an example of religious empowerment. These gifts, or charismata—tongues, prophecies, miracles, healing, wisdom, faith, and so on (see I Corinthians 12:4–10)—have received a great deal of attention in Pentecostal studies. In particular, speaking in tongues[4] is often used as the litmus test of Pentecostalism. Prophecies, uttered by pastors or common church members, often announce generally formulated threats to the well-being of the church, the community, or even the country or world, although very precise messages on concrete church matters are also transmitted. Ideally—or ideologically— these gifts are available to all believers, which is supposed to contribute to the establishment of a community of equals.[5]

The third essential characteristic of Pentecostalism according to Dayton is faith healing. The apostle James's appeal to the church elders to say a prayer of faith for the sick (5:14, 15) has inspired the widespread practice of faith healing throughout all Pentecostal churches and groups. Mass conversion rallies often use faith healing to attract people, and many conversion stories are based on healing experiences (for a detailed account, see Kamsteeg 1993). The last of Dayton's fourfold pattern is eschatology, in biblical terms, the Second Coming—or Return—of Christ, who will announce—or complete, depending on the reading of the Bible—the millennium. Few Pentecostals doubt this article of faith, yet much controversy exists about whether Jesus is to return before or after the millennium. This may seem an issue of only theological relevance but is in fact not without importance for daily Pentecostal practice; it has important consequences for people's behavior. Pentecostals who believe Christ will return before the millennium—the premillennialists—see no need to work for a better world, for this can only lead to frustration: Jesus is the one who will set in motion the construction of a better world. For postmillennialists it is the other way around: They are bound to collaborate in the establishment of "heaven on earth," and they see Jesus' life on earth as the starting point in this endeavor. The choice of one position or the other has important consequences for Pentecostals' social behavior, although it would go much too far to claim that Pentecostals behave on the basis of their corresponding theological convictions.

This controversy gains relevance in daily Pentecostal practice through the concept "world," which is a highly significant and concrete notion for Chilean Pentecostals, as for most of their coreligionists in other parts of the world. It refers to everything that is contrary to God's will, in which a true believer is therefore never to become involved. It is a term that is also used in a reductionist way to separate church matters from life outside the church boundaries. When these two sorts of interpretations are combined, the result is a strong fixation on church life and a categorical rejection of all other aspects of human life, such as politics, trade unions, sports clubs, and so on (paid work is the exception to the rule and is considered unavoidable). Thus, the notion "world" has a double meaning: It causes a defensive reaction, probably due to negative experiences (of discrimination and contempt) in daily life, but the proclaimed "retreat from the world" into a separate religious community is simultaneously balanced by the challenge to conquer the world.

Viewed from a theological perspective, in Pentecostalism "the emphasis lies on feeling, as opposed to the intellectual which is about understanding: a graphic, oral and narrative theology" (Alvarez 1992, 93). It could probably best be said that Pentecostalism is an experiential religion, in which doctrine only becomes important when it touches upon people's concrete life issues. Pentecostal "knowledge" is the knowledge of the heart, the theology of the heart, which is the fruit of experience, anecdotes, and testimony, combined with moral teachings passed on through preaching (Alvarez 1992, 93). This means that Pentecostals often do not have ready the theological distinctions made by Dayton, at least not in a well-articulated form. At best, they have a remote notion of the theological framework in which their experience may be embedded. Yet it is this emphasis on experience that makes room for variation and all kinds of personal meaning-making, despite the tendency toward uniformity stemming from the oral tradition and repetition. It is also this prevalence of experienced tradition over doctrine that makes it so hard to give a fitting sociological definition of Pentecostalism and to draw up a corresponding list of ingredients.

I have described Pentecostalism as an experiential religion that combines salvation, spiritualism, healing, and eschatology. Its various appearances always contain a specific blend of these four theological elements. From a sociological perspective, attempts have often been made to come to grips with Pentecostalism by way of a church-sect typology. According to most sociologists of religion, revivalist movements or sects[6] pass through a process of growth, which involves both institutionalization and a tendency to accept compromises with respect to the extreme positions adopted during the early revival period (Wilson 1978; Yinger 1970, 206–261). In Yinger's typology, the sect has a small number of adherents often following a charismatic leader who breaks with his/her church; its organization is simple, and its readiness to relate to the outside world is limited. Normally, the trend is that sects grow, become more complex and more willing to accept other values and practices than their own. Consequently, the charismatic leadership goes through a process of routinization (in the Weberian sense). Sects become established sects, denominations, and finally end as churches, which may cause a reaction: Another group separates, and the whole process starts again (Yinger 1970, 260).

The interesting thing is that the various appearances of Pentecostalism, the result of its great practical flexibility springing from the manifold spiritual gifts available, could be ranged under all four classifications in Yinger's scheme. Enormous Pentecostal churches may maintain the charisma of the small sect (like the Chilean Iglesia Metodista Pentecostal, IMP—Pentecostal Methodist Church), whereas a tiny group like the MIP has agreed upon an open and constructive attitude toward society. Although the Yinger model thus does not offer great possibilities for classifying Pentecostalism sociologically, it does provide useful categories for the study of Pentecostalism. As a model, Yinger's is too rigid and deterministic, but its suggestion of dynamism is attractive. If Pentecostalism makes sociological models waver owing to its flexibility, it is an excellent case for studying religious change. There are various areas where the usual but paradoxical combination of flexibility and rigidity, responsible for the many faces of the phenomenon (Droogers 1991), can be shown, for example, in evangelism, lay participation, and gender relations. These three issues receive emphatic attention in Pentecostalism, but in different ways, as I will briefly show.

Traditionally, Pentecostals have a strong proselytizing attitude. Well-tried techniques vary from door-to-door evangelization to street preaching, mass rallies, and campaigns, but these practices nowadays seem to have seen their day. TV evangelism, on the one hand, and social service, on the other, are also viewed as useful means for convincing people. Traditionally, Chilean Pentecostals operated like street-corner workers, who, during the weekly evangelistic parade through the neighborhood, read their open-air sermons and invited newly converted people to join them at the Sunday afternoon service in the church.[7] Pentecostal churches like the MIP, however, are aloof to such classical evangelization techniques. Although the same impulse to convince is present, conversion, a central theme in the classical approach, is mostly left out of the discourse. Proclamation and liberation have replaced this notion, and these are thought to be best achieved by practical services to both the church and the surrounding community.

Lay participation in the church is another area where huge differences in Pentecostal practice can be found. In Pentecostalism, individuals are personally responsible to God for their deeds, but strong emphasis is also placed on the fact that all men (and that includes women) are equal before God. This article of faith about the priesthood of all believers figures prominently in Pentecostal churches. In principle, all positions are accessible to all church members. In practice, this does not normally lead to democratic church rule; some are apparently more equal than others. Not a few Pentecostal bishops are notorious dictators within their own churches. Again, the MIP belongs to the countertendency and is probably one of the most democratically organized Pentecostal churches, although as we will see later, common practice leaves something to be desired.

Because of the emphasis on the aforementioned priesthood of all believers, women have often gained a much more active role in Pentecostal church life than for example is the case in traditional Roman Catholicism. They testify, pray, and preach, although preaching is often confined to the separate women's service. Pentecostalism is therefore even considered a "woman's religion" (Lawless 1988, 6). Pentecostal discourse on women and the family may have a significant emancipatory effect, because family morals are drastically changed in favor of women (and their children). Men are supposed to become responsible parents as much as women. Thus, family relations generally improve with a transition to Pentecostalism. This is one of a number of its important problem-solving properties. Despite this general trend, huge differences among Pentecostal churches exist with respect to this issue. Practice often does not follow discourse. In some churches, women's positions hardly change at all after a transition to Pentecostalism; they have no say in church life, except in their own women's group. Here too, the MIP has attempted to move further than the acknowledgment of a theoretical equivalence between men and women.

What I want to argue by referring to this variety in Pentecostal ideas and practices, is that there is no single form of Pentecostal church, no "real" Pentecostalism. The fact that so many Pentecostal churches are denouncing each other's supposedly Pentecostal character should be enough to make researchers suspicious of universal pretensions, although these mutual denouncements often have a background of power struggles (see Kamsteeg 1991). Subjective religious experience is such an encompassing element that it makes general definitions almost necessarily fall apart into Pentecostalisms with different measures of mutual correspondence. It is this dynamic aspect that I want to call attention to in this study of a Pentecostal church that in various aspects distinguishes itself from most other Pentecostal churches.

Chile's history of Pentecostalism is a long one. This means that a substantial number of the church members belong to the second, third, or even fourth generation of Pentecostals. They have gone through a process of socialization in Pentecostal churches from childhood, which the first converts did not. The important shifts of meaning that follow from being "born within the gospel," as compared with a radical conversion from, for example, Catholicism, is a theme that in Pentecostal studies has scarcely been tackled thus far. Normally, the emphasis on the Pentecostal conversion experience serves to explain why Pentecostals are not inclined to ecumenism. Yet Chilean Pentecostalism has a vast sector of adherents belonging to this religion by way of tradition. No exact figures are available on this issue, but many believers have grown up in Pentecostalism. This is true for most of my MIP informants. Among them, religious ideas that are less centered around individual spiritual experiences and more open to society and ecumenism could obtain a foothold. The elements advanced by Dayton have undergone a substantial change of meaning, which makes the MIP church an intriguing example of religious change.

Before starting the study proper, I think that dwelling for a while on a few central concepts is useful. First, I will briefly pay attention to the "confusion of tongues" over the terms *Protestantism*, *Evangelicalism*, and *Fundamentalism*, which all to some extent suffer from the same fate of generalization, exclusive definition, and random conceptual use as Pentecostalism. Then I will discuss the concept "prophetic," because it takes such a dominant place in my argument.

Nomenclature

The non-Catholic Christian world is like a big house with many rooms, each of them labeled with a tag that suggests its inhabitants' distinctive characteristics in comparison with those of the neighbors. Yet alongside the differences there are elements shared among groups of coinhabitants. Although they all call themselves Christians, various other labels are used. In the Latin American building, as anywhere else, we find Protestants, Evangelicals, Charismatics, Pentecostals, and Fundamentalists, to name the principal denominations. Each of these labels is invested with a set of more specific distinguishing features. In this study on MIP Pentecostalism, I select two terms in particular: *Protestant* and *Evangelical*.

The usual term in Spanish-speaking Latin America to indicate non-Catholic Christians is *evangélico*, but this is not a synonym for evangelical. Evangelicals, particularly in North America, clearly distinguish themselves from traditional Protestants by stressing personal salvation (through Jesus Christ) and the "born-again" experience. The latter does not figure prominently in mainstream Protestant churches, who trace their history back to the roots in the European Reformation. Usually, Evangelicals also reject most gifts (of the Spirit) that Pentecostals believe pertain to the condition of being born again. The Latin American concept of *evangélico*, however, is used to differentiate the non-Catholic Christians from Roman Catholics. The term, then, includes Protestants, Pentecostals, and Evangelicals alike. Its only clarifying aspect is the emphasis on the gospel (*belief* as the outstanding characteristic) against the supposedly "manipulatory" Catholicism (salvation can be *earned*).[8] *Evangélico* can therefore be considered an emic[9] term par excellence and, moreover, one that expresses militancy. In Latin America it is the umbrella term, like Protestantism in Europe and, although to a lesser extent, in North America. In academic social science vocabulary, at least in the Anglo-Saxon world, Protestantism is the common phrase to denote the non-Catholic Christians. Most analyses of the Latin American situation similarly apply the term (see Martin 1990; Stoll 1990). I therefore prefer to use the etic *Protestant* to refer to the sum of all non-Catholic Christians, whereas I use *Pentecostal* (etic and emic) when the reference concerns the specific subgroup. The term *Fundamentalist* has negative connotations and is, moreover, closely associated with North American church life. One of its principal elements, the infallibility and inerrancy of the Bible, can also be found among Protestants who refuse to be called Fundamentalists. I will therefore use the term very cautiously.[10]

Although I reject the possibility of using the emic word *evangélico*, I propose to accept another emic term, *prophetic*, because I think that a combination of its emic meaning and a particular sociological usage[11] leads to an appropriate description of the phenomenon that is the focus of this study. The sociological use of the concept "prophecy" relies heavily on Weber's classical analysis (1963; 1978). According to Long, however, Weber's interpreters have misunderstood his analysis, for they considered prophecies primarily as political phenomena, thus underestimating the religious meaning prophecy has as a resource for cultural and societal change (1986, 4). As Long sees it—and I think this is a useful point of view—it is best to look at prophets as actors who understand their task to be "to proclaim or demonstrate a divine message in the hope of submitting all of human life to a transcendent system of meaning" (1988, 4). Were prophets to succeed in getting their vision accepted, that would mean a religious change with a profound cultural impact. Whereas Weber understood prophecy mainly as a religious phenomenon of personal charisma, Long proposes to widen the concept and view it as a force challenging to the social order and an expression of, or resource for, building social solidarity (ibid., 4, 5). A similar suggestion is made by Bourdieu, who proposes to focus more on the unusualness of the situation in which prophets operate than on the extraordinary qualities of the latter (1971, 331–332). This may of course have repercussions in the political realm, but not necessarily. Long proposes a model of the characteristics of prophetic religion, according to organizational/institutional level, social resources, social location, and religious orientation (1988, 12). The specific blend of these characteristics accounts for the model's political and cultural drive and impact. Only the type of prophecy described as this-worldly and ethical (the adjectives are again taken from Weber) is likely to strive for social change and political action (ibid., 14).

In such a view, prophecy as a phenomenon gains prominence over the individual prophet, because its charismatic character is likely to become less pronounced in its orientation, religious as well as social and political. Defined in this way, it is very possible to discern prophetic religion, that is, a prophetic Pentecostalism in Chile. The Pentecostal tendency constituting the subject of this book can be considered an example of such a religious type. Its protagonists have themselves militantly adopted the label "prophetic." The connotations of social change and political action Long gives to the sociological (etic) meaning of the word come close to its Chilean (emic) usage, because sociopolitical action is exactly what Chilean prophetic Pentecostals stand for. I think that this particular case blurs the sharp contrast that is often made between emic and etic.

I wish to dedicate just a few more words to the term *prophecy*. Weber's treatment of prophecies puts a strong emphasis on the charismatic authority of people, that is, the specific and exceptional qualities with which leaders are considered to be endowed. In Pentecostalism, such qualities are believed to be bestowed on people through the gifts of the Holy Spirit, as we have seen in the previous section. Prophecy is just one of these gifts. For Pentecostals, then, prophecy is really an emic category. Most of the time, this gift is expressed during church services in which people feel they receive a divine message to be transmitted to the surrounding church community. These messages may concern a variety of topics, but talk of moral uplifting and general statements about the pernicious character of the world predominate. In the case of the MIP I am about to treat, an interesting mix of emic and etic prophecy arises. The prophetic response by MIP people to the situation created by the Chilean military coup in 1973, and to its favorable reception by a group of Pentecostal/Protestant leaders, was definitely not the kind of enthusiastic action Weber assigned to charismatic forms of organization. It was based on the discovery and acceptance of liberation as a core element in the theological reading of the Bible, particularly the Old Testament prophets and the book of Exodus. The hermeneutic Bible reading pertaining to this theology focused on the themes of liberation, oppression, and poverty (see de Wit 1991, 25ff). It was by inspiration from this theology that MIP leaders developed a discourse on liberation and people's participation in it, which in opposition to traditional Pentecostalism was called prophetic.[12] This emic use of the term *prophetic* comes close to the (etic) type of the emissary prophet discerned by Weber to indicate the God-sent proclaimer of messages confronting the established powers (see McGuire 1992, 227). Thus, the interesting phenomenon arises that a traditional Pentecostal device, the gift of prophecy,[13] is transformed into a this-worldly strategy, in which social and political claims are communicated to believers and nonbelievers alike.[14] It is molded into a weapon for the Pentecostal weak in the struggle for social justice.

Prophetic Pentecostalism: An Outline of the Argument

Having given a short introduction to Pentecostalism and its prophetic variant, I will now briefly sketch the book's main argument. In the first place, I study the vicissitudes of prophetic Pentecostalism in Chile, which implies a focus on religious change. My second aim is to assess a particular form of development policy, which explicitly tries to cause religious change, to alter Pentecostal ideas and practices. To tackle both closely related subjects, my strategy is the following. I start—in Chapter 2—with a broad overview of studies covering Latin American Pentecostalism, which serves as the background for a detailed presentation of the story of the Pentecostal MIP church and its development bureau, SEPADE, whom I consider to be the principal agents of prophetic Pentecostalism in Chile. Their genesis and development were complex processes, which I try to grasp by applying a practice approach, in which the roles of the structural conditions of context and of the meaning-making actors involved both receive due attention. This allows the researcher to alternate between a helicopter's view and a jeweler's-eye view of the world (Marcus and Fischer 1986). The position of the researcher in the process of science production and among (MIP) Pentecostals is discussed extensively following Bourdieu's infectious plea for scientific reflexivity. After explaining my choice for this research subject, and the conditions that affected this choice (research partners), I describe in graphic detail how I obtained the materials that served to help me reconstruct this part of Chilean church history.

In Chapter 3, I describe the genesis and development of Chilean Pentecostalism from what others have written about it. Consequently, it is more an account of Pentecostalism than one of acting Pentecostals; structure is paramount to agency. The growth of Pentecostalism is presented in close connection with Chile's social, political, and economic history. The participatory democracy that was strongly promoted in the working-class neighborhoods from 1964 onward provided a challenge for Pentecostals, to which a particular branch responded by developing an ever more open stance toward society. That brings me to the Misión Iglesia Pentecostal, which I present as an active defender of the latter position. I describe the history and present situation of this church from written documents but also from the lips of its principal actors. The turbulent period under the Pinochet regime provides an especially clear image of the complexity of the MIP's effort to cause shifts in Pentecostal signification.

In Chapter 4, I present a detailed analysis of Pentecostal politics in the La Victoria neighborhood of Santiago. Along with Chapter 5, this chapter constitutes the nucleus of the book, and the part in which most fieldwork materials have been processed. I have chosen the case of the MIP congregation in La Victoria because it is considered to have made the greatest effort toward Pentecostal renewal in this working-class neighborhood, which was itself a politically militant and well-organized place. I sketch the collision between a traditional Pentecostal worldview and the prophetic alternative over such issues as church practice, doctrine, and social behavior toward the population of the neighborhood where this church operates. I analyze the different choices made by different categories of church members: men, women, the youth, and those of its pastor. The MIP church is contrasted in a brief excursion with the neighboring congregation of the Iglesia Metodista Pentecostal (IMP). In the case study in Chapter 4, the efforts to establish a prophetic Pentecostalism and its results are caught in the act, as it were, which I maintain is the best—because it is dynamic—way of coming to grips with processes of religious change.

In Chapter 5, I turn from the church level to the nongovernmental organization SEPADE. This shift of attention is accounted for by stressing the organization's leading role in the propagation of the prophetic discourse. This role of religious renewal was also attributed to SEPADE by the outside ecumenical world (the World Council of Churches, [WCC]) and international development agencies (e.g., the Dutch ICCO). These multiple interdependencies—and the power relations involved—are dealt with by reconstructing SEPADE's history, institutional development, and impact on church positions and individual believers' meaning-making. The outcome of this Pentecostal politics as executed by SEPADE is critically evaluated, to contribute to the ongoing discussion among development agencies over the effect and impact of their policies. The functioning of the Pentecostal agency of development, SEPADE, is also used to stress the particularly complicated relation between culture (religion) and development.

In the concluding chapter, Chapter 6, the main findings, which have meaning in several distinct fields of knowledge, are presented. These fields are the study of religious change, Pentecostal studies, and development studies. I defend the view that the focus on people as meaning-makers enables me to show their active role in processes that are often portrayed as following a structurally determined course. I repeat the plea for a more balanced practice approach, which has important consequences for the nature of the scientific knowledge produced, as well as for accepted views on the topics I treat in this book. In an evaluation of the impact and strength of prophetic Pentecostalism in Chile, I also pay attention to the feasibility or plausibility structure (Berger 1967) of prophetic Pentecostalism, which leads me to a discussion of the prospects and perspectives of this type of Pentecostalism.

Notes

1. The names of all living people who appear in this book have been replaced by pseudonyms, except for those who explicitly consented to the use of their real names.

2. A Spanish version of Dayton's book (1991) is rapidly filling what has been experienced as a theological vacuum in the Latin American Pentecostal world. Chilean Pentecostal (and Protestant) theologians of the ecumenical tendency have warmly welcomed the book. It is thought to fulfill a useful emancipatory function for theologically interested Pentecostals, who are regularly confronted with disparaging remarks by Protestant coreligionists about the lack of theological foundations of the Pentecostal faith.

3. An often-quoted text in these testimonies is John 3:16, which reports how God offered his son Jesus in order to offer eternal life to all believers.

4. There is an extensive literature on this particular subject. Generally, a distinction is made between xenolalia and glossolalia. The first is the supposed capacity of believers who have been baptized with the Holy Ghost to speak in foreign languages they might have never heard of before. Glossolalia, the more common form of speaking in tongues, concerns the production of sounds that are believed to constitute a language that only God can understand.

5. A lot could be said about the use—and abuse—of these gifts. Since supposedly all believers are equal before God, all may receive these gifts. But it is not unusual for pastors or experienced—older—church members to serve as judges as to whether gifts are real, that is "from God." The speaking in tongues and prophesying are especially susceptible to abuse. I heard many examples of such abuses in my interviews.

6. In daily practice the word sect has a very pejorative connotation. Whereas believers avoid the term, their enemies—mainly the Catholic church—use it as a weapon in the religious struggle.

7. For this widespread practice, Chilean Pentecostals are nicknamed *evangelistas* (evangelists/preachers) or *canutos* (after a famous street preacher operating in the 1920s and 1930s called Canut de Bon).

8. Although Latin American *evangélicos* show no sympathetic feelings toward Protestant tradition and its representatives on the continent, it could be maintained that they constitute a real Protestant group, since one of their principal tenets is their unconditional rejection of the dominance of Roman Catholicism. It could be said that a major feature of Latin American *evangélicos* is their protest against exactly that Catholic hegemony.

9. The meaning of the epistemological terms (or constructs) emic and etic are usually taken for granted. We use them to refer to the way we understand phenomena. Yet in the past there have been lively discussions about the use and abuse of the terms ever since they were coined by Pike in 1954 and introduced in anthropology by Harris (1968). Without entering into the ongoing discussion (see Headland, Pike, and Harris 1990), I find the definitions given by Lett sufficiently clear. "Emic constructs are accounts, descriptions, and analyses expressed in terms of the conceptual schemes and categories regarded as meaningful and appropriate by the native members of the culture whose beliefs and behaviours are being studied. . . . Etic constructs are [accounts . . . appropriate] by the community of scientific observers" (1990, 130–131).

10. A discussion of the nature and spread of Fundamentalism would take us far away from the daily practice of Chilean Pentecostalism I intend to describe (for an extensive treatment of the concept, see Lechner 1991; Maldonado 1993; Schäfer 1994).

11. I realize that I set aside a vast literature on prophetic religion and movements, the discussion of which would hardly contribute to a better

understanding of the theme I deal with in this book. I describe the particular etic reading of the term *prophetic* by Long, to show that the emic reading
it receives from its users (although this is also contested, incidentally) has
explanatory value outside the realm of the actors who are directly involved.

12. These leaders applied the adjective *prophetic* to the Protestantism
they advocated, although they would certainly refuse to call themselves
prophets. Their rejection of the role of personal charisma in combination
with their plea for the renewal of an Old Testament tradition is illuminating
and at the same time adds a new dimension to the Weberian use of *prophecy*.

13. Persons who receive a prophecy, e.g., during a church service, are not
viewed as prophets, but as prophesiers. In emic terms, prophets are the
biblical persons indicated as such, while prophesiers can be chosen by God
to transmit a particular divine message. Prophesying is a temporary gift
bestowed on men or women, whereas the prophet is considered to be a
historical figure.

14. This comes close to the blend of rationality and enthusiasm in the
leadership roles of South African Zionism, as described by Kiernan (1976).
For him, the roles of prophet and preacher are separated because they imply
different, although complementary, kinds of action (see also Schoffeleers
1985 and 1988).

2

Studying Latin American Pentecostalism

Only a few years ago an overview of studies on Latin American Protestantism[1] would have started with a complaint on the limited appeal the subject had apparently had to social scientists. Lalive d'Epinay's writings on Chile (1969; 1975) and Willems's on Brazil and Chile (1967) have continued to be the texts of reference for all the work published since then. These subsequent publications lacked the scope and depth of treatment of their forerunners, and, moreover, they were predominantly concerned with statistics (how many Pentecostals are there really?) or pastoral strategies to fight the "sects," among which Pentecostals were commonly reckoned. Most of these books and articles were published either in Spanish or Portuguese (only occasionally in English), and they were hardly consulted by social scientists. Comprehensive, comparative studies on the topic were even more scarce.[2] Recently, however, the phenomenon has been tackled by two authors who, without explicitly pretending to replace what had been done so far, might put the founding fathers of Latin American Pentecostal studies in the shade for a while. The new Lalive d'Epinay and Willems are called Stoll (1990) and Martin (1990), and their books have received broad attention worldwide.[3] Both authors have a continental scope and focus on the tremendous growth—although varying widely by country— Pentecostalism has gone through during recent decades. In 1991, another book—in Spanish—on Latin American Pentecostalism appeared (Boudewijnse et al. 1991; an English translation was published in 1998), which stirred substantially less discussion. That book, which I took part in editing, combines an analysis of explanatory models of the Latin American Pentecostal phenomenon with various anthropological case studies. In the present study I continue the approach chosen for our 1991 book, which aims to bring together a structuralist and an actor-oriented viewpoint on Latin American Pentecostalism.

Interpretations of Latin American Pentecostalism

It is possible to discern great diversity in the theoretical approaches to the Pentecostal phenomenon. This may be because distinct visions of science lead to different conclusions, but researcher's ideological, including religious, biases have also strongly influenced the various perceptions of the problem (see the introduction to Chapter 3). Most explanations, for example, tend to concentrate on what religion—in this case Pentecostalism—*does* (occasionally to people, but more often to society at large) and avoid treating what it *means* to people. Very often Pentecostals themselves barely appear in the descriptions of the development of Pentecostalism. To some extent, this also holds true for both classics, Lalive d'Epinay and Willems, although less so in the case of the former than the latter. The new protagonists, Stoll and Martin, also seem to support a sociology of religion that leaves out the flesh and blood actors. One of the reasons for this may be that these studies principally focus on the macro (international) sociopolitical implications of Pentecostalism (the role and function of Pentecostalism). Of course such a general approach, which emphasizes certain structural characteristics of Pentecostalism, cannot simply be dismissed. In fact, I will give due attention to a macroperspective, but in contrast to the authors referred to, I prefer to look at the phenomenon from a different angle. In my study of the interplay of societal conditions and individual (Pentecostal) meaning-giving, I take up much of the discussions raised by practice theorists. That means, among other things, that I bring in the Pentecostal believers (actors) and their construction of meaning.

Before clarifying the theoretical perspective elected for this study, I first want to recapitulate the main line of argument of the authors mentioned earlier. This serves two purposes: First, it provides a general, though very concise perspective on Latin American Pentecostalism, and second, it gives me the opportunity to sketch the theoretical positions and their flaws, in order to subsequently delineate an approach that pretends to overcome some of these weaknesses.

The Classics

In the preface of his *Followers of the New Faith*, Emilio Willems declares himself a plain structural-functionalist (1967, v). In his book Willems investigates the function of Protestantism (Pentecostalism) in the sociocultural changes that took place in Chile and Brazil during the 1940s and 1950s. To Willems the sociocultural changes in both countries consisted of rapid industrialization and urbanization, which were the counterparts of the traditional rural-agrarian society that was in decline. Protestant individualistic ethic—here he refers to the same set of values and virtues Max Weber pointed out—apparently proved to be the right mix to accompany the changes described (ibid., 249–251). What Willems calls folk Catholicism no longer served the legitimating purpose it had in traditional rural society. From this perspective, turning Protestant was both an indication of, and a contribution to, the modernization process.

At least two unclear points can be discerned in this perspective. In his linear, evolutionist way of reasoning, Willems associates the rise of Protestantism with the emergence of a middle class in a period of rapid socioeconomic change. It is not clear whether this new middle class was in search of a new religion that fit its position, or whether embracing Protestantism and its ethics proved useful in ascending to such a middle-class position. Furthermore, there is confusion about the concepts Protestant and Pentecostal. Willems seems to use them interchangeably, and it remains unclear how Pentecostals, who usually belong to the lower social strata, fit in to his Protestant middle-class thesis. Willems seems to suggest that Pentecostals are gradually ascending to middle-class status. Although this is the aspiration of most, if not all, lower-class families, including Pentecostals, the realization of this goal is a different matter. Embracing the Pentecostal faith may for some people be inspired by hopes of socioeconomic advancement (Pentecostalism conceived as a vehicle of personal betterment); however, too strong an emphasis on this issue does not recognize the motives converts themselves provide. Because general and massive socioeconomic transformation does not occur as the result of the transition to Pentecostalism, but people continue to convert, Willems's modernization thesis needs to be relativized. Using an actor-oriented perspective might help to modify Willems's approach.

Similar to Willems, Lalive d'Epinay (1969; 1975) concentrates on Pentecostalism's possible contribution or hindrance to modernization. For Lalive d'Epinay the explosion of Chile's Pentecostalism between 1920 and 1960 is closely related to economic crisis, particularly in agriculture. For Lalive d'Epinay the rigidity of the *latifundio-minifundio* (large estate versus smallholders) complex from 1920 onward expelled vast numbers of agricultural workers who took refuge in the big cities, especially Santiago. They were not attracted by promising labor perspectives; their migration was more out of despair than hope, which Lalive d'Epinay takes as the principal reason for the state of anomie[4] these migrants brought to the cities. People lost their traditional system of meaning, which was closely integrated with the hacienda system and the authority of the *hacendado* (estate holder). According to Lalive d'Epinay, Pentecostalism offered the right solution to the discrepancy these people felt. The Pentecostal pastor is presented as the successor of the old *hacendado*. In that sense Pentecostal churches constituted a refuge for the disoriented migrant masses: The church saved them from societal alienation. In addition it also gave them a safeguard against the moral dangers of the world (*mundo*). To Lalive d'Epinay, then, conversion to Pentecostalism shows more features of continuity than of rupture with socioreligious tradition.

After these brief remarks on Lalive d'Epinay's characterization of the genesis (anomie) and structure (pastor-patron parallel) of Chilean Pentecostalism, I now come to the third principal theme in his work: Pentecostalism's function in Chilean society (1969, 106–158; 1975, 8, 9, 169ff, 273ff). From Pentecostalism's roots in anomie-fostering social conditions and in its authority structure that closely resembles the old hacienda relations, Lalive d'Epinay deduces a strong tendency to confirm the dominating social status quo. Pentecostalism's social ethics can be characterized by its rejection of participation in any of this world's action. According to him, Pentecostals often resort to biblical-theological grounds when justifying their positions, but their point of view is also built upon concrete (bad) social experiences (1969, 123, 278). Lalive d'Epinay even uses the words *voluntary segregation* and *apartheid* to designate the classic Pentecostal response to society and social behavior (1975, 122). The "world" (society "reigned by sin") is to Pentecostals synonymous with misery and corruption, to which the only correct answer is withdrawal, which means social (sociopolitical) passivity and disengagement (1969, 128). Yet to Lalive d'Epinay, in a special sense Pentecostals do have a social project: This sinful world will change when its inhabitants become converted believers. However, for Lalive d'Epinay this is largely a symbolic protest, lacking the means and ideas to effectively change the material conditions of the poor.

This relatively stable Pentecostal worldview (in the sense of vision of society) as Lalive d'Epinay describes it, is seriously questioned by Tennekes (1978; 1985). To him, Pentecostalism offers a series of practical solutions to people's daily problems, and there is more concern with the daily human practice of life than Lalive d'Epinay, in his premillennialist characterization of Pentecostalism, admits (1985, 114). The same holds true for the political conservatism of which Lalive d'Epinay accuses Pentecostals. This becomes particularly clear in a polemical debate over the implications of the support by Pentecostal leaders for Pinochet after the coup of 1973. Lalive d'Epinay maintains that this act of approval confirms Pentecostalism's propensity for isolating itself and reinforcing its anti-Catholic, politically conservative attitude. To him, the Pentecostals' first experience of being treated seriously by a secular government was widely felt and positively valued (1978, 84). Tennekes instead maintains that the Pentecostal masses have not exchanged their position of passive conformity and rejection of any worldly involvement for an active support of the military regime (1978, 78). To Tennekes, the political collaboration of a group of Pentecostal leaders was hardly representative of the wider Chilean Pentecostal population, whereas Lalive d'Epinay, on the contrary, suggests that not a few Pentecostals must have felt flattered by the preferential treatment by the Pinochet regime, which, moreover, constituted a good opportunity to challenge the hegemony of the Catholic Church (1978, 84).

In his 1985 book, Tennekes suggests that at another level some changes in Pentecostalism's social ethics and practice, although still very modest, are becoming visible (1985, 116–121). He quotes Lalive d'Epinay's suggestion that the growth rhythm of Pentecostalism in Chile started to decrease, when under the Christian-Democrat President Eduardo Frei, participation by lower-class people, particularly in neighborhood organizations, began to increase. Democratization of society, then, is considered to parallel stagnation of the growth of Pentecostalism, with its authoritarian church structure. For Tennekes, this tendency only became really manifest after 1970, when Allende started his "democratic route to socialism" (1985, 115).[5] The process of the democratization of Chilean society that started under Frei did have a parallel in Pentecostalism. In a chapter on ecumenism Lalive d'Epinay discusses the rather charity-like relief policies displayed by the Chilean Protestant interchurch organization ACE (*Ayuda Cristiana Evangélica*, Protestant Aid). He is quite negative about this organization, which he also thinks had only a very weak base in Chile's Protestant, predominantly Pentecostal, churches (1969, 179–186). Tennekes, though, points to ideological changes perceivable in some, albeit small, Pentecostal churches (notably the *Iglesia Wesleyana*). According to Tennekes, this-worldliness and other-worldliness (soul and body, spirit and matter, heaven and earth) in these churches ceased to be separate entities. The actual world became a place for action other than the type of proselytism that traditionally characterized the outward behavior of Pentecostal churches (1985, 116). For Tennekes, this new tendency was frustrated by the military coup in 1973, and he showed clear pessimism about the possibility for the development of a type of Pentecostalism open to sociopolitical involvement and action under authoritarian rule (ibid., 121). I continue to examine this issue, which was only tentatively touched upon by Tennekes.[6] In a sense the present book is also a response to Lalive d'Epinay's probing and rather negative remarks on the significance of Pentecostalism's early contacts with the international ecumenical movement (e.g., through the WCC; 1969, 185–186). Chile's turbulent (church) history since the period when both authors did their research demands a reassessment of the issue. That is exactly what this book aims to do; it provides a detailed examination, from an anthropological perspective, of what has happened within the prophetic brand of Chilean Pentecostalism during the last twenty-five years.

Recent Perspectives

In the preceding section I discussed the views of Willems and Lalive d'Epinay on Latin American Pentecostalism. Although their analysis was based on research in only three countries (Chile, Brazil, and to a lesser extent, Argentina), the outcomes have nevertheless often been generalized for the whole continent (see also Turner 1970, 213). In 1990, two books appeared (Martin 1990; Stoll 1990a) that explicitly focus on the entire Latin American continent. In his *Tongues of Fire: The Explosion of Protestantism in Latin America*, David Martin argues that the diffusion of, mainly North American, values has contributed to the kind of social differentiation in Latin America that creates the necessary social space in which voluntary religious groups (as he claims Protestant churches to be) can fruitfully develop. This process is said to have an essentially indigenous character now, but Martin—who speaks in fact quite positively of the whole phenomenon—takes much pain to show that the genesis of the movement shows a remarkable parallel to the way English, and subsequently North American, Methodism took off. The rise of Protestantism in Latin America is closely linked to the sociopolitical modernization, principally promoted by liberalism, which started to gain momentum after independence in many countries in the early nineteenth century. Methodism fit particularly well into this "program" because of its establishment of lay people as the principal actors on the religious scene and its promotion of schools, libraries, and mutual aid among its members. Pentecostalism, then, can be viewed as an instrument of the popularization of Methodist values and practices (especially with respect to leadership positions), which are made accessible to the Latin American masses (1990, 29–30, 42–46; see also Hollenweger 1982). According to Martin, in this process, Pentecostalism shows a capacity of adaptation to local culture and religious traditions (spiritual healing, oral tradition) far bigger than that of Methodism. In Pentecostalism, ordinary people leave the political, cultural, and religious status quo and create a free space where they run their own show, free of social and religious hierarchical mediations (Martin 1990, 280, 285). This "Pentecostal show" is characterized as "voluntary, lay, participatory and enthusiastic" (ibid., 274). The Roman Catholic Church most effectively represents hierarchical mediation—the opposite of lay participation—which is the reason why, according to Martin, Protestantism (Pentecostalism) had the greatest impact in those countries where "the church (i.e., the Catholic Church) has been drastically weakened and yet the culture has remained pervasively religious, as in Brazil, Chile and Guatemala" (ibid., 59).

Like Martin, David Stoll (1990a, 1990b) is preoccupied with the

recent spectacular Protestant expansion in Latin America. His interest is mainly in the—political—direction this movement is heading.
To Stoll, moral uplift constitutes the main attraction, especially of
Pentecostalism (1990a, 309, 310). He argues that conservatives,
pressing for personal conversion, are successfully appealing to the
apparently deeply felt moral crisis of Latin Americans, a feeling that
progressive Catholicism (liberation theology) tends to ignore or at-
tributes to repressive structural conditions. Stoll is pessimistic about
Pentecostalism's potential for social reformation.[7] He perceives
many benefits for personal survival that individuals, especially
women (he quotes Brusco 1986b) and lay people, may acquire by
changing their religion, but for the believers, collective struggle remains out of sight (Stoll 1990a, 315, 318–319). Protestant/Pentecos-
tal churches are seen as flexible survival vehicles in circumstances of
disrupting traditional social organizations (ibid., 331). Here Stoll's
conclusion resembles Martin's, although the former seems to regret
the massive attraction to Pentecostalism, which is received much
more positively by the latter.

The books by Martin and Stoll bear many valuable insights into
Latin American Pentecostalism. Yet what I think is missing in both
works is the interface between the structural effects of Pentecostalism and the level of those whom it concerns. Pentecostal growth
and its macro sociopolitical significance receive disproportionate attention. We hardly glimpse Pentecostal men and women struggling
and making meaning out of their life through their faith. After reading Stoll and Martin, the question remains where the concrete Pentecostal actors come in, a criticism I also made about Lalive
d'Epinay and Willems. A common feature in all these studies is the
focus on social and political structures and the (functional) role Pentecostalism as a phenomenon plays in them. The contents of Pentecostalism and its meaningful appropriation by people are hardly
touched upon. Yet there are other ways of interpretation, which do
pay attention to the religious subjects as meaning-makers. Obviously attention to the structural conditions under which Pentecostals live and practice their religion is important, but I want to
emphasize that structures can only be usefully studied if they are
treated *in relation to people*. To put it another way, to verify the
overviews obtained from the helicopter circling high above the land-
scape, the same helicopter should regularly touch down among its
inhabitants.

I therefore turn to Boudewijnse et al. (1991, especially the introduction and first chapter by Droogers) and Canales et al. (1991). In both works it is argued that we urgently need to return to the Pentecostal subject, without disconnecting it from the social context. The Pentecostal people consciously receive special attention in the book by Boudewijnse et al. Most of the contributions in this compilation of case studies are based on anthropological fieldwork, and subjective experience and paradox constitute the crucial concepts in the analysis. Pentecostalism is even called a paradoxical religion, although much of this paradox springs from the type of analysis chosen (and the person conducting the research) rather than from Pentecostalism itself (Droogers 1991, 36ff). Observers of Pentecostalism, whether they are scientists or not, generally suppose, or even require Pentecostalism and Pentecostals to be consistent, so that they can give straight answers to the problem of how to explain its growth or functioning.

Central to the findings of most chapters in the book, however, is the subjective experience of conversion. The mere centrality of this concept in Pentecostalism should make the analyst cautious about making general conclusions too hastily. Whenever attempts are made to answer the question of what Pentecostalism is, taking the fundamental religious experience of conversion as a starting point is essential. It is this experience that has to be taken into account when the wider implications, of what Pentecostalism does, are treated. This is the proposal made by Canales and others (1991, 16, 17). They see Pentecostalism as providing meaning to those who come to follow the movement (ibid., 35). Pentecostals name their conversion as the starting point for encountering new meaning(s) in their lives that apparently lack sense (for a similar approach see J. Sepúlveda 1992a, 85). It is at this level, during the search for the reasons why people have lost meaning,[8] that structural conditions come in. These latter conditions somehow determine the range of possible meanings and organize the search for them. Canales et al. name a few examples of these circumstances, such as the incapacity of the "popular subject" to live up to the dominating values and norms of the surrounding culture, which causes feelings of shame and frustration. In its most extreme form this may lead to what Lalive d'Epinay called anomie. Job insecurity, illness, individualism, and lack of class solidarity may also account for the absence of meaning that so many people belonging to the popular (lower) classes experience (ibid., 83).

This interplay between individuals looking for and appropriating meaning and the constraining (and enabling) structures given in any society is the principal topic of recent practice approaches. Their aim is to avoid structuralist, determinist analysis, without falling into the voluntarist trap. I will now dwell on this perspective, which I think is also a promising perspective for the study of the most recent phase in Chilean Pentecostal history.

A Practice Approach

Religious believers, be they Pentecostals or not, can be viewed as having relations at on least three levels simultaneously: with their God(s),[9] with their fellow believers, and with the society they live in (Droogers and Siebers 1991, 13–16). The separation between these three levels is of course artificial; in everyday life they are constantly mingling. Yet if we accept this differentiation of the religious field, we can also view these relations as expressions of the classic dilemma of structure and agency.[10] It seems sensible not to embark on this complicated matter without first giving a concrete example. I take it from my own research, and will come back to this case later (Chapter 4), where the argument will be considered more deeply. It concerns an event at the La Victoria congregation of the Misión Iglesia Pentecostal.

> On a Sunday morning in May (1992) the church members get together to celebrate their weekly Sunday class. In contrast to most Chilean Pentecostal Sunday classes, the MIP custom is to assemble in small groups to concentrate on a particular theme dealt with in a guide. This morning the topic is the annual ceremony of the Te Deum held during the week Chile's Independence is celebrated and consists of an intercession for the country's authorities and an evaluation of the past year. The Bible text related to the theme is from Mark 11:15–19, Jesus' cleaning of the temple. The discussion that follows is heated; in particular two young men attack the Te Deum ceremony, which they believe has served only to support the military regime, which neither God nor the Chilean people recognize as legitimate. They clearly understand the guide's reference as the Pentecostal Te Deum, constituted in 1975 in the presence of General Pinochet.[11] One of them even calls this a prostituted service for which a kind of temple cleaning would be very appropriate. Then an older brother asks why they, the youngsters, always have these severe criticisms? As he understands the Bible, "we ourselves are the temples, so the cleaning concerns us personally,

our hearts and minds, our relation to God. Instead of talking about politics, we would do better refreshing our personal relationship with God," he adds.

This concrete example from a Santiago neighborhood church shows us a clash of distinct religious—Pentecostal—perspectives. The actors whom it concerns explain Bible texts in different ways. They make their own meaning out of the same words they read in the same Bible. Is that because they are free to interpret that Bible how they like? Theoretically this may be so, but tradition has coined a specific line of interpretation as the right one. The older man in our example represents the classic Pentecostal viewpoint. The youngsters disagree with him and foster a deviant opinion. Yet for both parties it is true that although they seem to make their own meaning out of the events and texts, they do not do so in circumstances of their own choosing. The circumstances we are talking about here are, however, peculiar. Chile's democratic tradition had come to an abrupt end as a result of the military coup of September 1973, which had not left the Pentecostal churches untouched. Traditionally, Pentecostals, except a few, had tried to isolate themselves as much as possible from any direct social involvement; in fact this isolation was facilitated by the strong discrimination Pentecostals had to endure from the start, despite the separation of church and state since the 1925 constitution. After 1973, there was an official reaction by Pentecostals to the changed political situation. There were official statements of support for Pinochet and his coup by not a few churches, including the biggest, the Iglesia Metodista Pentecostal (Pentecostal Methodist Church, IMP). Yet during the years following the coup a counterreaction also became visible. This historical process is somehow reflected in the La Victoria example I have just given. We see in Chile's Pentecostal history, especially in the last two decades, a growing differentiation in the responses to the structural changes that took place in society. Individual believers increasingly felt pressed to make new and meaningful choices, while simultaneously they were heavily bound by social structures and religious tradition. Pentecostal actors also felt the power of their tradition, while at the same time they were challenged to amend the tradition in light of what was happening around them. In our example, the youth clearly took sides, while the older church leader seemed to avoid going into the wider sociopolitical dimensions of the historical process of which they were a part.

My example makes clear that this book pays close attention to the views and behavior of concrete Pentecostal actors. That does not mean, however, that a simple description will do. Actors' behavior has to be put into context. I will deal with this context first from a theoretical perspective, more exactly, practice theory. The principal concepts of this theoretical approach—structure, actor, process, and history—have only been tentatively, and implicitly touched upon. In the next section, I will further elaborate this framework, which is itself still very much in the process of construction, to analyze the development of Chilean Pentecostalism, particularly during the last twenty-five years. I do not pretend to give an overview of the complete field of practice theory—assuming such a field could be clearly defined. I will instead draw upon the works of a variety of authors, particularly on those of Sherry Ortner (1984; 1989a; 1989b) and Pierre Bourdieu (1977; 1990).

Structure, Culture, and Agency

Structure and agency, and particularly the relationship between them, have always been part of social scientists' agenda. Structural analysis tends to describe reality as a mechanistic model in which actors perform roles according to their formal positions in this "fabric." The structure of these abstract models is sometimes considered to be directly observable, although other analysts focus on hidden structures. Social class analysis is an obvious example of structural analyzing. Normally, in such analyses meaning is referred to in grand, theoretical terms (e.g., systems of meaning), while ordinary, everyday interpretations of experience are paid scarce attention (McGuire 1992, 27). Most of the time, the concepts of structure and agency have been treated as part of a series of analytical dichotomies, such as determinism-voluntarism, object-subject, and synchrony-diachrony. The resulting explanatory models were either "strong on institutional analysis" and "weak on action theory" or vice versa (Giddens 1981, 162ff). Put in other words, the discussion has for a long time been of an either-or character. Indeed, it makes quite a difference whether the emphasis is put on the mechanistic, determining role of class positions or on (individual) actors' decision making (Alexander 1990, 1, 2).[12] Until recently, most scientists felt obliged to choose one direction or the other of Giddens's theorem. Yet there is a growing awareness that both perspectives can be used fruitfully at the same time (Ortner 1984, 144ff).[13] We find an early application of such a synthesis-aimed perspective in Berger and Luckmann's classic work *The Social Construction of Reality*, where we read what almost sounds like an article of faith: "Society is a human product. Society is an objective reality. Man is a social product" (1991 [1966], 79).[14] This is in fact what we as human beings experience daily. During our lifetime we constantly waver between the sensation of freedom and feelings of constraint. Or in the words of Falk Moore and Myerhoff, "social life proceeds somewhere between the imaginary extremes of absolute order, and absolute chaotic conflict and anarchic improvisation" (1977, 3). The point for social scientists, then, is to find out where that 'somewhere' is. As Archer points out "social theorists are not just addressing crucial technical problems in the study of society, they are also confronting the most pressing social problem of the human condition" (1988, x). This implies that any theory that does not consider the fundamental issue of the interplay between structure and agency over time is thereby seriously diminishing its explanatory value. To apply these theoretical observations to concrete situations, and establish how, when, and under what circumstances actors can make a meaningful difference, is probably even more important than merely conceptualizing the problem of structure and agency itself (ibid., 76–77, 80).[15]

When we speak about Chilean Pentecostal men and women in the rest of this book, we realize that they are bound to a variety of structural conditions, yet they will still be considered meaning-makers, and more particularly religious meaning-makers (Crick 1976; Rostas and Droogers 1993; Hannerz 1992). We will portray their behavior within a particular historical setting, focusing on their religious roles. When we define religion as "a dialectical process of (re)production of religious—i.e., referring to a transcendental reality or supernatural—representations and practices" (Droogers and Siebers 1991, 2), we are immediately encountering the basic questions of practice theory. What part does the meaning-making actor play in this process? To what extent are actors producing, that is, consciously modifying, constructing, or inventing representations and constituting practices, and to what degree are they reproducing, repeating, and performing them? And if—as I think—believers are both producers and reproducers, is it still possible to separate them into different categories, or can only a gradual differentiation be made regarding the degree of (re)production? Another question concerns the relationship between religious beliefs and religious practices, and maybe even more urgently their relation to social practices. Religion may indeed constitute a relatively autonomous field of its own (Maduro 1982), yet the social conditions in which religion is embedded exert all kinds of influences on it (and vice versa). Nowadays, we have left the notion behind that religion and social structure are somehow congruent, and it has become less uncommon to look at inconsistency, paradox, contradiction, and so on (Falk Moore 1975, 217). Now that the nature of the relationship between the social and religious field, and the limits of autonomy of the latter have become diffuse, it is even more urgent to investigate them in concrete situations. It is therefore useful to provide some tools and concepts that may help to shed light on this complicated matter.

The subject of this book is a specific form of Pentecostal religion viewed from a practice perspective. What I explicitly do not want to do is merely list a series of actions by Pentecostals. Instead I aim to present them as actions that are only meaningful within their particular context. That is exactly what Sherry Ortner tries to do in her treatment of how and why Sherpa Buddhist monks founded their monasteries in the early twentieth century. Ortner's work leans heavily on Pierre Bourdieu, who is one of the leading practice theorists. I do not give an outline of both authors' views with supporting "evidence"; what I have done is borrow concepts and theoretical insights in an eclectic way. This choice stems from my wish not to build a closed and compact stock of theoretical assets that bears only a remote relationship with the rest of the book. I also think this would hardly be compatible with what practice theory intends to be. Besides, the absence of an outstanding representative of practice theory justifies such an approach. Practice thinking is scattered through the academic field and can better be considered an approach—a way of looking at things—than a well-established theory, as Ortner (1984) notices as well. Religious practices, like any human behavior, appear to a large extent to be predictable; that is, people will follow traditional ways of doing things. When we ask Pentecostals, for example, why they are behaving the way they do during their prayers, they will give answers like "because this is the way we Pentecostals do this" or "we always do it this way." When we want to give answers to the question of why people behave like they do, why they give this kind of answer, or even what is more important, why their behavior tends to be so tenacious and under what conditions change *does* occur, we need to resort to an approach advanced by the forementioned authors.

In her 1989 book Ortner maintains that "practice is action considered in relation to structure" (1989a, 12).[16] Analogously to Berger and Luckmann, Ortner characterizes the relation between the two as follows: "practice emerges from structure, it reproduces structure, and it has the capacity to transform structure" (ibid., 12). Since practice is what people do, it means that people's behavior is both structured and structuring. What then makes people's behavior often look like ordinary reproduction of common habits? And where can we locate the dynamism and flexibility that practice theory pretends to make visible?

In a 1989 article on ritual change among the Nepalese Sherpa, Ortner offers a clear practice analysis, which "examines the particular forms of human activity and human relationships prevalent in a society at a given moment, and attempts to distinguish the sources of cultural reproduction and cultural change" (1989b, 199). This characterization of practice makes clear that only in historical situations (the flow of events) can the interplay between structure and actor/agent be adequately treated. In her article, Ortner tries to grasp the mechanism by which Sherpa rituals have (not) changed. She uses the concepts "ideology" and "consciousness," together called "culture." Ideology, which is defined as the public symbolic order, or the order of official symbols and meanings, has a high degree of autonomy from the order of consciousness or taken-for-granted assumptions (ibid., 200). Both concepts (ideology and consciousness) are in themselves somewhat misleading; they have clearly different connotations. Because in Ortner's vision "consciousness" refers to structures of thought and feeling that operate largely unconsciously, I prefer to use Bourdieu's term *habitus* instead.[17]

Despite the confusing terminology she introduces, I think Ortner's division of the cultural domain into a public symbolic order (ideology in her terms) and habitus is useful. This separation may help, for example, to explain why changes in social practice do not automatically produce changes in the complete cultural domain. As Ortner argues, these cultural changes are in large part the result of specific cultural politics, "the struggle over the official symbolic

representations of reality that shall prevail in a given social order at
a given time" (ibid., 200). This cultural politics—which ultimately
aims to affect people's meaning-giving—takes place at a conscious
level and is dominated by a limited group of specialists. Its relation
to the habitus level, however, remains unclear in Ortner's article.
That also gives no clues for an understanding of the possibilities
and procedures of change in habitus. Nevertheless, I adopt Ortner's
analytical tools—which I will hereafter denote as habitus and cultural politics—in the analysis of the MIP/SEPADE case in the subsequent chapters. Before that, it is useful to relate both concepts to
the fundamental human capacity of meaning-giving.

Habitus and Meaning

The concept of habitus, coined by Pierre Bourdieu but wrongly
rejected by Ortner in favor of consciousness, is one of the key notions for the understanding of human behavior, of how individuals
behave in daily life where routinization and habitualization are so
common (Berger and Luckmann 1991 [1966], 70–72). In Bourdieu's
The Logic of Practice[18] (1990, 52–65), this concept is proposed to
mediate in and even overcome the structure-actor debate. Bourdieu's theoretical framework is composed of the trio, structures-
habitus-practices (the name of the central chapter in his book).
"Structures" refers to the *objective* conditions of action, "practices," to the interactional doings of concrete people. "Habitus" is
the key dialectical mechanism mediating between the two. It is constituted by

> systems of durable, transposable dispositions, structured structures
> predisposed to function as structuring structures, that is, as principles
> which generate and organize practices and representations that can be
> objectively adapted to their outcomes without presupposing a con-
> scious aiming at ends or an express mastery of the operations neces-
> sary in order to attain them. (Bourdieu 1990, 53; for a cognitive
> interpretation, see Layder 1981, 72, 73)[19]

Habitus, the incorporated social structure (Wacquant 1992, 17), has
no conductor and is performed in a practical sense manner; it offers
the limiting or allowing dispositions for a "feel for the game" (practical sense; Bourdieu 1990, 66). These dispositions (or propensities,
Bourdieu 1977, 214), categories, and schemes have a very large

influence on human behavior, although explicitly not in a deterministic way. They are like the stock of probable ways of conduct and even affect what we normally label as rational, consciously calculating behavior. Habitus gets (literally) embodied in people by means of socialization, the experiential learning processes that start during childhood (Bourdieu 1990, 66–79; Jenkins 1992, 74, 75).[20] It is there that habitus is turned into a set of permanent dispositions of *feeling* and *thinking*, although the exact procedures remain unclear to a considerable extent. It is exactly the hidden (while unconscious) workings of these permanently present dispositions that obfuscate questions about change, both in habitus and its ensuing practices, although Bourdieu himself claims that habitus is an open system, likely to incorporate new experiences and consequently open to change (Bourdieu 1992a, 87).[21]

Since habitus itself is difficult to locate (it is embodied somewhere in the mind of subjects or groups), it can only be deduced from a close observation of practices (of interaction).[22] This is one of the reasons practice theory is so concerned with the historical perspective (Ortner 1989a, 12). But even then it is still difficult to understand how habitus generates these practices (Jenkins 1992, 78–79; Layder 1981, 73). This hidden process is further complicated by the fact that habitus operates in an external social context, which puts conditions or constraints on its working. But if habitus produces practices, and is also limited in producing them effectively by external social constraints, is change still possible, both at the individual and the collective level (ibid., 79)? Habitus is said to be both durable and subject to change. It is on the one hand constantly reproducing structure, but on the other hand, subject to recreation and adaptation. Maybe habitus merely explains the fact that changes generally take so much time. In other words, habitus's main characteristic would be its slackening effect. That brings us back to the classic dilemma of production and reproduction, of people as subjects or as puppets in some sort of big game that they are not controlling themselves.[23]

If man is a meaning-maker, what kind of meaning does he or she make then? Certainly, meaning is always preconceived, mediated by habitus, and can therefore not just be associated with individual and unique personal experiences. Meaning is always personally appropriated, habitus serving as an important sieve: It produces a first sifting, deciding what is experienced as meaningful and what as insignificant. Signification outside the realm of shared meanings and "governed" by habitus and its connected practices always takes place within the (structural) context of the interrelated fields of politics, economics, religion, and so on. Yet it is the personal appropriation of meaning, or its reproduction in concrete practices, that allows for variation and even change in seemingly fixed significations. To what extent this is possible, and under what circumstances, remains one of the most intriguing questions to study, and one of the principal questions that should be constantly asked with regard to the habitus concept.

Anthony Cohen (1985) makes a strong argument for this way of looking at the meaning-making process. The shared use of symbols, rituals, and so on produces shared meanings to a certain extent, but leaves enough space to individuals—or subgroups—to generate their own meanings. Shared meaning creates the corporate community feeling or identity (relative to other groups); it differentiates one group identity from another. The uncontested possibilities of the individual interpretation of, for example, symbols satisfies meaning-making at the individual level and contributes to personal identity-building. The point is that both processes happen simultaneously, influence each other, and are put into a more structured outer context. So, in this process of meaning-making, people—collectively and individually—construct their identities, but they do so largely within the parameters habitus "prescribes." Both habitus and identity are concepts that are closely linked to a long-term historical or process approach. When I use them in this book to clarify a process that takes place within a limited period of time—the rise of prophetic Pentecostalism during the last thirty years—they are primarily meant as heuristic devices. Habitus, as a disposition generating "*meaningful* practices and *meaning-giving* perceptions" (Bourdieu 1986, 170; my italics), colored the reactions to changing circumstances that presented themselves during these years. The very "embodimentness" of habitus-constituted identities explains its continuity and the relative slowness of change of the ensuing practices.

The main concern in most theorizing about culture is to explain cultural change (see Archer 1988). The central questions of the practice approach advanced by Ortner ask when, under what conditions, and how this cultural change takes place. As we have seen, to Ortner these changes are the result of cultural politics. The dominant system of meanings, as well as the behavior rooted in habitus, is quite resistant to change. A similar argument is made by Tennekes, who—following Hanson (1975)—sees a "system of implicational meanings" as the heart of culture. When people are constructing meaning, they first do so by pulling from this stock of "ideas, representations, values, symbols and patterns of behavior" (Tennekes 1990, 34). Thereby, they contribute to the reproduction of culture as a system. Yet the answers that can be extracted from this cultural reserve, which is a model *of* reality serving as a pattern *for* behavior (Geertz 1973, 90ff), do not always suffice. This is particularly so if internal contradictions of the cultural system gain relevance under changing social circumstances (Tennekes 1990, 36, 43ff). Then, people (actors) may experience problems in confronting a meaningless reality, to which cultural ideas and concepts fail to provide sufficient meaning.

For Ortner (1989b), bringing about changes in the prevailing culture as a result of an experienced lack of meaning-providing is reserved to a body of specialists. Ortner's cultural change, then, is described as the result of (conscious) cultural politics, thus depriving large quantities of actors of the opportunity to contribute to this change and reducing them to mere reproducers of culture. The limiting function of Bourdieu's habitus may also be easily emphasized to neglect the actors' roles. Yet I think we cannot escape from trying to establish which (groups of) people have a larger say in the field of meaning-production, as long as it is understood that realizing these changes requires broader consent than the relatively small group of active policymakers represents. I would argue that cultural politics in Ortner's sense is particularly significant in times of manifest social and cultural disruption. Established meanings then become questioned and new meanings sought. In such turbulent contexts sociocultural interaction produces tangible outcomes in both the cultural and the social worlds (Archer 1988, xx–xxii, 304ff). These situations are probably most suited to demonstrating the tight relatedness between culture and social structure in sociocultural interaction. In such contexts power relations can be more easily demonstrated to be of importance in both culture and the social domain (ibid., 282ff; see also Asad 1983 and Tennekes 1990). Although culture (as a system) may have a strong conditioning character, it is never deterministic, precisely because the interplay between cultural and social practices prevents outcomes from being reproductions of previous situations. Changes within the religious field, in this case Chilean Pentecostalism during the Pinochet dictatorship, provide an excellent case in point.

This book is concerned with this specific religious field, which belongs to the cultural domain. What it is about, then, is religious practice, or, to be more precise, examples of Pentecostal practice, Pentecostal habitus, and Pentecostal politics. What I try to demonstrate is that the religious field, with its own margins of relative autonomy (compare Archer's cultural system, and Tennekes's "culture as system"), is susceptible to changes only to a degree that is strongly limited by habitus-dominated religious dispositions and practices. Reformulating this problem in actors' terms, I intend to clarify how (Pentecostal) believers manage to intentionally change religious beliefs and practices within the given habitus of that specific field and within a particular process of historical transformation. From Ortner I "borrowed"—with some amendments—the distinction between two aspects of human practice: the conscious meaning-making part of man and its habitus-shaped counterpart. Ortner argues that these are sides that all people possess, but she also maintains that there is a symbolic order subject to public debate, a domain of cultural politics where usually a small category of people struggle over hegemony. This theoretical model shows a close resemblance to Bourdieu's typification of the universe as divided into two spheres: that of the undiscussed (*doxa*) and that of discourse/opinion/argument (1977, 168ff). The latter can be subdivided into a dominating orthodoxy and a heterodoxy that questions both the taken-for-grantedness of doxa and the more explicit—and hence imperfect—variant of orthodoxy. Analogously with Ortner's (and Bourdieu's) analysis I propose to discriminate in the religious field between religious habitus and religious politics. Slightly adapting Ortner's definition, which I reproduced above, religious politics are the struggles over the official religious symbolic representations of reality that prevail in a given historical context (Ortner 1989b, 200).[24] This can well be comprehended as a fight over the prevalence of meanings. When, during the 1960s, Chilean sociopolitical conditions started to change, this inevitably provoked a reaction in the Pentecostal field. But initially this reaction was very tardy, because of the very tenacity of the Pentecostal habitus. Second, religious or Pentecostal politics as conducted by predominantly Pentecostal leaders, which was a struggle over religious identity as well as ove clearly diverging sociopolitical options, could not but have a relatively limited impact on the total habitus-dominated field (field and habitus are intrinsically related).

The working of the religious field in this layered construction retains people as active meaning-makers, as producers as well as reproducers, although habitus does clearly regulate their operational freedom. Although this may be held to be valid for Pentecostal believers, there is no reason not to consider the researcher him- or herself also as a meaning-maker. Precisely this consequence is extensively treated in Bourdieu's epistemological writings, where a fundamental discrepancy turns up in his views of the objectivity of (social) science. The epistemological consequences of a practice approach not only concern the knowledge about the research object; they are equally important, and directly related to, the knowing subject, that is to say, the researcher. I will now address a separate section to this topic, which will allow me to put the entire research into context and to expound on my research methods.

Research, Representation, and Reality: Between Objectivism and Constructivism

Our reach so often exceeds our grasp.

The present book relies strongly on anthropological fieldwork, which implies the application of familiar research techniques such as participant observation and interviewing. Consequently, I had to cope with the limitations of these methods. Working through some handbooks on methodology, I came upon an endless list of problems the researcher may be confronted with during the period in the field (Glaser and Strauss 1967; Russell Bernard 1989; Spradley 1979, 1980; Ten Have 1977; Wester 1987). Ten Have (1977), for example, wrote an introduction to—sociological—fieldwork, in which all chapters focus on "problems": of fieldwork, of relation, of observation, of analysis, of the investigator. He strongly advises the researcher to take note of all problems encountered, because even if a problem appears to have been solved, the resolution may have been successful only insofar as the problem was technical.

The fundamental point we have to tackle has to do with the nature of scientific knowledge, especially of the social sciences (including anthropology), where the investigator is his or her own research instrument. Generally, investigators give an account of all the pains they took to cope with "involvement and detachment" problems and how they tried to neutralize them as much as possible. Their methodological report is usually stored in a rather isolated appendix to the "real book," in which they offer an image of reality without paying due attention to how the picture was constructed.

Given the complexity and limitations of anthropological fieldwork, it seems justified to question the status of the account anthropologists present. In our attempts at "objectivity," what kind of knowledge is it that we produce; should we not show more modesty with regard to the presentation of the results? Anthropological accounts are often presented as very convincing representations of some remote, micro reality. It is common for monographs to be unique in the sense that no other publications on the specific tribe, culture, and the like have appeared (hence the temptation to present exclusive knowledge as objectively true). How then, are we to choose in this classic subjectivist-objectivist dilemma? Are we to follow the "natives," presuming that we are able to somehow interpret and express their view correctly, or do we keep to objectivist claims that pretend to provide a version of a particular social event or complex, which native participants by definition cannot produce? The same problem comes to the fore when we look at the peculiarities of the phenomenon of the so-called restudy. Complete field studies have been rejected on the basis of new (better) insights produced by restudies. The reason for such disqualification is the assumption that (the production of) knowledge is reproducible and that results are absolute. However, different results are not necessarily better; they may be the result of different methods employed, different theoretical orientations of the researchers, time differences, and so on. It is therefore questionable whether replication in the social sciences is possible at all (see Kloos 1988).

Practice theory tries to establish a bridge between the objectivist and subjectivist viewpoints. To illustrate this, I will place particular emphasis on Bourdieu's *retour réflexif* (reflexive turn), which urges reflection on the genesis of one's own descriptions and observations and objectification of the researcher's methodology and anthropological production process.

Underlying the problematic nature of social science research and the consequent limitations for anthropological research, are some fundamental controversies in the philosophy of science. Problems of description have given way to problems of reflection and representation. In modern social science most paradigms are characterized by a postpositivist stance (Guba 1990), which assumes that it is possible, despite many obstacles, to describe reality (society, culture, etc.) in terms of a reliable representation, if scientific standards of validity, probability, and others are satisfied. It is constructivism and particularly postmodernism that gives up the belief in the possibility of a valid representation of reality. In the anthropological discipline, George Marcus, James Clifford, Stephen Tyler, Michael Fischer—in a way all "followers" of the originator of interpretative anthropology, Clifford Geertz—are often presented as the main representatives (what's in a name!) of this last tendency (Geuijen 1992). They make a plea "to think of cultures not as organically unified or traditionally continuous but rather as negotiated present processes" (Clifford 1988, 273) and suggest presenting reality as polyphony, which ethnography should not try to reduce to its identity or essence (ibid., 53–54).[25]

The ontology, deconstruction, and eclecticism of what is called postmodernism, is often accused of leading to total relativism, although this criticism is explicitly denied by its exponents. To defend themselves against this kind of accusation, they propose that their work should be evaluated by reference to group criteria: "these facts on which a group—as big as possible, including the people investigated—can agree at a specific moment in time and space" (Geuijen 1992, 29). Although this is still a rather vague criterion—the reason why it is hard to define oneself as postmodern—there is in it an interesting plea to make visible the role of the person who conducts the research in relation to the people investigated. It also means that the researcher may, or even better, *must* appear in the story that is told, to clarify the elements of personal involvement and directive intervention, which in the end lead to the inquirer's creation (construction) of reality.

Practice theorist Pierre Bourdieu attempts to resolve several of the foregoing problems in his epistemological experiments. Although in many ways Bourdieu is far from a postmodernist, he fundamentally questions the position and behavior of the social scientist, including power relations, analyzing these within the general framework of the interplay between actor and structure (1990, 1, 20–21, 30–41).

As far as I can judge, Bourdieu does not give up wider pretensions of representation; what he explicitly aims at is preserving the gains of both the objectivist and the subjectivist view when he addresses the role of the researcher within the process of the production of knowledge (ibid., 25). This reflexivity (*retour réflexif*) is also common to many variations of postmodern thought, but it is especially well elaborated by Bourdieu. He rejects the tenacious view of the social scientist as a detached observer. He proposes an objective look at our research topic—which is the normal, positivist/objectivist stance—adding an objective analysis of this same objectivation process itself. This he calls participant objectivation (Bourdieu 1992b, 38). The pure subjectivist position is inaccurate and even illusory, because first, it is practically impossible to achieve the kind of doxic—that is to say, unreflective, "native"—experience that this stance requires, and second, it does not have the tools—which objectivism has—to analyze the same objective structures that would create the possibility of such an experience (Bourdieu 1990, 25–26). Objectivism, on the contrary, rejects the natives' points of view, the "accounts of the accounts which agents produce and through which they produce the meaning of the world" (Garfinkel 1967, 11; quoted in Bourdieu 1990, 26). Still, we need a view "from above" in combination with one "from below."

Bourdieu's "participant objectivation" or "objectivation of objectivation" is charming, although it is in no way easy to employ this methodological device in order to overcome the sterile objectivist-subjectivist debate.[26] It aims at combining a scientific objectivation of the object and the observer's relation to the object. The first remains necessary because "actors are unable to adequately describe and reflect on their own practice" (Jenkins 1992, 53). Yet, Bourdieu's participant objectivation implies that the observer is an actor him- or herself and hence should be observed too. To what degree this auto-reflection poses the same limitations as the objectivation of the research objects, remains unclear.

Bourdieu himself extensively treats this problem in his studies of the academic field. There, a kind of objective knowledge is produced, but when one looks at this production of scientific knowledge itself, it appears that this production responds to a large extent to its own interests; in that sense it cannot be considered objective. Although, as I pointed out, rigorous application of Bourdieu's epistemological/methodological standards is hard to realize,[27] I think that ideally every researcher should attempt it (Bourdieu 1989, 8–9, 179ff). For individual fieldwork situations, Kloos (1988) and many others have made similar pleas for reflexivity. In the remaining part of this chapter I shall attempt to reflect on my own work.

As anthropologist and meaning-maker one is caught in structural constraints very similar to those of the actors that have been chosen as research objects. Although reflecting on their own practice, researchers (themselves being the principal research instruments) are conditioned by habitus, as is any human being. At the same time, they try to make meaning out of other people's meaning-making. The story of a particular branch of Chilean Pentecostalism is presented in this book with the help of generally accepted conventions that to a certain degree respond to equally general demands for objectivity. An attempt is also made to make it clear that the results are construed as part of a personal meaning-making process of the observer. This is in fact the never-ending epistemological debate between constructivists and those who cling to some sort of postpositivism. My position comes close to what Kloos put forward in a concise article on knowledge production (1988, 233–237). His concern is not so much reliability, for the anthropologist in his construction of reality should take into account that he or she is part of that reality; he or she is "actor in interaction" (ibid., 235). *Credibility*, then, becomes the key word of Kloos's epistemological position, which means that the process of knowledge production by the researcher has to be visible, including the choices that are made. Yet, like the actors that are being studied, the researcher (observer) is also subject to structural constraints, basically set by the academic field he or she belongs to. Although Bourdieu is apparently claiming that he, which means in fact, all academics, can escape from this kind of restriction by turning to the "objectivation of the objectivation," I doubt whether that is really possible. The academic observer is definitely not the kind of superman required for such a job, which in fact Bourdieu himself "proved" in his *Homo Academicus* (1988). Such a position is also contradictory to practice theory as such, which takes the interconnection between structure (and constraint) and agency as its primary concern. Both the observer and the observed actors have to cope with structural conditions, but they also contribute to changes in structure. Most of the time researcher and researched are subject to different structures, but especially when doing fieldwork, the anthropologist may become (partly) involved in the same structural constraints as the research subjects.

What has been put forward on practice so far will be made more clearly visible in the rest of the book. The practice approach puts an indispensable check on the degree of representation of what follows, but it also delineates the representativeness of the story as it is presented. In order to clarify both aspects, I shall now give an account of the research process and procedures, which, I repeat, should be read as the researcher's attempt at meaning-making within the limited space the different habituses (including religious and scientific ones) set out. I therefore deal with the methods employed, but also with the personal involvement of the researcher during the accumulation of the material. I try to reconstruct the decisions I made during the fieldwork and reflect on the consequences for the outcomes of the research. This includes a comment, more particularly, on my role as a foreign believer and its consequences for the fieldwork procedure. This is in fact a self-examination of how I looked at Pentecostalism from a state of being partly in Pentecostalism, supposing that such a thing is possible at all.

Defining Methods and Employing Strategies

The following account of the actual carrying out of the research has to be understood against the background of the preceding epistemological remarks. Inevitably, a stylistic break takes place when moving from the theoretical level to the field procedures. Yet both levels are strongly interconnected and the breach is only intended to be observable in style. Although I may not employ most of the terminology previously introduced, this section in its personal exploration of the limits of participation closely follows the participant objectivation process advanced by Bourdieu. This reflection is also intended to display the coalescence of the different meaning-making processes at stake and their implications for the presentation of the research findings.

As will be pointed out in a later section my research project on Chilean Pentecostalism germinated from the close interaction between two Dutch research partners, ICCO (Interkerkelijke Coördinatie Commissie Ontwikkelingssamenwerking, Interchurch Organization for Development Cooperation) and the VRIJE UNIVERSITEIT, and the Chilean NGO[28] SEPADE (Servicio Evangélico Para El Desarrollo, Protestant Development Service). For my part, academic and personal concern were combined with an interest in development policy. The outcomes had to be somehow relevant to all parties involved, which naturally put some additional constraints on the choice of the concrete research topic. How I came to develop my final research agenda and finally conducted the fieldwork is described in the following subsections.

In the Field: In Search of a Topic

Once I arrived in Chile, the research proposals I had originally designed naturally acquired another dimension, because I was then to determine in concrete terms the particular field of study. But what were the criteria to be used for such delimitation?[29] What I had read about Chilean Pentecostalism suggested that there were two currents: a majority of traditional, spiritualist churches that officially did not speak on social issues but had been tacitly supporting the Pinochet regime, and, on the other hand, a small ecumenical, socially and politically involved minority, the voice of which was SEPADE. The first group had been described extensively in the classical studies on Chile by Lalive d'Epinay (1969) and Willems (1967). The second cluster had made itself known principally through the international contacts it maintained, for example, with the WCC in Geneva. In Holland, it was known because of its relationship with the Dutch Reformed Churches and ICCO, which was the principal donor to SEPADE, but little was known on the religious identity of the churches belonging to this prophetic wing of Pentecostalism.

To take some representatives of this group as the subject of research seemed both logical and attractive, because it promised a view on Pentecostalism other than the classic ones.[30] Although there were valid scientific reasons to concentrate on this topic, I want to emphasize that had I not established such close contacts with ICCO, the focus of the research might have become a totally different one. For the archive documents at ICCO (quite apart from the personal discussions I had at the Chile country desk) suggested the importance of this "other" Pentecostalism in Chile and, therefore, in a way forced me to take this as my central research topic. Although I am still convinced that it is indeed an important topic, if only because it offered the possibility of correcting the image of one monolithic

and uniform Pentecostalism, I realize that my final decision depended on the choice of ICCO as a partner and entrance into Chile,
thus permitting my exposure to its particular optical distortions.[31]

Given the close relationship with ICCO during the preparation of
the research and fieldwork, it may not be surprising that the first
contact I established after my arrival in Chile was with ICCO's principal partner in Chile, SEPADE. I also went to the services in some of
the bigger Pentecostal churches in the center and lower middle-class
suburbs of Santiago. These initial impressions confirmed the image
I had from the literature and documents: the separation into two
branches of Chilean Pentecostalism. Massive services showed me
Pentecostalism's spiritualist face, whereas the stories I heard at SEP-
ADE were about churches participating in community activities, food
aid, discussions on environmental pollution, etcetera. Of course this
made me very curious to know how the services in these latter
churches would be, what the members believed, and how they
viewed Pentecostals belonging to the other, more spiritualist, side.
At SEPADE I also discussed my research questions, my reading of the
literature on Chilean Pentecostalism, and my intention to study the
developmental aspect in Pentecostalism.

My Chilean partners in those conversations were Samuel Palma,
a sociologist who had studied in England for three years, and Juan
Sepúlveda, a theologian who had traveled to many parts of the world
as a result of his participation in WCC activities, including assemblies.
I was impressed by their scientific interest, their knowledge of the
subject, and their ability to analyze their own participation in a Pentecostal church, the MIP, from an outsider's point of view. This challenged my view on Pentecostalism, and I realized that this view
would have to be revised thoroughly if I was to take this kind of
Pentecostal as the subject of my fieldwork. It soon appeared that
both men welcomed the research topics I proposed, and they offered to comment on my work whenever I wanted and to help establish whatever contacts with churches I needed. I discussed the idea
of taking their church, the MIP, as a major focus in the research. They
did not see any problem if I decided to do so, but advised me not
to limit myself to that church, given the fact that it was a small, far-
from-representative church. On the other hand, it was explained to
me that almost any initiative, be it social, political, or ecumenical,
either came from that particular church directly or was organized
by it via SEPADE, which they presented as the brains and organizer

behind all public statements and acts that took place on behalf of the prophetic Pentecostal churches. According to both conversation partners, no other churches had the ideas or the capacities to implement them.[32]

During the first weeks of my stay in Santiago I elaborated my research strategy, consulting many more people from other NGOs, university departments, and research institutes. I heard severe criticisms of SEPADE, the MIP, and the so-called "gang of three families," who led this "numerically insignificant" branch of Pentecostalism. Yet I could also distill from the comments that indeed its influence was far greater than one would expect considering its numbers, but that it was rather doubtful whether it could still be labeled as Pentecostalism.

This clearly confronted me with a dilemma. On the one hand I could choose a neat and well-proportioned research population, the MIP, which possessed a development-oriented agency of its own and a vast network of national and international contacts. This seemed to meet all "conditions" set out in my research proposal. On the other hand, the same MIP people warned me not to limit myself to their church, and others even went much further and disqualified this church as "insignificant," "politicized," and "not Pentecostal." What could I do? Choose another (bigger, more representative?) church or find out about the MIP myself? I decided to do the latter and select some of the MIP's congregations to start the "real" fieldwork. Besides, I determined that it would be good to visit congregations belonging to other churches within the same prophetic group, in order to check the degree of representation of the MIP. I also decided to contrast the MIP findings with observations in some of the traditional Pentecostal churches in the same neighborhoods where I was to frequent the MIP congregations. Apart from this, I would study the content of the SEPADE development programs, especially insofar as these were conducted in and with the churches.

Doing Fieldwork among Pentecostals

My contacts at SEPADE led me first to the former squatter settlement, La Victoria.[33] The MIP congregation in this neighborhood was headed by pastor Erasmo Farfán, who at the time was also the director of SEPADE. According to my SEPADE conversation partners this was not an ordinary MIP church, because it had been strongly involved in the 1983–1985 protests against Pinochet, which had been a reason for much criticism by pastors and lay people from other MIP congregations. Yet they said La Victoria best represented the social and political development-oriented tendency within the church. They suggested visiting other, more typical, MIP congregations as well, to correct the image received in La Victoria.[34] I will describe my La Victoria experience to clarify the methodological research strategy I employed, although it cannot be considered totally exemplary.

When I first met pastor Farfán at SEPADE, he asked me if I would like to preach in his church when I came to visit it. He knew about my research beforehand and evidently assumed that I would be a fellow Protestant believer. Besides, his La Victoria church had been regularly frequented by foreign visitors; the international ecumenical contacts of the MIP assured a constant stream of visitors from abroad (often WCC missions), who were always invited to preach during one of the services. By offering me the same privilege, he forced me to identify myself and take a clear position.

My Peruvian experience with Pentecostal churches had taught me that this was a question that could be expected, and consequently I had thought of an acceptable response to this invitation. I knew that my host was aware that lay members in Europe do not preach in the mainstream Protestant churches, so this became my first argument. Second, I told him that I estimated that my Spanish lacked the subtlety I thought necessary for preaching. Third, I explained that I was to get to know church life as it normally was; I argued that a possible official role in the church (the logical consequence of regular preaching) might "disrupt" ordinary church life. I knew that my refusal of his offer, however politely it was presented, was in a way an offense, because for Pentecostals, the best way to communicate friendship and trust to outsiders (whenever they are Protestants) is to lend them the pulpit to deliver a sermon.[35] But pastor Farfán accepted the arguments for my refusal. Consequently, my entry into the church was that of a friendly newcomer, who took a place at the side of the ordinary believers and behaved as most of the church members. During my first visit I was invited to greet the congregation, but no expectations were raised toward a future structural function in the church.

This did not mean that I did not get involved in church activities. Within the limits of what was possible (the most pressing one being time) I participated in church events outside the regular services. I normally attended the services once a week—for I had to visit other churches as well—and I regularly went to the Sunday school meetings in the morning. In La Victoria this last activity required active participation. Additionally, I joined the youth group that met on Sunday afternoons. There I was received warmly and after a while I almost came to be considered one of them, although I never became an official member.[36] Furthermore, I spent some time attending meetings of the distinct church departments, and I also participated in the few happenings that occurred on a national scale. I will concentrate here on the first three levels of intervention in the local church (services, Sunday school, and youth group), in order to show how I worked, and then reflect on my own position and role and their consequences for my findings.

Worshiping in La Victoria

The Sunday afternoon service is the best visited service in all Chilean Pentecostal churches. The majority of the church members come, but it is also the service at which outsiders, mostly curious visitors, assist. The latter pop in and participate as long as they feel comfortable, and at the level they themselves choose. They do not know the songs, the way of praying, the customs of kneeling, the exclamations, etcetera. Some try to adopt the "rules of the house," but most of them just remain on their seats for the time they stay. This is what I did at first, but when I started to attend more often, I decided to adapt my behavior to the local customs; because I had presented myself as a fellow believer, why would I not share the prevailing church practice? So I knelt, sang (using the book of hymns), raised my hands, saying "praise the Lord" (*gloria a Dios*), uttered my approval, clapped my hands, etcetera. What I did not do is shout Hallelujahs, pray loudly, or weep. In short I refrained from the most typical characteristics of Pentecostal worship.[37]

Why did I try to act like an ordinary church member? First, for me it was a quite natural thing to do. I felt no personal barrier to participation; I had already done so during my Peruvian research, and I supposed that it would be appreciated by the people. Second, full participation changed my position; I was still viewed as a foreigner but one who at least apparently could share similar experiences. In personal conversations I was told that my behavior made me more trustworthy, which made access to people easier. Third, I adopted not only some of the classic worship techniques but also the "vices" people demonstrate during their church attendance. I no longer felt ashamed when I arrived late, or when I wanted to ask somebody something or even have an interview during the service; these were things people were very much accustomed to (except for the interviews of course). Pentecostal services are moments when all kinds of businesses are done; my research job fit perfectly into the normal church practice. In short, by adopting some of the Pentecostal "virtues," I felt that I could also practice some of its "vices," whenever I thought they could serve my research purposes.

Learning during Sunday School

During the Sunday school meetings, I participated in a much more direct way. The worship part very much resembled the usual practice in the services, but a substantial amount of time was dedicated to Bible study. After the communal worshiping, the church was divided into various groups, according to sex and age, which discussed parts of the Bible along the guidelines of a specific manual. These discussions were quite participative, although not all—especially not the women—entered the discussion to the same degree.[38] For me, these sessions were extremely illuminating. Although Bible texts always constituted the terms of reference, contextualization was one of the principal goals of the discussion. This varied from an application of Bible texts for one's personal relation to God to profound discussions on the implications of biblical notions and stories for social practice in today's Chile. Here I felt free to offer my opinion about the views expressed by the church members, and I was often asked to give my interpretation of texts and of the ways these were treated in the manuals. Discussions were lively, and I learned a lot about people's opinions, experiences, and personal histories. These sessions also provided me with the opportunity to introduce themes that were of special interest to me. When I was asked, for example, to expound on certain passages from the Sermon on the Mount (Matthew 5), I once gave a radical social interpretation, referring directly to local circumstances in Chile, and La Victoria in particular. By doing so, I consciously provoked a discussion that was most clarifying as to the behavior of the La Victoria church during the strongest years of repression under Pinochet. In short, religion, politics, and talks on social justice often merged during this weekly discussion hour.

Discussions with the Youth

From various sides I had heard that the La Victoria youth group had radicalized politically during the Pinochet regime; this had been a hot issue at the MIP annual assemblies, especially during the early 1980s. The group itself was just emerging out of a prolonged crisis that followed the years of popular protest. During my stay in Chile (August 1991 to August 1992) the La Victoria youth were reorganizing themselves (parallel to a reorganization at the national level), but the reorganization was being watched closely by the *Junta de Oficiales* (church council). The active social and political behavior of the church youth had meant a profound critique of the spiritualist position that was defended by other groups within the church, including the church council. The youth had been accused of "depentecostalization" and politicization. In reaction, the greater part of the youth had turned their backs on the church, whereas others continued attending, although lowering their profile considerably. I was able to observe the return of some of the former dissidents to the church during my research period.

The group was a rich source of detail for several reasons. The youth could tell me endless stories of social and political conflicts within the church. In addition, they were struggling with their Pentecostal identity, in which they wanted to combine social involvement and spiritual inspiration. This struggle was reflected in the agenda of their activities. One day they discussed the local drug problems, another day the rise of Satanic sects, and at another opportunity they spoke about their personal relation with God, Jesus, and the Holy Spirit. I was pressed to participate actively in the discussions, in which it was impossible to take a neutral stance. On one occasion I spoke about my research and my participation in the church and my personal feelings about that. I felt that this was highly appreciated, because by expressing my own views and personal feelings, I behaved like one of them. I was in fact considered a member of the group, although this was officially impossible because of my not being an official church member. This position facilitated the introduction of themes and questions of my personal research agenda. I imagine that the fact that I was a Christian,

although not a Pentecostal, was an advantage; many of the youngsters were not quite sure whether they were really Pentecostals or
"just Christians." The discussions we had on this kind of problem
were most illustrative for the effects of social involvement on Pentecostal identity and religiosity. The following is an example of the
outcomes of my active participation in the group.

During Christmas 1991, I participated in a theater play that was
performed in the church. It was a critical piece about the celebration
of 500 years after Columbus, which one of the former political activists in the group had written. They asked me to play the role
of the missionary who was to meet an Indian woman during an
evangelization campaign. My script was that of the classic evangelist
with only one goal—to convert as many Indians as possible. Yet the
Indian woman in the play was to remind me of all the horrors the
first Catholic evangelization had brought them and to clearly set
out the conditions under which she was prepared to accept Christ.
The majority of the La Victoria people seemed to appreciate the
content of the play—which was indeed a severe critique on ruthless
evangelization—and they apparently valued my participation in it.
This performance happened only four months after my first visit to
the church, and I had gladly accepted the opportunity, because I
thought this was the perfect occasion to make a substantial contribution to church life and my own research project. Thus, in the
hope of gaining some popularity, I really made an effort to learn the
text by heart, expecting that this exercise would pay off one day in
benevolence toward collaboration in my plans. I still think that my
performance was indeed appreciated and that it contributed to gaining some extra confidentiality and cooperation.

Institutional Context

Apart from being my principal introduction into the Chilean
Pentecostal field, the Pentecostal NGO SEPADE also became one of
my specific research targets, because I gradually started to conceive
of the institution as an important instrument of Pentecostal politics
(see Chapter 5). Consequently, I went to SEPADE frequently during
the period of investigation. I participated as an observer in parts of
its program (youth and neighborhood projects), especially those
that were concerned with Protestant, and particularly Pentecostal,
churches (seminars, courses; again, see Chapter 5). Third, at SEPADE

I maintained a close professional relationship with the two academics (mentioned earlier) with whom I regularly discussed the direction and progress of my research, my findings, my interpretations, and my dilemmas. I also tried to fill what I considered shortcomings in my material by exposing them to additional inquiries.

Consequently, my relation to SEPADE was rather complicated. It was simultaneously my way into the churches, in a way my research partner, and also a subject to be studied. What complicated—and sometimes facilitated—my work even more, was that several people I met in the churches also worked at SEPADE. The La Victoria church in particular, which I described before, provided several of its (lower) employees. I suppose that most SEPADE functionaries are still wondering about the kind of a job I actually did. I maintained a rather fluid relationship with the majority of the staff, which was in part the result of the fact that to different people I emphasized different reasons for my behavior. Probably the only person who was well aware of my broad set of objectives was SEPADE's new director, Samuel Palma. Others variously thought I was a Dutch pastor, a theology student, an anthropology student, a missionary, a tourist, a fellow believer, and who knows what else. It is difficult to evaluate the consequences of this relatively unidentified status, but during the fieldwork I had the feeling that this chameleon behavior enabled me to maintain distinct relations within the SEPADE network. As an example, SEPADE's receptionist initially treated me rather formally, but when I later discovered that she belonged to the La Victoria church, we developed an entirely different relationship. We used our lunch break at the SEPADE office to chat about church problems and the latest rumors, but on those occasions I needed to obtain some practical detail, she could also lobby easily on my behalf.

My frequent contacts at the SEPADE office and my participation in SEPADE activities meant that I was considered by people from other NGOs to be a SEPADE employee. As long as they shared the same sociopolitical line, there was no problem. But the critics, and there were many, sometimes treated me rather hostilely, or tried to convert me to their points of view. Because I was Dutch and ICCO-Holland was SEPADE's main sponsor, I was somehow also viewed as a representative of the Dutch "development circuit." I am well aware that people sometimes tried to give as negative an impression as possible of SEPADE, in the hope of diverting financial aid to their organizations. People belonging to the SEPADE network may have put forward favorable results, with the same implications in mind.

The church people also often thought that I belonged to the SEP-
ADE personnel, which had both positive and negative consequences.
There was a clear suspicion that I would pass information to SEPADE
regarding the functioning of its projects in the churches. It was
feared that if, for example, participation in a youth program was
minimal and I reported that to some SEPADE officer, this would have
consequences for the continuation of the program. For this reason,
people were somewhat reluctant to permit me to visit church-
SEPADE activities. Conversely, people also saw me as a channel
through which they could express their critiques and frustrations
with these same programs. These comments were extremely revealing as to the impact of the SEPADE social policy within the churches.
For example, I noticed that people's participation in church projects
often directly served their practical interests, which considerably
handicapped the SEPADE staff in their efforts to reach other, less material, goals. It was also interesting to record people's comments on
the social impact of the messages that were given during the church
services or at the Sunday school.

There is one other aspect of my relationship with SEPADE that I
want to mention. During my stay in the field I was visited by several
representatives of the Dutch donor agencies ICCO and SOH (Stichting
Oecumenische Hulp, Dutch Interchurch Aid). I knew beforehand
that ICCO functionaries might be interested in what I would "discover" in Chile, but when I had settled in Santiago and had established my working relations there, I considered it a kind of betrayal
to pass information about SEPADE, its employees, or the churches in
general directly to outsiders, which is how I started to think of the
ICCO people (this had clearly not been so during the period of the
preparation of the fieldwork). I was not asked to deliver confidenti-
alities, but I still felt a little uncomfortable about my role. I was not
sure about the consequences of my passing on detailed information,
although I realize that financial support to organizations like SEPADE
does not depend on the single opinion of an outsider, however well
informed he may be.

Playing Practice: Role and Research

To close this report on some aspects of my research among Chilean Pentecostals, I want to focus briefly on the role the anthropologist plays in his or her specific field of interest. I deliberately use

the word *play* in order to indicate the multifaceted position of the fieldworker who takes part in several plays at a time. He or she is involved in the play of his or her actors, playing the role of observer. Yet the interaction with them also entails a personal (human) interplay. Since there are several stages (or fields in Bourdieu's sense) on which the anthropologist plays his or her parts, he or she obeys different rules and conventions (or habituses). I use the play metaphor—which comes close to being metonym—to indicate the different positions and loyalties the researcher has to combine in his or her fieldwork. I think it is a good metaphor, because the play is usually serious. This is true for the fieldworker, as well as for those he or she is studying. I particularly want to stress this, because the objection of "betrayal" can be expected when one declares one has played several roles during the fieldwork. The role of active participant in the Pentecostal churches I visited may especially provide grounds for disapproval.

Yet, in my role of professional anthropologist I try to work seriously. After all, I am in the first place responsible for the task with which I am entrusted, for the scientific contents of the research, and for the financial resources endowed. I believe that my active participation in church activities falls within the same category of serious fieldwork. It is in a way the consequence of the fact that the anthropologist is his or her own research instrument. There are serious epistemological consequences of that fact, which I dealt with previously, but it also means that the anthropologist's total personality, his or her opinions, and his or her prejudices are involved. This issue can best be clarified by seeing the professional anthropologist as a meaning-maker. My different roles, then, are part of my condition as meaning-maker, which includes my anthropological behavior. By taking the position that I am describing, the artificial contradiction between the researcher as anthropologist and as human being is lifted. My attempt to practice an anthropology that includes the people in scientific reports, by listening to them and considering their testimonies as valuable and as counterbalancing structural analyses and theorizing, can be seen as my personal meaning-making as well.

I feel my role as a believer still needs some further elaboration. I arrived in Chile to study Pentecostalism, and I played the role of a Protestant believer simultaneously. Hence, I participated actively in all kinds of Pentecostal practices, which I felt was the way I could

come closest to people's experience of their Pentecostal faith. I made
a conscious decision to do this, but I must admit that it was not
always easy. Whenever one joins a church, maybe not as a regular
member, but as a kind of fraternal fellow, one tacitly accepts its
values. I can say that my values often collided with those of the
brothers and sisters with whom I was talking. Some of them expected that and wanted to hear comments. Although somewhat hes-
itatingly at the beginning, I normally entered the discussion quite
straightforwardly. If I had not done so, I think that in the long run
my position might have lacked credibility to the people I investigated and become insupportable for myself (also as a researcher),
with all the negative consequences for the research. I am convinced,
however, that the same demand can be made to the anthropologist
who chooses to identify him- or herself as a nonbeliever.

There is another aspect to this "playing a role." I was tempted to
stop being a fellow believer, but I did not really feel the impulse to
do so; that might have seriously damaged the trust I had been trying
so anxiously to gain, revealing myself as a "traitor." But my reason
for continuing was in fact more positive: I believe that I did not do
so badly. In general, I think that in the first place people did like it
that I participated in their church life; second, I myself felt quite
happy in my role of a believer, and I was easily able to meet the
requirements this role brought with it (sufficient biblical knowledge, ability to adopt the Pentecostal "slang," among others); third,
I value the fact that my embracing the role of fellow believer considerably facilitated my entry into the Pentecostal field. I think I got
access to people that otherwise would have opposed my questioning, although I realize that the reverse has also happened occasionally. This is, in my opinion, proof of a harmonious coexistence of
personal and professional involvement.

When I evaluate my position in the Pentecostal field during the
year I was in it, I conclude that my adopting different roles proved
to be for the greater part successful; I felt myself at ease doing what
I did, and I think that I learned a lot about my specific research
topic. I suspect that this same success helped me to grow into my
role, or better, both roles—that of the so-called professional anthropologist and that of the believer—merged into one single role of the
participant observer. I imagine that this "conversion to participation" is, however, by no means unique, but is inescapably the experience of most anthropologists.

Finally, it should not be surprising that my "insider" position caused a sort of group loyalty, but my writing a book about those people with whom I shared so many experiences, inevitably created a distance from them. Sometimes I felt that this gap hampered the writing, but in general I think a certain degree of detachment is fruitful during the writing process. I have nevertheless made an effort to avoid absolute objectivation of the behavior of those Pentecostals, some of whom I have come to know quite well. In this section, which is in fact my personal *retour réflexif*, I have tried to reconstruct the participant objectivation process underlying the present work. It is an attempt to make visible the process of scientific knowledge production and its limits, a glimpse at an endeavor that can be characterized as "work-in-progress."

Technical Approach of the Fieldwork

In the section entitled Research, Representation, and Reality, I discussed the representativeness of the present investigation and I located it somewhere on the scale that runs from construed to objective reality. In order to account for the credibility advanced by Kloos (1988) I want to give a brief overview of how I technically did my research. In my one-year stay in Chile's capital, Santiago, I settled in a middle/upper-class suburb, which meant that I did not live in the neighborhoods in which I did my actual research. Field observations, then, are limited to the times I was present in those neighborhoords, and although I made lengthy visits to the churches I selected for studying, no doubt much of the daily life of its members has escaped my direct attention. It also means that I only superficially knew the neighborhood life in general, which I must admit is a significant omission. It means, among other things, that my argument is principally built upon discourse analysis and interviewing that have not been exhaustively confronted with daily practice.

Another limitation concerns the number of people I was able to talk with. I limited my participant observation to three different congregations: La Victoria and José María Caro from the MIP, and San Miguel from the Iglesia Wesleyana, although the book principally draws on my experience with La Victoria. In total I paid more than a hundred visits to activities in these communities (services, Sunday School, youth group, special occasions). At these occasions I not only participated in the particular activity of the moment, but

I always "arranged" informal chats with some of the people present. I also conducted some thirty in-depth interviews with church members, both leaders and ordinary people. Men are overrepresented on my list of interviewees, although women dominate the church membership. The gender identity of the researcher is no doubt partly responsible for this. My access to women was simply more difficult than to men, and in leadership functions, men clearly outnumbered women. Although my interviews were mainly with men, my informal talks were most often with women.

Apart from the churches, I spent considerable time in the SEPADE organization. I had talks with people from all the projects executed by the NGO, and I took part in several of its activities. I dropped in at the office about three times a week, on the grounds of which I was jokingly called a SEPADE volunteer. Sometimes I came across church people at the SEPADE office, but most of my work there remained hidden to most of the ordinary church members. Yet, as I already indicated, I was occasionally labeled as a SEPADE officer, a role that referred to a particular, somewhat bureaucratic pattern of behavior. With the SEPADE staff I also conducted a series of lengthy interviews, most of them during two successive sessions, which gave me a fairly balanced view of activities, motivations, and policy appraisal among the personnel. With the SEPADE leaders I had many additional talks—most of them informal—about church policies, NGO strategies, and not least, on my own research findings.

When I speak about interviews here, I mean formal talks that were recorded on a tape recorder and later transcribed completely by a research assistant I contracted for this purpose. In sum, I have thirty-six transcribed interviews, which constitute about 800 pages of text. The other talks, varying from short chats to lengthy conversations, I later recorded in separate files, on the basis of my memory and the short notes I had made on the spot. These latter files constitute about seventy-five documents (300 pages). Field observations were recorded separately in "observation files" (about 100). These contain the accounts of all the activities (by church and NGO) in which I participated or which I was able to observe. All the material gathered in this manner was ordered in my personal computer, with the help of a word processor and a qualitative database program. The latter gave me quick access to the data I produced and a constant overview of what I was doing during the actual fieldwork and after. On my return to Holland, this way of storing my fieldwork notes proved very useful during the writing process.

Besides the data I recorded and produced myself, I examined a vast number of books, papers, copies of archive documents (the latter from SEPADE as well as the MIP), leaflets, newspaper reports, policy documents, and the like. I did this partly in Santiago, but I reviewed a considerable collection of material, which I was unable to see there, after my return. This holds in particular for the many policy documents I collected at the SEPADE and ICCO offices. I also conducted many interviews (which have not been recorded on tape) with staff members of the latter organization during the entire research process from 1988 until the completion of the first draft of this book (spring 1995).

Notes

1. My choice of *Protestantism* as the overall term is explained in the introduction. Nevertheless, the Latin American *evangélico* will be used in specific cases. When I speak about Pentecostals, which is in the greater part of the book, I of course use the corresponding terminology.

2. Droogers (1991) published an extensive bibliography that confirms this statement. Especially during the 1980s, however, several more complete works were published: Glazier (ed., 1980; articles on different countries in Latin America and the Caribbean); Butler Flora (1978; Colombia); Brusco (1986; Colombia); Muratorio (1980; Ecuador); Hoffnagel (1979; Brazil); Tennekes (1985; Chile); Rolim (1985; Brazil); Annis (1988; Guatemala); Mariz (1994; Brazil); Kessler (1967; Peru, Chile).

3. The book titles probably make for much of the interest. Stoll's book is called *Is Latin America Turning Protestant?*, and Martin's *Tongues of Fire: The Explosion of Protestantism in Latin America* equally attracts attention.

4. Absence or disturbance of collectively appreciated norms responsible for social consensus; see also Merton's *Social Theory and Social Structure*, 1949.

5. Within Chile, there is no general agreement over Pentecostal growth figures during the successive governments of Frei, Allende, and Pinochet. Sepúlveda (personal communication) confirms the view provided by Tennekes, and I am inclined to follow him.

6. Tennekes, who is a professor of anthropology at the same university (VRIJE UNIVERSITEIT) that sponsored my research, has for a long time been the only Dutch scientist publishing on Chile's Pentecostal movement. His research, which ended in 1973 just before the military coup d'état, hints at the emergence of a more socially committed type of Pentecostalism. My research focuses explicitly on this last tendency.

7. Hence he pays practically no attention to Protestant resistance to the

Chilean military regime (Stoll 1990a, 316). The way he treats the successive ecumenical attempts in Latin America suggests that these have been totally insignificant (ibid., 130ff).

8. The authors consider this search for meaning in daily life as the central motive of all types of popular religion.

9. This relation to God(s) and other supposedly supernatural beings is of course of a different order than the relations to fellow believers and society. To speak about the former relation is in fact to speak about people's testimonies about it. The supernatural is to me a virtual reality, for it is mediated by people; God(s) cannot be interviewed. My position on this point of debate in the social sciences is that the relation with the supernatural world people claim to have belongs to the meaning-making dimension of people. For them it is a directly experienced world. When we claim to take the people researched seriously, we are obliged to take this virtual world seriously. For research purposes, then, this relation people declare they have with a supernatural domain cannot be omitted, but approaches that present supernatural beings as performing actors are missing the point just as much as those that do not consider this complicated issue worth treating at all.

10. Archer (1988) argues that the culture-agency dichotomy runs parallel to this structure-agency question. To her, structure:social actor (the domain of the material aspects of life, notably including interest and power) = culture:cultural actor (the world of ideas, 1988: ix). This is a fruitful parallel, especially because she aims to bring both worlds together by focusing on sociocultural interaction. Yet the comparison tends to equal culture and symbolic structure, which echoes a mechanistic view in which human signification appears to be strongly reduced. I will come back to this point later, when dealing with Sherry Ortner's work.

11. The tradition of holding a Te Deum is in fact much older. It has been celebrated in the Catholic Cathedral since time immemorial; in 1971 Allende changed it into an ecumenical service (see also Chapter 3).

12. Alexander (1990) argues that culture relates to the order corresponding to meaningful action, as opposed to the mechanistic order. His article gives an overview of analytic debates, which is rounded off with a plea for theoretical eclecticism and the acknowledgment of the mutual influence of culture, social structure, and action.

13. The same sterile dichotomy dominated at the epistemological and methodological level (see the section on research and representation).

14. These authors only occasionally employ the concepts "religion" or "culture." Yet their focus on the reality of everyday life of ordinary members of society and their "common-sense knowledge" in fact includes what is often defined as culture. It is because of this hidden nature of culture in Berger and Luckmann's work that I prefer to use the more explicit insights of Ortner, and to a lesser extent, Tennekes.

15. A fundamental question remains as to whether the complexity of reality should be reflected in a scientific model that is equally complex, covering the mutual connection of every facet of this reality. Archer, for example, is very emphatic in her distinction between the cultural system and sociocultural interaction. Although in daily reality both categories are inseparable, they must be separated analytically in order to have any explicatory value at all (1988, 78–80). Archer accuses practice theorists like Bauman (1973) and especially Giddens of neglecting this—to her—fundamental scientific truth. Archer rejects their views because they create a sort of black box from which only unaccountable inferences are made. For that very reason, she would probably also reject Bourdieu's *habitus* concept.

16. In her 1984 state-of-the-art article, she defines practice as "all forms of human action" taken under specific conditions of asymmetry, inequality, and domination (1984, 149ff). The strong emphasis on power relations implied in this definition is less pervasive here.

17. Ortner rejects the term *habitus* for the very reason that it is too cognitive (1989b, 209). I doubt whether characterizing Bourdieu's habitus concept as cognitive is correct; however, changing it with "consciousness" is certainly more confusing than illuminating. Probably Ortner's "consciousness" corresponds to Giddens's "practical consciousness" (as opposed to discursive consciousness; Giddens 1985), which indeed comes close to Bourdieu's habitus concept.

18. This book is a revision of the 1977 *Outline of a Theory of Practice*.

19. Note that there is not just one habitus; different social groups, operating within different fields, may be submitted to different habituses. This is important for my argument, for it enables me to speak of a Pentecostal habitus.

20. Similarly to Bourdieu, Connerton, in his *How Societies Remember* (1992 [1989], 72ff) marks down "bodily practices" as one of the principal means human beings incorporate culture. This learning process takes place at both the unconscious and the conscious, intentional level.

21. Establishing Bourdieu's line of thought is hampered by his—deliberately?—opaque formulating. The very vagueness of Bourdieu's habitus concept, especially with regard to its genesis and possibilities of change, points to the primacy Bourdieu gives to structural analysis over an actor-oriented approach. Giddens (1985), emphasizing human beings as knowledgeable agents, which puts him more on the side of action theory, describes change as dependent on power relations—power as the capacity to achieve outcomes, which themselves rely on access to (allocative and authoritative) resources (ibid., 256–258). Therefore, Giddens is more of an action theorist, which also applies to Ortner; her cultural politics also implies the emphasis on power relations.

22. For some critics this makes a strong argument for considering

Bourdieu (like Giddens and his duality of structure) as ultimately advancing a sophisticatedly designed, actor-oriented perspective, despite the strong emphasis on the structural properties of the habitus (Layder 1981, 73–74).

23. Layder proposes to distinguish different types of (contextual and interactional) structures, the former lying beyond the reach of actors' creative doings, while the latter are subject to individuals' influence (1981, 91ff).

24. Bourdieu also seems to recognize the possibility of strategic calculation working upon habitus (1990, 53), but this is never a direct transformation of habitus itself. The relation of actors to habitus is one of determinism. Habitus is not produced by men but by "conditionings associated with a particular class of conditions of existence" (ibid.). The doxa-orthodoxy-heterodoxy model also points to at least two categories of actors (orthodox and heterodox) who are consciously manipulating and trying to exert power over others.

25. In a provocative article, Robert Pool argues that postmodern ethnology is largely a construct of its critics. Pool quotes Marcus and Fischer (1986) to prove that what these so-called postmodernists strive for is simply reflecting on the quality of their representations and does not mean a rejection of representation as such, leading to an anything-goes relativism (1991, 321–323, 327). I agree with him in the sense that it is too easy to avoid the principal discussion at stake by stigmatizing some of its instigators.

26. Yet it bears in it the danger of endless regression. Suppose that scientists were able to objectively take into account their own objectivation process. Whose task would it then be to study the reflection of this reflection, and so on?

27. This even proves hard for Bourdieu. For example, he declines theories that consider people as rational and conscious decision makers, but he seems to make an exception for himself—and colleagues—as a scientist.

28. This abbreviation stands for *nongovernmental organization*, which is a general term without a clear meaning. It is used especially within development policy to designate Third World organizations (partners) that claim to contribute to development and are often sponsored by Western relief agencies. There are several words in vogue that pretend to be more precise, for example, the term *NGDO* (nongovernmental development organization). Although this term may be somewhat more to the point, I still prefer the more commonly used NGO.

29. In this process I chose to be guided by the so-called grounded-theory-approach (Glaser and Strauss 1967), which tries to avoid both inductivist and deductivist biases. In this approach, the research starts with certain general questions, based on the existing literature on the theme. The basic idea is to avoid research being nothing more than filling pre-established theories and concepts. Ideally, a theory grows out of a constant, systematic, and recurrent search and comparison of material. In the case of

anthropology, it can be considered an actor-oriented approach, since theory is built stone-by-stone, using concepts that during the time of research are transformed from general, almost empty notions into a well-documented framework. This approach values the existing tension between the perspective of the observer and the observed as a positive, fruitful one. Although the final results cannot always satisfy all parties, the people who are the subject of the research should be able to identify with the results to a certain degree (Wester 1987).

30. Representatives of other, often bigger, Pentecostal churches thought that research on such an insignificant group was useless. For those people, who measured success by the number of church members, I was really wasting my time. For example, I once met a pastor at the printing office of the Iglesia Evangélica Pentecostal (IEP), where I tried to obtain references to the 1952 schism between the IEP and the MIP. I wanted to search the IEP journal *Fuego de Pentecostés* to trace back the MIP's history, hoping to find some material on its first historical period. The pastor-editor of the journal, however, could not see the use of digging up the sources of the old controversy, which to him had proven utterly irrelevant. He was absolutely certain that his *Fuego* magazine would not contain any reference to the events I was looking for, although he was himself only remotely aware of the story. "We do not pay attention to schism," he said, and his assessment turned out to be right. Additionally, he even tried to disqualify any research in the Pentecostal field: "What is the sense of holding interviews and doing research? The only thing you get are different visions and interpretations. Who is to judge if these are true or not? Not the scientist, but only God knows!"

31. ICCO of course chooses its partners not on the basis of a general scientific interest, but on the similarities of objectives of development policies.

32. The close cooperation both men offered me during the time of the fieldwork does not mean that they agreed to my analyses. In fact, both severely criticized the contents of the present book.

33. This is in fact the oldest squatter settlement in Santiago, dating from 1957. It has become the symbol of popular protest, because its neighborhood associations were extremely combative, especially during the Pinochet regime when La Victoria regularly became a battlefield between the military police and the "subversive" inhabitants (Espinoza 1988).

34. After a while, I indeed started to visit another MIP church in the José María Caro neighborhood, which showed less outspoken social opinions and behavior. Still later, I joined several congregations in other churches (of both "wings") in the same or adjacent districts (*comunas*).

35. Later, when I went to other churches of the progressive variety, I always repeated the same story in response to the constant invitations. In the traditional Pentecostal churches, however, I was never invited, not even to address myself to the gathered members, to explain the reason of my

visit. The big Iglesia Metodista Pentecostal (IMP) is especially keen to control every detail during the services. In that church, uncontrollable speeches by a foreigner who is hardly known do not fit into the scheme of things. Much distrust exists as to the possible ecumenical inclinations of any foreign visitor.

36. I still remember vividly the moment that the group members exchanged birthday presents, which they do once a year. Although I had been participating in the group for almost a year, I was not asked to buy someone a present, and no one bought me one. It was one of those moments when I felt that my belonging to the group was never—and could never be—as complete as I assumed. I concluded that the anthropologist's fate is to remain in a position somewhere between the stranger and the native.

37. Not every church member showed the same level of Pentecostal behavior. Some indeed showed a great fervor, whereas others were even "colder" than I was as a North European Protestant.

38. In other churches, notably the IMP, these groups are headed by a "professor" who generally delivers a minisermon that the other participants are obliged to listen to. The contribution of the others normally does not go beyond a personal testimony at the end of the session. There is no discussion about the content of the leader's presentation.

3

The Vicissitudes of Chilean Pentecostalism

This mainly historical chapter starts with an exploration of the various interpretations of Chilean Pentecostalism, that is, the variety of meanings the respective interpreters (Pentecostals and non-Pentecostals) have attributed to the behavior of Pentecostal people. These interpretations are contrasted with the structural conditions Pentecostals live(d) in. The actor-structure duo then receives attention. I also pay attention to the other hobbyhorse of practice approaches: the reflection on the position of the researcher.

Practically all studies on the topic have been carried out by people who were somehow doing their job from a religious (Christian) inspiration or involvement, alongside, or sometimes instead of, academic interest (Vergara 1962; Kessler 1967; Lalive d'Epinay 1969; more recently Galilea 1987, 1991 [with Father Poblete]; Canales et al. 1991; Sepúlveda 1992a, 1992b; Ossa 1991; Lagos 1988). As far as I know, Willems (1967) and Tennekes (1985) are the only observers who explicitly limit themselves to a sociological approach, although the latter author does not hide liberation theology sympathies (1985, 121). My observations on the dominantly Christian background of the authors writing on Chile's Pentecostalism do not aim to disqualify the results of their studies. My intention is to stress that they have all, although in various degrees, served other than purely scientific purposes and that their respective points of departure have colored their interpretations. In other words, the scientific efforts at explaining Chilean Pentecostalism all, although in varying degrees, served purposes of personal or institutional meaning-making. In several cases this signification meant an effort to guide the meaning-making of (groups of) Pentecostals whose conduct was initially only the object of explanation. I maintain that this characteristic of the research on Chilean Pentecostalism only emphasizes the construed character of knowledge production. Let me elaborate this suggestion in more detail by characterizing the above-mentioned studies.

Father Ignacio Vergara did a pioneer job in the study of Chilean Pentecostalism. He is said to be "surprisingly objective" in his approach to Chilean Protestantism (Lalive d'Epinay 1969, xxi) in his book, which tries to provide a historical overview of Protestant, including Pentecostal, denominations. On the other hand, the same Lalive d'Epinay questions this objectivity by quoting a 1955 publication in which the Catholic Vergara regards Protestantism as a decisive stage on a road that is leading man toward atheism (and communism), because it "shatters the religious unity of a nation and introduces both the idea and the possibility of choice" (ibid., 40).[1] Whether this assumption is correct or not, is not our primary concern here, yet it clearly shows the Catholic hegemonic worldview emanating from it. It is the same spirit that can still be traced in those works by Catholic scholars that consider sects and other movements a "huge pastoral problem" (Santagada 1989, 37; for Chilean examples, see Urrea 1992 and Muñoz 1989). They express the growing anxiety by the Catholic church, and more particularly of its bishops, over the growing Protestant movement, which is considered a threat to the Roman Catholic monopoly in Latin America. In Chile, the work by Galilea and Poblete is based on the same pastoral motive. When Lalive d'Epinay considers Vergara's 1962 book to have made a valuable contribution to the writing of Chilean church history, that is probably only because he found a considerable amount of "data" in it that saved him much trouble.

About Lalive d'Epinay's own "objectivity" the following remarks can be made. The first pages of his *Haven of the Masses* make it clear that the research project he carried out in Chile was instigated and financed by the World Council of Churches (WCC), in close collaboration with the Concilio Evangélico de Chile (CEC, Protestant Council of Chile) and the Comunidad Teológica Evangélica de Chile (CTE, Protestant Theological Community of Chile; Lalive d'Epinay 1969, xiii, xvii). It was to fit into a series on *Churches in the Missionary Situation: Studies in Growth and Response*. The explicit aim of Lalive d'Epinay's study is sociological in its attempt to give a complete picture of Chilean Pentecostalism based on a representative survey. The emphasis on church growth and the generalized conclusions from Pentecostal pastors' opinions, cast around the hypothesis of the "sectarian" character of their attitudes, can hardly be considered objective. Moreover, Lalive d'Epinay openly acted as a WCC representative, which cannot but have produced divergent views among Pentecostal pastors and lay people, who are generally not very enthusiastic about this organization. These remarks do not mean to invalidate Lalive d'Epinay's findings, after all his research methods meet generally accepted standards. I simply wish to put this research into context.

Kessler's work is clearly a mixture of theology and church history, so it is full of moral and theological statements and judgments. The author provides many detailed historical insights that are not found in any of the other writings on Chile's Pentecostal movement, but he is constantly evaluating the behavior and opinions of these early actors in the light of his personal idiosyncrasy. One of his final chapters, for example, deals with the three main problems he discerns (division, nationalism, and native ministry), and it starts with a theological appraisal called "divisions among God's people." This subjective stance that Kessler takes is far from surprising, because he mentions that he received a divine calling to work in South America a few years after having "committed his life to Jesus Christ and His service" (1967, 369). Again, I want to stress that I am in no way against this kind of meaning-making, although it is definitely very different from mine.

A motivation totally different than Kessler's is found in a book called *En tierra extraña II* (Canales et al. 1991). The title of this book refers to the way Pentecostals view the world surrounding them: as a "strange place" in which they no longer fit after conversion, but where they have to create a meaningful life. The authors of this book—all of them sociologists—make a plea for focusing on the meaning-making Pentecostal actor instead of remaining caught in structuralist analyses; the authors want to make a contribution to the fusion of Pentecostal identity with what they consider to be the essential part of poor people's identity. It is hoped that such "reconciliation" will create greater solidarity between Pentecostals and non-Pentecostals in the specific area of social action and the struggle for social change. This last goal springs from the authors' close relationship with the development agency SEPADE, which

explicitly advocates the Protestant social participation in its program of action. This gives the book an additional function as an
instrument of institutional Pentecostal politics. Sepúlveda, who has
worked as a theologian at the same SEPADE institution, takes great
pains in his work to prove the significance of the change conversion
to Pentecostalism causes in people's lives. He even maintains that
Chilean Pentecostals have shown more awareness of social problems
(alcohol abuse, the ill-treatment of women) than their fellow Latin
American believers, although he realizes that this has not exactly led
to a massive struggle to bring about social change. Most of his work
is an attempt to give Chilean Pentecostalism proper (Pentecostal)
theological grounds for social action. Various contributions to the
first editions of the journal *Evangelio y Sociedad* (Gospel and Society, published by SEPADE; see also Sepúlveda 1994, 48) bear witness
to this. So, Sepúlveda's analyses are always colored by this long-
term project. They can be characterized as the conscious meaning-
making efforts of a Pentecostal actor within a particular institutional
setting, a theme I will further elaborate in Chapter 5.

Similarly, Ossa (1991), a Lutheran pastor who worked for several
years at another ecumenical NGO[2] in Santiago, wrote a book—called
Lo ajeno y lo propio. Identidad Pentecostal y trabajo—to demonstrate the hidden—and growing—force of a prophetic tendency in
Pentecostalism, a theme that shows a clear parallel to that of the
present book. His opinion, that around 20 percent of the Pentecostals are open to ideas of social change and share antiauthoritarian
attitudes, seduces him into predicting that this group may in the
future put its stamp on Chilean Pentecostalism (ibid., 33, 34). Con-
trarily, Lagos (1988), a Baptist lawyer and sociologist, who also
served as counselor for religious affairs in the Aylwin government,
concentrates on the political conservatism of Pentecostalism in his
attack on the legitimacy of those Chilean Pentecostals who, united
in the Consejo de Pastores (Council of Pastors; from now on Consejo), claimed to represent all Chilean Protestants in their adherence
to the Pinochet military coup and the subsequent regime. These
authors, then, can be considered making consciously political and
religious statements in their work; they are meaning-makers and
opinion-leaders who exert considerable influence in the religious
(Protestant-Pentecostal) world. This Pentecostal policymaking
theme will be treated more extensively in the following chapters,
particularly in Chapter 5.

From this introduction to the religious background and motives of the different writers on Chilean Pentecostalism we may conclude that all construct their vision of the phenomenon according to their own—Christian—idiosyncrasies. Sometimes, theological appraisals are made (Kessler, Sepúlveda, the Catholic authors), whereas others have their research questions and focus molded by their social and political preferences (Lalive d'Epinay, Canales et al., Lagos, Ossa, and Tennekes). Moreover, the Chilean researchers in particular are closely related to the Pentecostal movement itself, often having to make strategic decisions concerning its course. I consider it my task to "deconstruct" part of this Pentecostal meaning-making at the ideological (political) level and relate it to the indeterminacies and inconsistencies of Pentecostal believers at the congregational level. Both aspects—which I referred to in Chapter 2 as Pentecostal politics and habitus—are to be envisaged within the context of the twentieth-century history of Chile. This context, indispensable as it may be, is described relatively briefly in the first, more general overview of Chilean Pentecostalism I give, but given more weight toward the end of this chapter, where the roots of the main topic of this book, prophetic Pentecostalism, are looked at. In Chapter 4, which is more ethnographic, the contextual emphasis will remain prominent.

From Revival to Mass Movement: Pentecostal Growth 1909–1973

Although the events that marked the beginning of Pentecostalism in Chile are not the principal subject of this book, they certainly need to be discussed. Probably all eyewitnesses are now dead, and churches' archives are difficult to enter. Consequently, I did not take great pains to tell the story from the lips of its protagonists: In the following historical account few Pentecostals will be quoted. When I do quote them, it will appear that they themselves often resort to abstract generalizations and structuralist explanations. So in a sense, I deal more with Pentecostalism than with Pentecostals. This shortcoming—at least from a practice perspective—will become less noticeable toward the end of this chapter and in the following two.

The Pentecostal Takeoff

Chile's Pentecostal movement is generally interpreted as an autochthonous movement. Outbursts of Pentecostal "revival," or "revitalization," are reported to have occurred in several other parts of the world around the turn of the century (the United States, India, Europe). Chilean Protestant believers must have known of some of this "new spirit," at least toward the end of the first decade of this century (Orellana 1989, 21). Still, both foreign and national observers confirm the national origins of Chilean Pentecostalism. The Chilean theologian Sepúlveda (1991b, 6) considers the *pentecostalismo criollo* (indigenous Pentecostalism), as it is generally called within Chile, the first really national expression of Protestantism. To Hollenweger, the Pentecostal Methodist Church that took shape in September 1909 was even "the first theologically and financially independent Protestant church in the Third World" (1982, 176). The "heroic" details of the *avivamiento* (revival) that took place during the years preceding 1909 in the Methodist church at the port of Valparaíso—conducted by the U.S. minister, Willis Hoover, who had lived in Chile since 1889—and subsequently in the two main Methodist churches of Santiago, are vividly described in Hoover's own memoirs, which serve as the primary source for all later interpretations (Corporación 1977[3], Vergara 1962, Kessler 1967, Lalive d'Epinay 1969). Another detailed account of the first stage of Chile's Pentecostalism is provided by Zenteno (1990). In a special issue of *La Voz Pentecostal* (*The Pentecostal Voice*), the official periodical of the IMP, strong emphasis is put on the role of the two Santiago congregations in the constitutional phase of the new church. It is stressed that Hoover and his Valparaíso church only joined the IMP after it had been established in Santiago (1990, 19). This emphasis must be appreciated in light of the later church schism of 1932, when Hoover was forced to leave the IMP and established the IEP. Both churches, which are now by far the biggest two in Chile, claim to be the heirs of the pioneers.

In Hoover's account of the events (Corporación 1977), we come to know him as a strong promoter of the spiritual fervor practiced by the first Christian communities from the New Testament (the so-called baptism of the Holy Spirit, see I Corinthians 12 and 13) and as a defender of Chilean national ministries against foreign—North American—missionaries. Both issues met strong resistance within his own Methodist church, but it could easily have caused the same reaction in other historical Protestant churches (as in part it did in the Presbyterian church). For these churches were run predominantly by non-Chilean leaders and they served an audience that was for the most part of non-Chilean descent. Besides, they were Protestant in their religious practice: Complying with church doctrine was of central importance, and the worship went according to an established liturgy highly limiting the possibilities for the expression of religious experience as an important act of faith. It was against this "cold" and formal practice of what had become of Methodism that people started to revolt. Methodism's spiritualist past became a constant term of reference in this search for spiritual—Pentecostal—renewal (Hollenweger 1982).

As Hoover comments, in his personal report on the beginning of Pentecostal history in Chile, Pentecostalism was a movement that had started well before September 1909, which is generally celebrated as the real "takeoff" of Pentecostalism. Methodist Chileans in the Valparaíso church as early as 1902 appeared eager to reintroduce the spiritual practices of the early Christian churches in Europe into their Sunday school sessions (Corporación 1977, 25, 26). Methodist pastor Hoover and his wife had also received various messages about revival movements in other parts of the world during the years preceding the Chilean schism. Frequent and varied spiritual manifestations (tongues, dreams, visions, weeping, etc.) occurred in the respective two Methodist churches of Santiago and the one in Valparaíso during these same years, and these churches saw their regular numbers rise spectacularly (ibid., 41). These diverging religious practices resulted in a split in the membership of the two Santiago churches. When both Santiago churches in 1910 decided to form the Iglesia Metodista Pentecostal (IMP, Pentecostal Methodist Church), Hoover abandoned his ministry in the Iglesia Metodista Episcopal. In his letter of renunciation—after an unsuccessful attempt at reconciliation during the Annual Conference of February 1910—Hoover explicitly mentions his faithfulness to the principles of John Wesley, the founder of Methodism (ibid., 63, 66; see also Orellana 1989, 45, 46).[4] By that time, members of the Santiago and Valparaíso churches had already made visits to other parts of the country, especially in the south, in an attempt to push the movement forward. Apparently, these same Chilean people asked Hoover to stay with them.

For Kessler (1967, 288ff), Hollenweger (1982, 176–177) and Lalive d'Epinay (1969, 65, 66) the newly established church was a clear continuation of the Methodist mother church, at least as far as its organization. To all of them the movement was in the first place a spiritualist revival of Methodism carried out by national Chileans, despite the leading role of Willis Hoover as a North American and his explicit denial of any nationalistic motives for the separation (Corporación 1977, 66). Sepúlveda advances the same vision of Chile's national Pentecostal origin (1991b, 6; 1992b, 11, 14). He also maintains that the key conflict was cultural and not over doctrine. Because the first Pentecostals simply copied the Methodist articles of faith and were only pretending to return to the sources of Methodism, Sepúlveda postulates that Chilean Pentecostalism from the beginning singled out its specific experiential practice (hence cultural) as preeminent over doctrinal questions, in contrast with what generally happened in many North American brands of Pentecostalism. The Methodist annual conference of 1910 condemned the revival and Hoover, as its visible organizer, because the revivalist practices would be anti-Methodist, antibiblical, and *irrational* (my italics; Corporación 1977, 59). Here, we do not need to decide which of the two parties was more faithful to Methodist tradition. What is important, however, is that the Methodist revival meant a shift away from doctrinal correctness toward religious experience. To most authors on the subject, this was exactly what opened the way for massive conversion to Methodist Pentecostalism by lower-class Chileans, because the emphasis on experience is supposed to link well with "popular culture." For Sepúlveda (1992b, 14, 15) and others (e.g., Lalive d'Epinay 1969, 14; Canales et al. 1991, 23–26) this accounts for the establishment of an autochthonous Chilean brand of Pentecostalism, and it also explains the later expansion rate.

Although the birth of Chilean Pentecostalism still needs careful historical research, it is by far the best documented part of its history.[5] The period of more than twenty years from the start to the first big schism in 1932, for example, is either left almost untouched (Vergara 1962, 118; Lagos 1988; Sepúlveda 1987, 256ff; Sepúlveda 1992b, 39) or treated superficially by concentrating on growth figures (Lalive d'Epinay 1969, 15ff). For most authors, the big schism of 1932 is, as it were, the second highlight after the heroic start in 1909, the third focal point seemingly being the Pentecostal reaction to the military coup of 1973 and the subsequent developments. Since the present work does not aim to fill the historiographical gap but focuses on the most recent phase of Pentecostalism, I will make only brief mention of the intermediate years from 1909 to the 1960s. Some contextual remarks on the development of wider Chilean society will also be made, because Pentecostalism and Pentecostals obviously cannot be treated as if they evolved independently of the socioeconomic and political setting.

Socioeconomic and Political Context

> During the first decade of the new century, which brought great political, economic and social transformations along with scientific and technological progress, humanity—infatuated and tormented—was to experience the big changes of modern man. . . . But it was also during this decade that God in His great mercy started His work of changing the religious and Protestant map of Chile, because in 1909 the Pentecostal revival took place in our country. (Zenteno 1990, 9, 10)[6]

The above quotation, taken from the IMP's eightieth anniversary edition of its periodical, shows a clear sensitivity by Pentecostals to the close links between church history and the development of Chilean society in general, a connection conceptualized as a divine intervention in human history. The early expansion of Pentecostalism referred to in the previous text depended on unorganized evangelistic efforts, which often caused quite brutal reactions. This period of "heroic" evangelization, taking place in semi-clandestinity—because until 1925 Roman Catholicism was the only officially recognized religion—is depicted in this same publication (as in many others) as a kind of religious intervention in Chilean society, an effort to "win Chile-for-Christ." I will now briefly sketch the socioeconomic and religious characteristics of Chile during the Pentecostal takeoff in 1910 and the following five decades of steady growth.

When Pentecostalism started to spread through Chile from 1910 onward, urbanization and industrialization were already easily observable features. According to the CEPAL[7] (1972, 47), in 1920 28 percent of the population lived in cities of more than twenty thousand inhabitants, and 30 percent was employed in the (semi-)industrial sector. According to the same source, by 1950 the urbanization rate had risen to 40 percent, although the number of industrially employed Chileans stayed at the same level as in 1920. The national census even shows that in 1930 the total population was 53 percent urban, rising to more than 70 percent in the 1970s (Drake 1993, 89). Even if these figures, especially on industrialization, are taken as only indicative of socioeconomic trends, it appears that a huge gap exists between industrial employment and the urbanization rate. This gap is filled by a relatively strong and diversified middle class (public services and state apparatus) and an ever-growing share of un-, semi-, or informally employed people (Pinto 1974, 6, 16–17; Salman 1993, 143–144). These last groups predominantly inhabit the urban peripheries, the *poblaciones* (working-class neighborhoods).[8]

According to census figures Pentecostals are particularly numerous in the big cities' working-class neighborhoods. The Concepción region with its vast coal mine areas, is a stronghold of Pentecostalism. The 1970 census suggests that around 15 percent of the population was Pentecostal by then, and as much as 24 percent in 1988 (INE 1970; PRESOR et al., 26). The percentage of Pentecostals in Santiago is considerably lower, even lower than the national average, yet the exceptional size of Santiago is responsible for the fact that in absolute numbers most Pentecostals do reside there. Santiago's growth rhythm, however, is significantly above the national average (INE 1970). Somewhere between 1930 and 1940 the Pentecostal numerical growth became significant (see Sepúlveda 1987, 258; Lalive d'Epinay 1969, 22–23). The 1970 census shows that more than 6 percent of Chile's population was Protestant, and the latest census (1992) gives a percentage of around 13.2.[9] This growth can undoubtedly be attributed partly to the extraordinary evangelistic zeal of Pentecostals, who themselves consider church growth a direct spiritual blessing, as an "expression of God's will." Although the proselytizing drive of Pentecostals is certainly accepted by most social scientists as an important factor for the explanation of Pentecostal growth, observers tend to focus more on the extremely benevolent reception of the Pentecostal "message." A wide range of explanations for this ready acceptance of Pentecostalism, especially among the poorer social strata, has been given, practically all of which include a lengthy treatment of the social, economic, and political context in which this growth occurred. After a brief summary of the main arguments presented, I shall go deeper into the question of what kind of social objectives Pentecostals were advancing, or, in other words, what purposes they were aiming for through the expansion of the movement.

Practically all sociological explanations of Chilean Pentecostalism consider its growth to be a phenomenon intimately related to the transition from a traditional agrarian to an urban, industrial society. Willems (1967) and especially Lalive d'Epinay (1969) are the most sophisticated proponents of this argument. There can indeed be little doubt about the coincidence of an accelerating Pentecostal growth and the aggravating economic crisis Chile experienced in the late 1920s and 1930s. Chile's primary exports—copper, nitrates, and agricultural products—suffered rapidly declining demand after the 1929 worldwide economic crisis. As a highly export-oriented country, Chile was heavily affected by this crisis (Blakemore 1993, 83–84). The period following the economic crash of 1929 is characterized by a turn to production for domestic markets. The import substitution model of industrialization, which was also applied in several other Latin American countries, was introduced in Chile at that time (Pinto 1974, 10; Drake 1993, 89, 96). This industrialization process, in combination with the shrinking labor market in agriculture and mining, contributed to the increasing urbanization rate. The cities, and Santiago in the first place, had to face a massive influx of migrants from the most affected regions in the north and south. In fact, the urban population grew faster than both employment through industrialization and the expansion of the service sector, including the state bureaucracy. Job opportunities worsened, while the demand for work increased. A steadily increasing number of Chileans faced impoverishment in the suburban neighborhoods.

Lalive d'Epinay, like Willems, views the "collapse" of the traditional (rural) ruling classes and the massive migration to the cities by the rural proletariat as the principal reason for the expansion of Pentecostalism, because the latter provides an alternative set of values as well as practical and economic tools for coping with their situation, for all those who suffered the consequences of migration and impoverishment. The new situation of migrants in the city is characterized as one of anomie, or lack of life-orienting values (1969, 15, 32). For Lalive d'Epinay, this moral crisis is closely related to the crisis in the traditional hacienda system. The argument is, then, that the Pentecostal community and its pastor replace the traditional agrarian hacienda "community" with the *hacendado* (a hacienda owner) as the main provider of norms and authority (ibid., 33). This historical simultaneousness of the hacienda breakdown and the Pentecostal takeoff is, however, seriously questioned by the Chilean historian Salazar (1986, 1–2). He argues that the hacienda system had already lost its significance toward the end of the nineteenth century.

Tennekes also proposes drawing attention away from the supposed anomic situation of possible converts; he focuses on the effective problem-solving qualities of Pentecostalism and the Pentecostal community (1985, 77). According to Tennekes, Pentecostalism, like "popular Catholicism," concentrates on the solution of people's daily problems, although in a much more encompassing way than its Catholic rival. Sepúlveda (1989, 84, 85) and Canales et al. (1991, 75–80) also severely criticize the usefulness of the concept of anomie. According to these authors, what the increasing urban impoverished masses had to cope with was not so much the absence of norms as the lack of normative standards that could really be met. The modern society that gradually started to take shape from the beginning of this century onward stressed new values—especially the accumulation of material goods—which many people with a deteriorating socioeconomic situation were incapable of living up to. Failure,[10] then, became an increasingly widespread feeling. The capacity to provide an adequate and twofold answer to this crisis of meaning, is held responsible—at least during the initial phase—for the success of the Pentecostal message and its messengers (Sepúlveda 1992a, 85). The double answer to the experienced meaninglessness Pentecostals proclaimed consisted of a confirmation of this feeling and the subsequent replacement of the common cultural answers to it by a concrete offer of salvation. This offer was both material and spiritual: It gave new prospects to life, on earth as well as in heaven (Canales et al. 1991, 79).

Because of the emphasis on meaning Canales et al. and Sepúlveda stand for, their view is in fact nothing but an alternative anomie approach. Yet I think it is an approach that is more useful for research, because there is certainly an important shift of focus. The anomie concept of Lalive d'Epinay and Willems mainly serves to explain Pentecostal growth at the societal level: What are the consequences of massive conversion to Pentecostalism for the surrounding society? It is a generalization, which largely neglects the Pentecostal actors themselves. The "alternative" anomie approach brings in the subject; consequently there is much more room for variation and shade. Like their predecessors, however, Canales et al. and Sepúlveda think Pentecostalism constituted a meaningful offer to people who lived a particularly anomic life. Let us take a look at how this new meaningful religion took shape in twentieth-century Chile.

The accounts of the revival in the Methodist church, which started in Valparaíso but quickly spread to Santiago and other places, show that many practices of a strongly emotional character found expression at the regular church services and the special prayer sessions and night watch services that became increasingly popular (Corporación 1977; Kessler 1967). The practices observed consisted of visions, dancing, weeping, laughing, shouting, gesticulating, speaking in strange languages, prophesying, and also cases of spiritual healing. These manifestations were interpreted as signs of spiritual renewal, as "gifts of the Holy Spirit" very similar to those that are reported in the second chapter of Acts of the Apostles. According to Reverend Hoover's autobiography, it all started in 1902 during a course for Sunday school teachers. On one occasion, Hoover writes, one of the "brothers" asked him "what is stopping us from becoming a church like the primitive church?"[11] Hoover then says he answered that there was "no other obstacle than the one within us" (Corporación 1977, 26). Hoover's testimony makes it evident that from then on the search for revival was a constant preoccupation, which in 1909–1910 culminated in a series of tumultuous services. An ever-bigger number of the Methodist brothers and sisters reacted with enthusiasm and started to take part in the manifestations, both in Valparaíso and in the two Santiago congregations. The initial revival and the beginning of the spread of Pentecostalism are described in detail by Hoover as well as in Zenteno's triumphant history of the movement.[12]

Obviously, the emotional upheaval in the Methodist churches did not go unnoticed in the neighborhoods, the inhabitants of which began attending the services, which caused a considerable growth of the congregations. On the other hand, the phenomenon stirred commotion in the church's neighborhood, and also among the Methodist church leaders (except Hoover; Kessler 1967, 122, 123). The supposedly "irrational" behavior of the dissidents was strongly repudiated by the majority of the church representatives—under strong pressure by the North American bishop and some of the pastors near him—and the "Chilean rebels" saw themselves as forced to leave the Methodist church (Vergara 1962, 115). The conflict, then, gave birth to what in 1929 was officially registered as the Iglesia Metodista Pentecostal de Chile.[13] Until 1925, when in the new constitution the separation of church and state became established, the expansion of the movement met strong resistance and

overt hostility. Nevertheless, the strong evangelistic zeal—the principal method being street campaigning—emanated to many church
annexes, which were established all over the country, especially in
the south (Zenteno 1990, 24, 25). All sources agree that no foreign
missionary intervention (or financial support) was involved in this
whole process, which is seen by some as the principal reason for
Pentecostalism's success (Vergara 1962, 117). Within the Pentecostal
communities, faith and all action emanating from it became all-
pervasive; daily church services, prayer sessions at home, and ex-
hausting evangelization efforts left no time for anything else besides
work. This self-imposed isolation from the mundane world, in combination with strong militancy, meant that public opinion regarded
Pentecostals as eccentrics and seduced Lalive d'Epinay into labeling
them as people who had withdrawn into their own "haven" (hence
the title of his book *Haven of the Masses*). It is this strong concern
for its own religious community and personal salvation that is at
the core of the traditional Pentecostal meaning-making. Within this
tradition, pastors were (and still are) not required to have a solid
theological background but to possess a convincing spiritual testimony and calling, in combination with a flourishing congregation
of believers that was growing and evidently manifesting spiritual
qualities. In such a context, charismatic leadership was quite common and practically all of the numerous Pentecostal churches have
their outstanding heroes. These same leaders are the protagonists
of a long series of church conflicts, often resulting in division and
separations, the principal one being the 1932 conflict within the IMP.

The picture we get of this conflict largely depends on the sources
consulted. Visions of the 1932 schism, for example, are often diametrically opposed. Kessler portrays Hoover as an autocratic leader
who held on to power far too long, although undoubtedly motivated by a sincere concern for the well-being of his church (Kessler
1967, 307). Those who came after Hoover, however, are characterized as ambitious and longing for power; the leader of them was
Manuel Umaña (ibid., 305). In IMP official history, the latter has
practically replaced Hoover as the "founding father" within the IMP
(Zenteno 1990, 27, 37). The opposite has happened in the church
history depicted by the IEP (Corporación 1977). There, the name of
Umaña only appears on the list of ordained pastors and his—
prominent—part during the first twenty years is not mentioned
at all. Umaña is not even chastised for being power hungry or

schismatic; he is effectively erased from the church books. The fact that Hoover's moral conduct was questioned (he was accused of having practiced homosexuality) is strongly emphasized in the IMP church history, and the subsequent division is interpreted as the result of the Devil's constant and pernicious divisionist efforts. Reference is then made to the first epistle of John, chapter 2, verse 19: "They went out from us, but they were not of us; for if they had been of us, they would have continued with us; but they went out, that it might be plain that they all are not of us" (Zenteno 1990, 26).[14] Painful as it may have been for some, the schism in 1932 stood at the beginning of a decade of rapid increase in the growth rhythm of Pentecostalism, which according to Tennekes could be considered to follow a "cell division" model (1985, 21); the schism just described is a good example of this process. In an attempt at self-criticism during the writing of the history of his own IMP church, Orellana identifies three structural "weaknesses": the lack of theological formation of the church leadership, the limited preoccupation with church administration, and the neglect of maintaining a united movement (1989, 74–75). Yet, the quantitative success that followed the crisis apparently confirmed those who had engaged in the conflict in their conviction of having acted justly. Following the separation of church and state, and the official registration of the IMP in 1929, evangelization became ever more open. It is during the decade of the 1930s that street campaigning was developed as the principal method of enlarging the church (Zenteno 1990, 28–29). It is common practice, even today, to spend Sunday afternoon at outdoor preaching, either in the wider surroundings of the church or in more remote locations. Near the hour of the principal late afternoon service the "brethren" used to perform a parade-like march into their churches, loudly singing and bringing the newly won converts to the "community of believers." Obviously, not all of those who are received in the churches after these conversion rallies effectively become church members. There are, however, no figures available on the effectiveness of the church evangelization efforts, yet the steady growth rhythm from 1930 onward shows that this method yielded clear results.

Growth is the key word in all the publications made by individual churches and church leaders (Corporación 1977; Zenteno 1990). Reading the pastors' biographies in the IEP's own church history documents, one is left with the impression of a movement, the progress of which cannot be stopped (Corporación 1977). The prophecy of a "Chile-for-Christ," that is attributed to the IMP leader Umaña (Zenteno 1990, 37), was certainly one most Chilean Pentecostal pastors have fostered and to some extent must still be fostering today.[15] Lalive d'Epinay also asserts that the principal difference between Pentecostals and their Protestant fellows concerns preaching in the street. For the former this is a regular practice, whereas the latter only consider it an occasional duty, the exertion of which is hardly ever observed (Lalive d'Epinay 1969, 59, 61).

Explaining the growth rates, then, was the most logical asset social scientists (and theologians) could choose. Above (and in Chapter 2) we have discussed several answers that have been given to the question of why this tremendous growth took place. Willems pointed at Pentecostalism's suitability for providing an ethic which facilitated the transition/adaptation to modern society and its exigencies. Lalive d'Epinay's anomie hypothesis rather pointed to the opposite function of Pentecostalism, providing a means of survival by copying older authority structures into the new (religious) setting. Tennekes focused on the practical meaning of Pentecostalism for solving daily problems. This notion of religious problem solving, so familiar to "popular Catholicism," was transformed in Pentecostalism: Conversion to a "new—spiritual—life" (Tennekes 1985, 84) turns the somewhat manipulatory practice of asking the saints for favors (in 'popular Catholicism') into a permanent and all-embracing practice that enables people to cope with their problems in much more encompassing ways. Canales et al. (1991) take this argument further and stress Pentecostalism's capacity to supply people with a new and meaningful identity.

Hence, most authors on the subject agree that Pentecostal growth is fastest during periods of manifest lack of answers to the experienced meaninglessness. Likewise, the presence of clear alternative possibilities of experiencing community should produce the opposite effect. Sepúlveda (1992a, 85) "proves" the value of this statement by pointing out the declining growth rhythm of Pentecostalism during the 1960s. In another publication (1991) this author labels the period between 1964 and 1973 as one of increasing opportunities for "social participation," especially by peasants and *pobladores* (neighborhood dwellers). Although since the 1930s the Chilean state had played an ever more directive role with regard to its subjects, and consensus and dialogue were key concepts (Salman 1993,

144–145),[16] sociopolitical development during the 1960s and early 1970s altered this situation considerably. More people became involved in politics, especially at the local level, where political antagonism also increased. Sepúlveda argues that Pentecostalism was affected by this process in two distinct ways: one tendency proved susceptible to a cautious opening of itself to social involvement while the majority of Pentecostal churches only strengthened their traditional standpoint (1991b, 15–16). We will see later that Sepúlveda—and others belonging to the former tendency—saw the new course that part of the Pentecostal movement took as a return to the very roots of Pentecostalism, as an attempt at reconciling the individual search for meaning with the urge for social and communal solidarity. That is also one of the reasons why Sepúlveda argues for focusing on the quality of Pentecostal growth, that is, what growth should be aiming at (1992a, 88). The whole effort to constitute a prophetic Pentecostalism can be considered an attempt to answer that question.

Pinochet and the Pentecostals

On September 11, 1973, the Chileans were confronted with a violent military coup d'état against the government of the socialist Allende. A long democratic tradition was broken, and for more than fifteen years Chile was to suffer under military rule. Much has been written on the background to this event—economic recession, political clientelism, foreign pressure, and so on—but one of the principal reasons was the increased aversion to the all-pervasive state influence and the consequences of an over-developed participatory democracy. Particularly during the second part of the Allende government, political polarization in Chile reached a climax. The economic elite, the middle classes, and the military felt increasingly threatened by what they experienced as rapidly spreading chaos. The result of this we now know. All this did not pass unnoticed by Pentecostals, as the following quotation shows. "The serious socioeconomic crises the nation went through during this decade [the seventies] caused a rapid growth of the [Pentecostal] Church all over the country, because it provided the only correct answer to solving man's problems: the Holy Gospel of our Lord Jesus Christ" (Zenteno 1990, 35). This observation, taken from the IMP's own church history, demonstrates that the leaders of the biggest Chilean

Pentecostal church were well aware of the relation between society and religion. In a following paragraph, the author of the text mentions the inauguration of the *catedral evangélico* in the presence of General Pinochet, thus implicitly presenting the military coup as the solution to the state of paralysis Allende's government had produced.[17] The period of economic transformation following the coup is characterized as one of prolonged crisis, which was, however, inevitable given the "chaos" that the Allende government had left behind (ibid., 34). The year 1980, when Pinochet's regime had its new constitution recognized in a plebiscite, is viewed as the beginning of a new phase of "modernity," which coincided with "substantial results of the Gospel in Chile" (ibid., 35).

From an altogether different point of view, Sepúlveda (1988, 242ff) also labels the beginning of the military government a watershed. First, he argues that the Pentecostal movement raised its growth rhythm (numerically) when compared with the Frei-Allende period. The 1970 census counted 6.18 percent Protestants in Chile; in 1992 this number was 13.2 percent. For Sepúlveda the slackening of Pentecostal growth during the 1960s was more than recompensed during the subsequent almost two decades of military rule. Democratic political participation and the struggle for progress at the grassroots level, which had offered themselves to increasing numbers of lower-class people during the Frei, and especially the Allende, government, disappeared as an alternative means for achieving social goals. Spiritual solutions to the increasing daily problems presented themselves anew under the military regime. People again took refuge in traditional Pentecostal churches, although not in search of new values and orientation, as Lalive d'Epinay (1969) would have it, but rather desperately seeking meaning in a situation of constantly worsening living conditions. The military scorn for politics and social organization in general, expressed in the abolition of political parties and lower-class organizations, linked up well with the manifest Pentecostal distrust of "worldly" solutions advocated by grassroots organizations. The Pentecostal tendency to teach a noninvolvement in secular forms of organization was aroused again, as will be shown in the next section.

On the other hand, the "social awakening" in some parts of the Pentecostal movement during the 1960s became more frequently expressed, although it should be noted that a large number of Pentecostals never became "converted" to social activism. Some churches, and notably the Iglesia Wesleyana, had preached a "social gospel" as part of the spiritual renewal as early as the 1930s (see Ossa 1989). This Wesleyan renewal was rooted in experiences in the coal mines of southern Chile, where trade unionism was strong, even among Pentecostals. The specific social changes in Chile during the Frei government, however, had an even bigger impact on Pentecostals. Participation in all kinds of grassroots organizations constituted a competitive attraction to the same people the Pentecostal churches were dedicating their evangelistic efforts toward. This meant that Pentecostal churches lost a substantial number of believers to secular organizations, although in some Pentecostal churches new voices, preaching social commitment, were heard. The appearance of aid agencies like ACE (see next section), and the corresponding foreign contacts, contributed to making these voices resound more loudly. Those Pentecostal churches that went in search of the compatibility of belief and social organization later combined this endeavor with active, prophetic, and anti-Pinochet stances. The rise of this prophetic Pentecostalism is the subject of a later section, which will be followed by a much more detailed section on the roots and subsequent development of the MIP, the Pentecostal church of which some congregations will be the focus of attention in the next chapter. I start, however, by introducing those Pentecostals who defended the traditional Pentecostal position of nonintervention in "worldly" matters by stressing their obedience to this same worldly authority, which was apparently in no way considered inconsistent.[18]

What is described in rather generalized terminology, was of course achieved by religious—Pentecostal—actors, who tried to make sense out of the radical sociopolitical changes occurring under the Pinochet regime. How religious meanings were used (and shaped) in the circumstances of that day is the most challenging question to be asked.

The Consejo de Pastores

Protestant—and Pentecostal—interdenominational organization has no strong tradition in Chile (as in many other parts of the world). Although it is quite common to speak of a Pentecostal movement, also by Pentecostals themselves, efforts at organization-building, or even regular contacts between churches, have been weak. The first substantial Protestant association was created in 1941 out of a prayer group by Methodists, Presbyterians, and Baptists: the CEC (Lalive d'Epinay 1969, 176), which for almost twenty years dedicated itself primarily to organizing evangelistic campaigns (Palma 1988, 29). During the 1960s internationally sponsored relief work (by the WCC among others), executed by the Ayuda Cristiana Evangélica (ACE, Protestant Aid, at first as a special department of the CEC), took the place of evangelization. Although ACE experienced a boom during the 1970s and early 1980s, the CEC itself fell into oblivion. Hardly any other efforts at Protestant organization—except some at the local level—were attempted during the period before the military coup (Sepúlveda 1987, 264, 289).

Several of the recent authors on Chile, however, perceive the development of two increasingly divergent tendencies within the Protestant world (Sepúlveda 1988, 243; Canales et al. 1991, 31), which were already pointed out occasionally by Lalive d'Epinay (1969, 222). Sepúlveda, himself a clear exponent of the ecumenical and social action approach, seeks the roots of this division in the social turmoil Chile experienced during the 1960s. The hopes and perspectives of democratization and socioeconomic progress that were awakened by Christian Democracy under Frei definitely also had some attraction to Pentecostals. Frei's program of organization of the working-class sectors dedicated much attention to their marginalization and lack of voice. In order to "uplift" the masses, the government created the *juntas de vecinos* (neighborhood councils), mothers' and youth clubs, and an extensive housing project (Angell 1993, 149, 150; Aylwin et al. 1985, 309). Membership of the respective neighborhood organizations, and also of the agricultural cooperatives that grew out of the government's land reform, rose spectacularly. Also, the membership of the traditional trade unions increased noticeably.[19]

Pentecostal churches and individual believers were affected by these developments. Most churches opted to strengthen their tendency to isolate themselves as much as possible from society, whereas other churches started to rethink their social function. The MIP example that is looked at later will show this process in more detail. Individual believers felt challenged by the new and growing opportunities for social and material improvement, but most of them were hesitant, because participation in the new organizations was as time-consuming as church life, and what seemed even more discouraging was that such involvement went against the negative worldview that had been preached in their churches of old. Still, the churches felt the pressure by some of their members to permit participation in social organizations; moreover, they saw public interest in street evangelization waning.

The military coup in 1973 only hastened the process of existing tendencies, as they are labeled by Sepúlveda (1987, 269ff). Two days before the coup, Catholics and Protestants held a public service together to ask that "God be with Chile." The military overthrow of September 11, 1973, was received with relief by most churches, including the Roman Catholic (Lagos 1988, 98, 99), although after a few weeks critical remarks started to be heard. This criticism soon became embodied in the Ecumenical Committee for Peace in Chile (Comité Pro-Paz), founded on October 6, 1973 (Lowden 1993, 192). The chief participants in this organization, besides Catholics, were mainly traditional Protestant denominations and a few Pentecostal ones (among them the MIP). The committee's tasks were to provide legal aid to people who were directly affected by the coup and to press for explanation of disappearances. The military regime saw these activities as increasingly threatening its legitimacy and finally forbade its operation. Subsequently, the archbishop created the Vicaría de la Solidaridad (Vicariate of Solidarity, from now on Vicaría), which continued the committee's activities, although henceforth protected by the church's immunity (ibid., 200, 201).

The majority of the Protestants, however, were taught in their churches more than ever to refrain from any social and political involvement. The growing political polarization of the preceding ten years was viewed by most of them as negative and was therefore rejected. From such a perspective, the military coup, which immediately banned all political activity, was causing effects that Protestants could not but welcome. Although this in fact meant a recognition of the coup, there were no major public statements on the issue before December 1974.[20] Then, at the occasion of the opening of the Pentecostal "cathedral" built by the IMP, General Pinochet was invited to assist at the opening service. As appears from non-published correspondence (Lagos 1988, 155), Pinochet promised to come on the condition of public recognition by the Protestant churches of his military regime. This "demand" was conceded two days before the service at another meeting, when the group of Protestant church leaders who were later to constitute the Consejo pronounced the following: "The military intervention by the Armed Forces in the historical process of our country was the answer of God to the prayers of all believers who consider Marxism to be the highest expression of the Satanic forces of darkness" (quoted in Sepúlveda 1988, 274).[21] This public statement of adherence to the military regime was apparently clear enough to induce Pinochet to personally assist at the opening of the Jotabeche cathedral by the IMP, on the occasion of which he expressed his gratitude toward "the Evangelical Church as a whole" and assured the congregation that in Chile "all churches are equally respectable" (Lagos 1988, 170; the author provides an extensive analysis of biblical references made on both sides—government and churches). This Protestant "success" in establishing a relationship with the authorities encouraged them to expand and institutionalize this contact. Hence, in June 1975 the Consejo was formally founded to provide "the solution to practical problems of its member churches at the social and legal level, for the purpose of which a dialogue—independent, open and fruitful—with the government of our nation is maintained" (from the newspaper *La Tercera*, October 8, 1977, in Vicaría 1978, anexo 11, doc. 3). The Consejo explicitly saw itself as the only representative of *the* Protestant church, which supposedly had one single voice and opinion (Lagos 1988, 187).[22]

What, then, made an important sector of the Chilean Pentecostal leadership decide to seek favor with the political (military) authorities? Several answers can be given to this question. Pentecostals, although very critical of the world they try to convert, are traditionally also authority-abiding. Expressing their loyalty to the authorities was especially attractive in this case, because the military had reversed the tendency of the previous governments to enlarge social participation in Chile by the previous governments. This tendency had negatively affected Pentecostal growth (as discussed previously); a return toward a situation of social stability, which the regime promised, must have been quite attractive, especially when the Protestants were finally promised some form of recognition and even concrete material benefits. In a situation in which relations between the regime and the Roman Catholic Church were tense, Pentecostal leaders—for the most part strongly anti-Catholic—must have felt this was their opportunity. The regime's benevolence toward the Protestants can be seen, then, as a signal to the Catholic Church that its religious monopoly was no longer unquestioned.

The Consejo's main activities during the first half of the period of Pinochet's rule were the Pentecostal Te Deums and the constant efforts to gain better legal status, and special benefits, for churches and pastors. Traditionally, the celebration of Chile's independence (1810) had also been publicly commemorated in a special religious service in the Roman Catholic cathedral in Santiago. Protestants had never taken part in this so-called Te Deum, except on the two occasions (1971 and 1972) when president Allende reshaped it into an ecumenical meeting. Under Pinochet the Consejo invented the Pentecostal Te Deum, which from 1975 onward competed with its Catholic rival. These services have been held uninterruptedly since then and continue to be held until the present day; they have been incorporated into the government's yearly Independence Day protocol. Year after year, the Consejo—usually from the mouth of pastor Francisco Anabalón or the IMP bishop (from 1985 onward) Javier Vásquez—expressed its unconditional support for the military regime in this public service, which was fully broadcast by the respective mass media. This last aspect is particularly appreciated by the IMP in the main building where the Te Deums are celebrated. The Te Deum, like the building of the huge temple (cathedral) in which it is held, is said to be the fulfilment of a specific prophecy by bishop Umaña:

> In this place we shall have a Cathedral having exits to all four streets boarding it. And here Thanksgiving (Independence Day) services will be held, as in the other Cathedral, and the president of the Republic will come with his Ministers and Ambassadors. The streets will be full with cars. (Zenteno 1990, 43, 45)

The same source describes in vivid detail the row of important people from state, diplomacy, army, and commerce who have attended in all the years the service has been held, thus swelling with pride that finally the country could witness the "extraordinary spiritual qualities of the Protestant services" (ibid., 44, 45). In a way these public appearances, then, can be seen as compensation for all those long years of discrimination and persecution, or in the words of Zenteno, "the country could see the truth; yes, the Protestant, mainly Pentecostal truth of the people leaving oblivion after 66 years of express denial by the authorities, but now entering a phase of recognition of the fact that it constitutes a significant part of the

Chilean population" (ibid., 46). In addition to the public "facelift" for Pentecostalism that the Consejo and the IMP aimed for during Pinochet's regime, they also tried to obtain new rights and additional material benefits. Concrete form was now finally given to the free access to medical care for church ministers already legally established under Frei, although the Consejo managed to have this privilege restricted to its own members. This was for a while a carefully cherished result, but when the whole medical sector was later handed over to private enterprise, the obtained prerogative disappeared again. Talks on improving the legal status of Protestant churches as compared with that of the Roman Catholic Church never brought concrete results, any more than did the efforts to gain entry into the field of religious education at the schools and colleges (Palma 1988, 142, 143).

The precise result of the Protestant collaboration with the regime is difficult to measure. Although the yearly Te Deums were obviously demonstrations of strong Pentecostal mobilizing power, and many people aspiring to attend the services had to be disappointed, it would be too hasty a conclusion to infer that the believers belonging to either of the approximately thirty churches of the Consejo were in the main supporters of the regime. Several sources indicate that Pentecostals show hardly any or no preference at all for authoritarian rule in general, or the Pinochet regime in particular (Tennekes 1985; Concepción 1988; Fontaine and Beyer 1991). What this case does show, is that Pentecostal leaders themselves are often quite authoritarian people, keen to play the role of representatives of their followers. In the case of the Consejo this can be easily demonstrated, but the same holds true for its opponents, whom we will pay attention to now.

A Prophetic Response

The Consejo's claim to representing the entire Protestant population of Chile was given much support in the regime-friendly media for obvious reasons. The image of a vast population of Protestants showing gratitude for the blessings of the military regime could not but be welcomed by Pinochet, whose relationship with the Catholic hierarchy was tense during almost the entire period of his presidency.[23] The present section aims to demonstrate that different, critical voices were also heard among Protestants/Pentecostals. This "critical" Protestant tendency (Lagos 1988, 25) has been labeled prophetic by others (Seibert 1989, 46; Sepúlveda 1991b, 22), because of its propensity to denounce the military regime's abuses in a way similar to the appearance of the prophets of the Old Testament. For someone like Sepúlveda such a critical-prophetic stance was in accordance with the growing awareness among the Chilean subordinated masses and their increasing opportunity to participate in social and political matters (ibid.).[24]

Although opposition to the legitimizing position the Consejo took has been present in Protestant circles from the beginning, it should not be forgotten that the differences and contrasts among the different Christian churches with respect to the sociopolitical situation on the eve of the military coup were not that big. As has been mentioned, there had been a massive meeting of Catholics, Protestants, Jews, and Orthodox believers right on September 9, to "pray for peace in Chile." On the Protestant side, representatives of both later opposing tendencies signed the summons to the event.

Yet soon after the coup the diverging expectations of the various participants became clear. While the sector that later became the Consejo welcomed the coup as an answer to prayer, those who opposed the coup started to get organized on their own. The result of these efforts was the AIECH and the Comité Pro-Paz. The first, the Asociación de Iglesias Evangélicas de Chile (Association of Evangelical Churches in Chile), was founded in November 1974 by several traditional Protestant and Pentecostal churches many of which had joined the CEC in order to "establish a mechanism facilitating mutual understanding, exchange, cooperation and the execution of united programs among the Protestant churches of Chile" (Lagos 1988, 183). Most of the churches belonging to this AIECH had a more or less ecumenical attitude, although it should also be noted that the majority of them had shared the strong ideological criticism toward the Allende government with those churches that after the coup came to defend the Pinochet regime in the Consejo (Seibert 1989, 47; Lagos 1988, 243).[25] During the AIECH's almost six years of existence, various public statements were made by this organism, the majority of which challenged the hegemonic position of the Consejo. Apparently, internal cohesion among these churches was scant; by 1980, the year of the plebiscite over the regime-dictated constitution, the AIECH disappeared as a result of internal power struggles and quarrels over its position toward the plebiscite (ibid., 54; Sepúlveda 1991b, 23).

Some of the AIECH members had been participating in the Comité Pro-Paz, an ecumenical organization including the Catholic Church, which started to work for the benefit of the victims of political persecution within a month of the coup. Although at first both Protestants and Catholics played a waiting game regarding the outcome of the military overthrow, as soon the manifestations of the repression became more clearly visible, part of the Protestant churches—headed by the "progressive" wing of the Lutherans and their leader Helmuth Frenz—started deliberations with Cardinal Silva Henríquez, which resulted in the establishment of the Comité Pro-Paz. This committee soon grew into a substantial institution with a staff of 200 in 1975 (Lowden 1993, 194), not least because of substantial funding by the WCC. One of the major concerns of the committee was to gain solid information on human rights violations that could be brought to court. On the other hand, the committee, which had started its work maintaining a low profile, increasingly made public addresses critical of the regime's abuses. Lowden meticulously describes the details of the growing tension between the committee and the military regime, which finally ended with the closure of the committee, which was, however, soon to reappear under the charge of the Roman Catholic Church. The committee's institutionalized successor, the Vicaría, became one of the strongest moral opponents of the regime during the rest of the military rule (ibid., 197–200).

The base for this strong social commitment was liberation theology, which, however, has been the subject of severe internal disagreement—particularly over its political overtones—ever since it was introduced. Liberation theology, the "option for the poor in their struggle for justice," had been gaining strength in Latin America, particularly since the Medellín bishops' conference of 1968, but its impact has been different in the respective countries of the continent. It seems that the Chilean Catholic Church was among the most progressive in this respect (Smith 1990), but there were different positions within the Chilean hierarchy, which is reflected in its successive public declarations, showing growing criticism toward the regime after a first statement that included recognition of the necessary role the armed forces had played in ending the threat of a Marxist dictatorship (Correa and Viera-Gallo n.d., 94–96).

The later public role played by Cardinals Silva Henríquez and Fresno should not be minimized, but the bulk of the Church "opposition work" was done in the parishes and through the Vicaría (see also Lowden 1993 and Salman 1993, 210–217). Although there were periodical conflicts between the hierarchy and the regime, they always kept on speaking terms.

It is difficult to grasp the weight of the Protestants within the two organizations—the Peace Committee and the Vicaría—in which liberation theology was strongly supported. Lutherans were clearly the most involved (and hence persecuted), and only a few Pentecostal churches participated, among them the MIP. Their degree of adherence and participation is, however, hardly documented, which may be because Protestant opposition to the regime, ecumenism, and social involvement took a course separate from the Catholic Church from 1975 onward, when several Protestant ecumenical agencies were established or reestablished (SEPADE, ACE, FASIC—Fundación de Ayuda Social de Iglesias Cristianas, Social Aid Foundation of the Christian Churches).[26] Protestant, and Pentecostal critical stands were more publicly heard during the 1980s, when from 1982 onward the Confraternidad Cristiana de Iglesias (CCI, Christian Fraternity of Churches) became the critical opponent of both the military regime and the Consejo.

In its first attempt to write its own history, the CCI locates itself as one of the last stops on the road to Protestant unity (CCI 1987a) and ecumenism. To raise a public and prophetic (ibid., 2) voice against the violation of human rights was considered one of the primary tasks of this interchurch council in 1982. This task was constantly performed during the period that started with the national protests against the regime from May 1983 onward (Ossa 1992). According to the 1982 declaration (CCI 1987a, 2), the formalization of the organization had no priority and was continually delayed. It was not until 1985 that the CCI became legally established by the ten participating churches, among which were several of the smaller Pentecostal denominations (Iglesia Pentecostal de Chile—IPCH, Pentecostal Church of Chile—Iglesia Wesleyana, MIP).[27]

As was the case with the Consejo, the rise of the CCI is closely related to the period of military dictatorship. Yet reference is also made to the diminishing effects on church growth of the socially turbulent years between 1964 and 1973 when social participation became increasingly normal. Whereas some churches turned to classic, isolationist religionism, the document states, others became supporters of the struggle for social change. Simultaneously, the winds of ecumenism were believed to be blowing more strongly (ibid., 4).[28] As its main result the 1987 document lists the CCI's public acceptance as an organization representing an important section of Protestantism, thus breaking the image of a homogeneous evangelical movement unconditionally supporting the military regime; second, it lists the achievement of great progress in involving its church members in the several dimensions of its work (ibid., 3). A wide variety of activities are said to have generated these results: demonstrations of solidarity with victims of repression, hunger strikes, support of social organizations, public statements on important issues, ecumenical celebrations, and cooperation with other churches and organizations in working groups. The same document points to the principal challenges—one could also translate them as "weaknesses"—for the near future: ecumenical activity among churches at the regional level and the improvement of communication between the leadership level and the "grass roots" of the churches.

The current president of the CCI confirms that the gap between leaders and church people among its member churches has still not been bridged.

> At the moment we are in the middle of bringing the CCI closer, through services, to its base which is the churches . . . although we may have been just a group of individuals, we made institutions take on their responsibility, for example to sign a letter to Pinochet in a period of strong repression. (Carlos, June 24, 1992)

His predecessor was of the same opinion when he declared the first priority of the CCI for the near future to be "spreading the spirit of ecumenism among the people at the base" (José, May 12, 1992). It is clear that the CCI always conceived of its role as a prophetic one, which must be taught to its member churches (although by now it is recognized that the time for prophets has passed since Chile returned to democracy). The fact that only a few people from the member churches have ever been really involved in CCI activities is explained as follows:

> I have always said that the prophets of the Bible do not represent the majority either; the prophetic element always consisted of only a few

people. . . . Moreover, to take up a prophetic role in the past [he means under the military regime] was difficult, given the fragile legal position of the [Protestant] churches. . . . It required some homogeneity of the church and a well-determined leadership to raise a prophetic voice and struggle for it. (Carlos, June 24, 1992)

When I confronted one of the prominent laymen of the MIP with this view and asked him about the inclination of common church members to speak out in public against the regime, he gave another interpretation of the limited participation in, and enthusiasm for, working on behalf of the CCI:

Of course [not all people can be prophets], but leaders do not always think the same as those at the base. This is a big truth and it worries me. I am not against ecumenism, but I have my own thoughts about it. There are many things that should be changed [in the practice of ecumenism], but the professionals tend to overrule the people at the base, who are seldom consulted. (Juan, November 9, 1991)

The clearly problematic relations between the group of Protestant and Pentecostal leaders and those believers they say they represent is particularly noticeable when it concerns the defense of a discourse on the prophetic social and political role of the churches. This theme will be elaborated in more detail in the next section and especially in the following chapters. In the case of Pentecostals in particular, it proved difficult to bring about changes in religious experience and practice. The weight of the Pentecostal habitus—which regulated how and what meaning was made by believers—clearly counterbalanced, or retarded, the impact of the prophetic discourse that was propagated during the twenty-year period of the contextual changes Chilean society went through.

How, then, did this discourse of the prophetic tendency in Pentecostalism sound? I look at some examples of how the people leading the CCI expressed their prophetic message on the occasion of some specific actions. In the first public statement by the CCI (April 1984, in the middle of a raging economic crisis and people's uprising) it described its mission as one of "both announcement of God's Word, as well as profound concern for all problems affecting the quality of human life, be it individuals or groups of people" (Ossa 1992, 19). In the same document, the unjust character of the economic system and its consequences for the poor are denounced. Near the end of the declaration several detailed demands are made to the military, for example, the right of dissent, with a clear reference to the large-scale protests that were going on in those years (1983–1984) (ibid., 20). After this first publication, several other statements were issued, for example, when individual people (priests, e.g.) fell victim to oppression by the regime.

In 1985, the year of the official constitution of the CCI, the Chilean economy started to recover slowly from the crisis that had begun in 1982. The people's protests, which had defied the regime during the preceding years, now gradually lost their attraction (for the complex of reasons for this, see Salman 1993). Human rights violations became less noticeable, and for a while the earthquake of March 1985 received the full attention of the Protestant churches. The relief efforts were coordinated by an Interchurch Emergency Committee, which was sponsored by the WCC, and goods were distributed by the CCI.[29] It seems that this particular activity was the necessary final push for the establishment of the CCI officially in November, perhaps because three more churches made overtures to it after contacts had been established via the Emergence Committee (Ossa 1992, 26).

In an open letter (dated August 29, 1986) to Pinochet (CCI 1987b, 27), which was—after a public lecture during a church service—personally delivered by CCI leaders to the presidential palace, testimony is given of the situation of the poor among whom they claim their churches are working. The letter speaks of hunger, unemployment, undernourishment, disease, a deficient school system, and the consequent social diseases springing from them, such as prostitution, drug addiction, delinquency, and suicide. Contrary to what commonly happens in Pentecostal public preaching, the blame for all this misery is put not with man and his/her "wicked nature," but with the state (i.e., the military). This situation is said to be "against God's will." As a result of this deplorable situation people are desperately seeking relief, which they find refused to them through all regular channels, the letter goes on, and finally they turn to the churches, hoping to find solutions these churches are not primarily destined to provide, but which the state is denying them.

The church leaders continue to denounce the state's prohibition of its citizens, defending their rights, and they condemn the imposition of laws that "consider defenders of communal rights to be delinquents." On this instance, reference is made to the general protests of 1983–1984 and they quote the Old Testament prophet Isaiah when he exclaims,

Woe to those who decree iniquitous decrees, and the writers who keep writing oppression, to turn aside the needy from justice and to rob the poor of my people of their right, that widows may be their spoil, and that they may make the fatherless their prey! What will you do on the day of punishment? (Isaiah 10: 1–3)

This quotation is followed by a description of good state governance, based on the words of the same prophet,

Behold, a king will reign in righteousness, and princes will rule in justice. Each will be like a hiding place from the wind, a covert from the tempest, like streams of water in a dry place, like the shade of a great rock in a weary land. (Isaiah 32: 1–2)

The government then, is called to take this responsibility, perform its tasks properly, and pay honor to justice, because "the effect of righteousness will be peace, and the result of righteousness, quietness and trust for ever" (Isaiah 32: 17).

If no attention is paid to all these warnings, a spiral of violence is foreseen and the government is held responsible for the consequent bloodshed. For the subscribers to the letter, the only real solution and opportunity for the government to "avoid God's wrath," is

Opening the doors to full civil participation in the search for a consensus over the reconstruction of a land of brothers which, for the moment has stopped being such a land. In the name of God, giver and supporter of life, we [the pastors] proclaim the urgent necessity to reestablish a participatory, pluralist and democratic society, based on respect for human rights. (CCI 1987b, 4)

This strongly worded letter was written after a month of intensive church labor in "the campaign of prayer for peace and reconciliation in Chile," and in my opinion it gives a synthesized view of how the CCI saw its role in Chilean society during the Pinochet years. The CCI and its representatives occasionally, but explicitly, saw themselves as prophets who were calling for biblical justice. God is conceived by them as having a relationship with mankind, where mankind is clearly considered to comprise both the individual human being and the people as a group, as a community. It is to this belief in a God defending His people that the CCI is turning in its policies in general, as happens in the letter just referred to.

The question could be raised as to whether the theology hidden in the document I have just quoted played a role of any significance in the Pentecostal churches that were in the CCI. Most Pentecostals certainly interpret the message of social responsibility the letter radiates in a different manner than the church leaders were hoping for on this occasion. The common Pentecostal testimony contains an account of how a personal conversion to Jesus makes the new believer leave his/her state of misery and depression; responsibility, then, lies with the individual. If and how this typical Pentecostal experience is turned into or reconciled with a concern with the community surrounding the group of believers are questions we can only answer by studying in more detail one of the churches belonging to the CCI tendency. A first attempt is made, when in the next section of this chapter, I study the origin and development of the MIP. One congregation will be examined in greater detail in the next chapter, and I dedicate a separate chapter to this church's NGO SEPADE. The MIP can be considered one of the strongest pillars of the CCI, not least because it offered its staff know-how and international contacts through the SEPADE agency.

Contesting Classic Pentecostalism: The Emergence and Development of the Misión Iglesia Pentecostal (MIP)

The preceding sections have focused mainly on the institutional history of Protestant social and political involvement. Protestant and Pentecostal believers other than church leaders hardly appear. This will change from now on. I have argued that structural changes in Chile's social and political development since the 1960s created a context in which a particular segment of the Pentecostal movement developed an awareness of its social responsibility. The political emphasis on social participation by the lower classes between 1964 and 1973 had a noticeable impact on Pentecostals (see previous section entitled Socioeconomic and Political Context). Those Pentecostals and other Protestants who were attracted by the perspective of combining spiritual salvation with social action, and who had begun preaching what may be called a social gospel in their churches, were shocked by the military coup in 1973. Their dreams of a more egalitarian and participatory society, much in accordance with their spiritual and ecclesiastical practices, were broken. As was the case with the Chilean opposition in general, it took the critical Protestants several years to recover and establish an organized "resistance."

Classic Pentecostalism, that is to say its leaders, which had always fought social participation outside the church boundaries but had nevertheless been experiencing competition from social movements and growing political activity among those social classes that were also the target of its conversion efforts, were quick to take advantage of the new situation created by the regime. Because Pinochet's regime had big problems with the Catholic Church, traditional Pentecostals tended to view him as a natural ally ("the enemy of your enemy is your friend"). Moreover, this "friend" stirred hopes of ending the discrimination Pentecostals had been experiencing from the very first moment they started growing. In a way, then, the separation between different Pentecostal tendencies, which originated in the 1960s, became more marked after 1973. I will now turn to one particular member of the prophetic tendency to show in more detail how this process of cultural and religious change took place, but it will also become clear that the antagonism was not absolute. The story of the MIP, which I turn to now, will be followed up in the next chapter when I present some of its congregations, believers, and their respective religious and social positions and behavior. Thus, the case of prophetic Pentecostalism is narrowed down to the case of the MIP.

Origins and Main Characteristics

From its very start in 1952, MIP founders have emphasized that they never planned to establish a church of their own. In fact, the separation from the IEP is presented as circumstantial. The written testimony of one of the present MIP leaders, Narciso Sepúlveda, who was also involved in the incidents leading to the separation, relates the illegitimate procedures that were followed at the appointment of a new pastor in the principal IEP congregation (Palma 1988, 204). In a small document written for the occasion of the twenty-fifth anniversary of the MIP, the same Narciso Sepúlveda states that 120 people manifested their solidarity with thirty other church members who had been expelled because of their opposition to the applied procedure of appointment (SEPADE 1984). Several of the older still active MIP members told me that this schism took place amid a lot of tumult, which even stirred the attention of the local press.

The way MIP members tell their history suggests—quite stereo-typically—that there was no other option than to leave the mother church on that specific occasion, but that separation was never actively sought. Those who left had "only defended the proper application of church rules," as their view has it. In an interview in the same book in which Sepúlveda tells his story (Palma 1988, 199–218), the current superintendent of the IEP mother church presents the division as a tragic incident, but one that does not depart from the normal pattern of division that characterizes Pentecostalism, which is a struggle for power (Palma 1988, 28). It is, of course, difficult to know what actually happened: Both sides have interest in presenting their version as the true one. The reason why I mention these different visions of the start of the MIP is that it immediately reveals one of the principal issues of the new church.

From the beginning, the MIP has presented itself as an explicit antisectarian, "open-door" church, thus distinguishing itself from other Pentecostal churches, which are viewed as conservative and exclusive. The name the local MIP church buildings carry is always just "Evangelical Church" (*Iglesia Evangélica*), without additional indications, in order to "avoid misplaced self-esteem." This "symbolic construction of community" (Cohen 1985) with other Protestants can also be found in the MIP statutes on church and ecumenism (MIP 1977, 3). The theme of ecumenism, still rather rudimentary at the beginning, has gained weight over the years and is now one of the spearheads of the MIP's official discourse. It was, however, not only that relations with other churches changed profoundly, but almost every characteristic of traditional Pentecostalism, of which the IEP was a clear example, was radically transformed, at least on paper.

In general, Pentecostalism is often described as a lay people's religion, but in most churches the prominent role of the laity is not formally determined. The MIP has given a formal say in church administration to all its members, who can even be elected by the general assembly onto the church board, the highest executive organization the MIP recognizes (see the statutes, MIP 1977). Another peculiarity of this church is that women are given status equal to men at all levels, which means that women can be pastors as well. This "concession," made in 1963, created manifest tensions in the local congregations, which saw quite a few of its male members resent the decision, frequently resulting in their withdrawal as members (see also the next chapter for effects at the local level). In fact, the MIP has had only one female pastor during its forty-year history, and just one lay woman has been elected onto the church board.[30] Overcoming traditional gender roles is apparently not an easy job. My impression is, however, that MIP women play a role in church life that is more clearly visible than in other Pentecostal churches. Here, I refer not only to religious manifestations but, more precisely, to aspects of organization.

At the level of doctrine, two major shifts took place within the young MIP. The emphasis on studying was strong from the start, and studying meant not only the "traditional" Sunday schools and Bible studies but also learning and theology teaching; preparing oneself theologically was also strongly encouraged at the academic level. Together with the Pentecostal IPCH and other Protestant churches, in 1966 the MIP became involved in the establishment of the CTE, the first interchurch theology training center in Santiago, which now has several theologians among its members. The dissatisfaction with the knowledge and especially the understanding Pentecostals have of the Bible and of theological issues must have been manifest at the moment of the split from the IEP in 1952. Listen, for example, to one of the dissidents of that day mocking his former brothers, sisters, and pastors.

> Look, once a preacher called V. announced the Bible text of his sermon from the apostle James, and then he stood for two, three, four minutes, or maybe even more, trying to find the letter of the apostle James, and then J., the assistant-pastor had to find the text for him. . . . It really was a spectacle. Happily it was on a Tuesday, or Thursday, not on Sunday. . . . And what was even worse, they defended their ignorance by asserting that "the more ignorant you are, the more the Lord is able to use you as His instrument." (Francisco, May 14, 1992)

The dissatisfaction with the educational and theological level in the IEP church has been confirmed to me by several of the older church members who were present at the time of the separation. The shift toward more theologically reflective preaching and teaching has had profound effects on the MIP membership. Although there are noticeable differences among congregations, in general an appreciation has grown of a theological argument in the preaching. Consequently, the preaching has in some congregations become the main channel for teaching the brothers and sisters new elements and interpretations of the Bible (for the effect of this kind of preaching, see the sections on the church in the La Victoria neighborhood in the next chapter). In fact, many of the prophetic Pentecostal themes and issues were propagated through Sunday school classes, special training seminars, and incidental theological courses.

A final shift of attention in the MIP, away from classic Pentecostalism, was its growing concern for social responsibility and service. There are no clear references to these issues in MIP documents before the early 1960s, but in 1963 the biblical foundations of the social responsibility of the church were recorded in a document prepared for that year's national convention. In that document it is stated that

> The social responsibility of the church is fully justified in the attempt to establish the best conditions for this proclamation of the gospel. . . . These conditions not only comprise the freedom and right of proclamation, but also better social circumstances in the actual world in order to increase susceptibility to the gospel. On the other hand, the social action should also be the consequence of the new life of the believers, producing good fruits and maintaining a living faith which is translated into works. (Based on James 2: 14–20; MIP n.d., 73).

The social action that was to start first concentrated on education and basic needs. In the 1977 revision of the MIP statutes, following the 1963 intentions and practical outcomes, it states that "Centers of education and social service shall be created at the regional or national level, as a testimony to Christian care for the community, without any intention of proselytizing" (MIP 1977, 40). The MIP effectively started a school (in the southern Hualpencillo), and its social action commission started to collaborate with ACE but also installed permanent bodies of lay people in each congregation to assist the poor within their community (MIP n.d., 75).

The fact that the social theme became prominent during the 1960s can be explained as the MIP's reaction to the rapid social changes that were taking place as a result of the execution of the Christian-Democratic political program of participatory democracy (Sepúlveda 1987, 269). Some of the MIP leaders played an active role in this "social awakening." Víctor Pavez, one of the early church leaders, who also contributed to the document on social action, had been delegated to the WCC assembly in New Delhi in 1961, at which

occasion the MIP entered the WCC.[31] Pavez, the MIP president at that
time, was presented to me by several people as not particularly enthusiastic for the ecumenical cause, but willing to see if WCC membership could increase his power. The first contact with WCC
activities went through the previously quoted Francisco, who first
came into WCC circles during his stay in Uruguay, where he worked
as a missionary (for Francisco's role in the foundation of SEPADE,
see Chapter 5). Another pastor, Narciso Sepúlveda, also pressed for
WCC membership on the basis of his work in the ecumenical ACE
from 1960 onward (Palma 1988, 206). The social action theme, then,
took shape, at least within a small circle of MIP leaders, under the
influence of international, or internationally sponsored, ecumenical
organizations. From the early 1960s onward, these leaders spread
the social action message among their congregation members, where
it gradually obtained a foothold among some of the membership.
After the military coup of 1973, social commitment became institutionalized in separate institutions, first the Comisión Técnica Asesora (CTA, Technical Advisory Commission, 1975) and later SEPADE
(1978). With the increase of foreign aid, this last church body gradually gained more and more momentum and also became less dependent on the MIP itself. In Chapter 5 I will pay special attention to
this process, which had an important impact on the church as a
whole. Many church members participated in one or more of the
SEPADE projects (food aid, health, education) besides their regular
church attendance. The religious messages transmitted also focused
increasingly on themes like community, charity, sharing, politics,
and so on. The story of the introduction, elaboration, and transmis-
sion of these themes and the concrete actions pertaining to them
requires close attention, because it reveals the process of religious
change and the conscious politics promoting it; I shall look at this
subject in the next chapter(s). I now return to the origins of the
church, because I think that many of the previously mentioned
changes in Pentecostal doctrine and practice that the MIP brought
about had their roots in the period of rupture.

The 120 members who left the IEP in 1952 were dominated by
young, relatively well-educated people, who had often served as
Sunday school teachers. As one of the initial separatists declared,
"The pick of the bunch left: there was an ordained pastor, the head
of the Sunday School department, the head of the Youth Group,
several members of the church council, almost the complete body

of teachers and also some lay men who were running an annex of
the main church. . . . Their educational level was also above average"
(Francisco, May 14, 1992). Another witness of the early events
points to the theological skills of the people who left, compared
with the general practice of preaching which was, as he states,
guided by the biblical principle that reads as follows. "And when
they bring you before the synagogues and the rulers and the authorities, do not be anxious how or what you are to answer or what you
are to say; for the Holy Spirit will teach you in that very hour what
you ought to say" (Luke 12: 11–12). According to my interviewee,
most Pentecostal churches, including the IEP, applied this principle
to preaching and used it as a pretext for neglecting theological argument and exegesis. He assured me that most of those who left were
at variance with the common practice of preaching in the IEP.

Some other characteristics of the IEP that are presented by the MIP
separatists as motives for their discontent also appear in Kessler's
representation of the conflict. Kessler argues that the IEP developed
a relatively democratic system of church rule. The annual conference, at which all churches are represented, has the ultimate responsibility in most church matters. In that sense, the IEP differs from
the IMP, in which decisive power is given to the bishop. This leads
Kessler to the suggestion that the IEP is

> Governed autocratically within the local church, but democratically at
> higher levels. It has avoided the concentration of power right at the
> top . . . , but has given more power to the local pastor. The result is
> that the struggle for power has often been transferred to the churches
> themselves. (1967, 314)

The MIP separation seems to be a case in point. Although the official
MIP version speaks about the incorrect procedure that was followed
for a pastoral appointment, the witnesses I spoke with were also
prepared to admit that power struggles and frustrated expectations
did play a role. Kessler also mentions the desire to break with the
rule of noncooperation with other Christian bodies (ibid., 315), but
as is the case with many retrospective explanations, subsequent developments may have been mistakenly held as primary goals. Nevertheless, the relatively big changes in the traditional Pentecostal
doctrine and pattern of behavior that were made soon after the
schism suggest that there were—at least among the leaders—

adherents of ecumenism, interchurch relations, theological education, etcetera. On the other hand, the changes only became
substantial during the 1960s. It was then that the MIP moved into the
ecumenical world and became a member of the WCC (together with
a fellow Pentecostal church, the IPCH). The social commitment ma-
terialized when Church World Service and Lutheran World Relief
helped to start social work in Chile, which led to the foundation of
ACE; the MIP immediately began cooperating with it. In the field of
(theological) education, the MIP executive committee soon decided
to form a training school for its members, but theological preparation developed more widely when MIP members started to participate in the CTE theological programs.

Theology, ecumenism, and *social action* were the key words that
gradually came to be associated with the MIP. The previous paragraph suggests, however, that these three pillars were given a
stronger and more institutional foundation by the support of international agencies, which also brought the necessary resources to
sustain them. It is this interplay between the aspirations of (some
of) the MIP church members and the supply of material, training,
and financial means that created the kind of prophetic Pentecostalism the MIP represents.

Growth and Setbacks

In the 1977 document that is quoted from previously, reference
is also made to the evangelistic strategy employed by the MIP. It says
that from the beginning there was a decision not to aspire to church
growth at the expense of other churches, that is, other Protestant
churches. Expansion had to come from natural growth of the already existing churches and the establishment of new ones as a result of missionary work. Existing congregations belonging to other
Protestant churches could only apply for membership after a proba-
tional period, in order to provide assurance that they really shared
the so-called "Spirit of the Mission." As I was told by several of the
pastors, this specific politics of growth was explicitly to avoid the
common Pentecostal practice of proselytism, which went as far as
"stealing converts" from other Protestant, and even Pentecostal,
churches.[32] In fact, this meant that quantitative growth was never
the main purpose of the MIP. In retrospect, it is clear the MIP has
never been a numerically significant Pentecostal church during its

forty-year history. In 1954 its central church building was opened, and by 1963, there are reported to have been eighteen churches, forty groups and more than ten thousand members (Kessler 1967, 319).[33] Santiago was (and is) the stronghold of the MIP, although for a while the Southern Concepción and Los Angeles regions were also of importance.

The present president of the MIP tells a story of slow but steady growth until 1968, when a huge scandal concerning the president of that day caused a major split in the central MIP congregation. Rumors and accusations of homosexuality led to intense internal quarrels, legal fights, and church separation. By the time the church had recovered from this blow, Chile had experienced the military coup. The social consequences of this event made the MIP turn to a more active social policy and also a publicly critical stance toward the regime. According to church president Farfán, the church inescapably had to pay for its social commitment. In 1983, the biggest congregation—of around fourteen hundred people in *Curacautín*—broke away for fear of state repercussions as a result of the MIP's social activities and public appearances in the anti-Pinochet opposition. The decade of the 1980s showed a further decrease in numbers, which is also perceived by the church leaders as a consequence of public opposition to the regime. During the 1992 general assembly, chaired by La Victoria's pastor and MIP president Erasmo Farfán, the MIP's secretary reported that 1,927 people could be considered church members. Of those, 764 were full members, 432 were on probation, 731 were children. Additionally, 194 were categorized as "adherents" (irregular visitors). Although exact figures on the MIP's earlier numerical strength are lacking, the conclusion can be safely made that by now support for this branch of prophetic Pentecostalism has become progressively weaker. Not much has been done so far to reverse the tide. The MIP's evangelistic zeal gradually decreased as the emphasis on the social dimension of the gospel became more prominent. Church growth, which has never been the strongest side of the MIP, was no longer of much interest for most church leaders during the period of dictatorship. During the 1992 general assembly it was put on the agenda again, but not without hesitation. Most significantly, the special commission on evangelism and mission had not produced its annual report, for the simple reason that no action at all had been undertaken.

During the period when I conducted my fieldwork, the almost

two thousand MIP members were divided over seventeen congregations. Of these, seven were situated in Santiago (Colina, Lo Aranguiz, La Victoria, Ochagavía, José María Caro, San Gregorio, Lo Espejo); three were in the countryside south of Santiago (San Vicente de Tagua Tagua, La Vinilla, Pichidegua) and another seven could be found in the Concepción-Los Angeles region (Hualpencillo, Talcahuano, Los Angeles, Curacautín, Victoria, Antuco, Lonquimay).[34] The La Victoria and Ochagavía churches are considered to be the most advanced communities, whereas Colina and San Gregorio in Santiago, together with most of the others outside Santiago, are viewed as more traditional. This characterization of congregations seems to be more or less intuitively shared by most MIP members, although it is only explicitly given voice by some of the present church leaders (personal communication with Samuel Palma and Juan Sepúlveda). The next chapter will show in more detail what shape the prophetic character of the MIP took in a specific congregation, what people took part in it, and with what purpose. During my fieldwork I studied two congregations in particular, La Victoria and José María Caro. The former takes a central position in the following chapter, whereas the latter will only occasionally be referred to. The reason for this is that it was only in La Victoria that I managed to make an in-depth study of all facets of prophetic Pentecostalism.

Notes

1. David Martin's argument (1990) about Protestantism creating "free social space" seems to be an echo of Vergara's concern.
2. Its name is Diego de Medellín. This NGO concentrates on research and teaching theology and Bible courses for lay people from both Protestant and Catholic backgrounds. The spread of liberation theology ideas and practices is an explicit goal of the institution, which uses its own publishing department for this purpose. One of the MIP's leading figures works in the theology department, and there are close links with the MIP-governed NGO SEPADE. Foreign support (also from Dutch agencies) enables its existence.
3. Hoover started to write his historical account in 1926 (Kessler 1967, 114), apparently pressed to do so by believers he befriended. I use the 1977 version that appeared in a volume on the history of the Iglesia Evangélica Pentecostal (IEP, Evangelical Pentecostal Church). The small booklet by Hoover has greatly contributed to the view of him as the pioneer of Chile's

Pentecostalism, although the initiative for the search for revival most probably came from the Chilean church members.

4. Hoover's wife is reported to have played a decisive role in his decision to stay with the Chilean brothers and sister in revival (Corporación 1977, 377). Women's role in the spread of Pentecostalism is now slowly becoming recognized and studied (see Sepúlveda 1992b, 39–41). Orellana (1989) significantly dedicates his thesis on the start of Pentecostalism in Chile to women in Pentecostalism.

5. Vergara identifies one of principal issues at stake: Who was leading the movement in these first years, the people from Santiago or those of Valparaíso? Additionally, the involvement of Rev. Hoover and other pioneers is still a point of debate. It can be noted that much of this historical dispute can be attributed to power struggles among the early leaders. Although Hoover seems to have been the undisputed leader during the early years, he gradually acquired competitors, which finally created a situation that led to a breach of the movement into two parts in 1932. Both churches from then on took separate paths—the IMP and the IEP—and claim their version of the history of the movement to be the accurate one. It is an apologia that is endlessly repeated in Pentecostalism's subsequent history. The various interpretations of the past can be seen as so many efforts at meaning-making. Zenteno 1990 and Corporación 1977 both present a historical account of their own church beginning in 1909. Both churches, the IMP and the IEP, consider themselves to be the only legitimate bearers of the Pentecostal tradition.

6. All translations of Spanish texts are mine.

7. Comisión Económica para América Latina (Economic Commission for Latin America), a United Nations organization.

8. There is a wide range of other names for these urban working-class neighborhoods, like *campamentos* (encampments), *villas* (villages), *callampas* (mushrooms), which all have their specific connotations related to the historical period in which they took shape. *Poblaciones* (populations) is the most generally used term.

9. The 1992 census had only just appeared at the moment of writing of this chapter. That 13.2 percent of the Chileans consider themselves Protestant confirms the various estimations by authors writing on the subject; their estimates ranged from 12–16 percent (e.g., Sepúlveda 1987; Ossa 1991; Fontaine and Beyer 1991; Lagos 1988). The most recent (before the census came out) figures on Protestantism in the urban context are provided by a Centro de Estudios Públicos (cep, Center for Civil Studies) survey (Fontaine and Beyer 1991), which used a reliable sample and recognized research methods.

10. These feelings of shortcoming, failure, and shame are given a central place in the authors' characterization of "popular culture" and "popular

religion." Pentecostals use an appropriate language to express these feelings and promise a new life in which this misery ("the valley of tears") can be left behind (1991, 78–79).

11. This story shows a remarkable resemblance to what happened in the Bethel Bible College of Topeka, Kansas, United States of America, when in December 1900, a woman was reported to have received the Holy Spirit, which led her to speak in the Chinese language, after the question had been raised among a group of students about the significance of the second chapter of Acts. The "spiritual answer" to this question is often regarded as the beginning of Pentecostalism worldwide (Dayton 1987, 179).

12. The IMP history by Zenteno repeatedly uses the word *movement* (1990, 7), which, during the account, becomes a synonym for the particular IMP church. The Corporación document (1977) does not make this implicit equalization. In practice most Pentecostals seem to be vaguely aware of their belonging to a movement, although day-to-day reality shows tremendous fragmentation and competition. Priority for most Pentecostals certainly lies with their own community of believers, which is only in a much later instance associated with something like the Pentecostal movement as a whole.

13. In fact, this name had been in use from the beginning in 1910, except for the very first months, when it was called Iglesia Metodista Nacional.

14. The translation is from *The Holy Bible* (Revised Standard Version, Thomas Nelson and Sons Ltd., 1952).

15. For example, the church order of the Misión Evangélica Wesleyana Nacional (National Evangelical Wesleyan Mission, henceforth Iglesia Wesleyana), which is often included among the prophetic Pentecostals, prescribes that its believers collectively invoke God to help with the conversion of Chile ("Oh Lord, give us Chile-for-Christ within this generation"; see Misión Evangélica Wesleyana Nacional 1990).

16. Except for a brief period of military dictatorship, democracy reigned in Chile this century until 1973. Traditionally, there were three political tendencies with more or less equal strength: conservatives, socialists, and Christian-Democrats. Absolute majorities were scarce, so political compromises were always required. Political solutions were reached on the basis of numerous ad hoc coalitions.

17. At the inauguration itself (December 1974) the opening discourse read in the Jotabeche temple postulated: "Given the historical process of our country, the military coup was God's answer to the prayer of all believers who view Marxism as the zenith of the Satanic force of darkness" (quoted in Lagos 1988, 157).

18. "The Pentecostals don't *have* a social policy, they *are* a social policy!" This provocative affirmation (Gros 1987, 12) suggests that the very reasons for Pentecostal conversion and growth have to be sought in the

social circumstances of believers, something that is said to be better understood by anthropologists than by fellow Christians. That does not alter the
fact that there is considerable divergence in the social conduct Pentecostals
display.

19. For an exploration of the genesis of poblador activism during the
1964–1973 period, see, e.g., Salman 1993: 262–282.

20. At a lower level, that is between local church leaders and military
government officials, there were mutual declarations of respect and support
(Lagos 1988, 154).

21. Many more instances of adherence to the regime could be quoted
from interviews in the media, eyewitness reports of demonstrations—
among which are the Te Deums' television recordings—and official documents of the Consejo (Lagos 1988; Vicaría 1978). Even during the 1989 Te
Deum, just a few months before the presidential elections in which he was
defeated, Pinochet was said by the preaching pastor "to possess a special
place in our hearts," because of the "wise statesmanship" he demonstrated
by attending this [Te Deum] service (personal recording).

22. On the list provided by Lagos (Vicaría 1978, 47) the IEP and the IMP
are together by far the biggest Pentecostal churches in Chile. The Consejo's
claim to represent *all* Protestant churches in Chile is not so surprising, or
misleading, then, as its enemies often declare it to be, which does not mean
that it is a correct representation.

23. During the 1989 Te Deum, which was broadcast on television, the
bishop of the IMP in a gross exaggeration still boasted that four and a half
million Protestants supported Pinochet's regime (personal recording). The
presidential elections in December of the same year proved that reality was
different.

24. Smith (1982) used the same term *prophetic* with respect to the speaking out of the Catholic hierarchy in defense of human rights and later the
development model applied by the military regime. According to Lehmann,
the word *prophetic* has become common currency in Latin America to indicate this kind of religious protest. He particularly refers to Catholic base
communities—*CEBs*—in this respect (1990, 111).

25. This last characteristic is an example of the widespread feeling of
political ambiguity shared by many Chileans and Chilean organizations in
1973. The social and political climate at that time must have been one near
to resignation, which caused people to accept the coup, hoping that it
would be a short interlude before reestablishing democracy. Such different
social actors as the Roman Catholic Church and the Christian Democratic
Party shared the initial acceptance of the military overturn, which was only
gradually replaced by a more critical spirit (de Kievid 1993; Lagos 1988).

26. Lowden's article (1993) is the first major effort in this direction after
Lagos's book, which concentrates mainly on the legitimating discourse of

the Consejo and much less on its Protestant counterparts. Recently, a history of the Vicaría (Pastor et al. 1993) appeared, which pays only brief attention to Protestant involvement. The history of the CCI is still in process. I consulted a first draft (Ossa 1992), which treats the period prior to its formal establishment only superficially.

27. Parallel to the constitution of the CCI the Consejo Latinoamericano de Iglesias (CLAI, Latin American Council of Churches) was founded, which maintained close relations with the WCC in Geneva. The CCI members practically all joined the CLAI, although membership of the WCC remained limited to the Pentecostal IPCH and MIP, together with some traditional Protestant churches. MIP leaders such as Sepúlveda played a crucial role in the corresponding networks. In 1992 the Comité de Coordinación Evangélica (CCE, Protestant Coordination Committee) started to operate, in which the CCI and the Consejo worked together—in spite of big ideological differences and confrontations in the past—with Baptists, Methodists, Anglicans, Presbyterians, the Salvation Army, and nonorganized Pentecostal churches, for the attainment of better legal status for Protestant churches. Up to now the committee has not dealt with any other issues than that which result from a practical interest shared by all participants.

28. The source of these remarks, the 1987 CCI document, appeared when Juan Sepúlveda (MIP) presided over the CCI. It can hardly be a coincidence that the given analysis is roughly the same as those that he provides in other publications (see, e.g., Sepúlveda 1991b).

29. In the constitution of this committee, Marta Palma played a decisive role. This former SEPADE cofounder, employee, and prominent member of the MIP had recently been appointed to the WCC staff bureau in Geneva. This appointment emphasized the importance of ecumenical "family ties," thus enlarging the importance of the relatively small MIP church.

30. In 1994 another woman—the wife of an already ordained pastor— was appointed as pastor.

31. The MIP and the IPCH, which became a WCC member on the same occasion, were the first Pentecostal churches ever to join this organization. According to several people I spoke with, Víctor Pavez and Enrique Chávez, who went for the IPCH, seem to have taken the decision to join the WCC practically on their own account (see also Palma 1988, 162).

32. "Stealing" converts from the Catholic Church is thought of as less harmful, although explicit anti-Catholic preaching is repudiated by the church board. At that level, ecumenism goes as far as considering it a possible role of the Pentecostal church mission to stimulate nonpracticing Catholics to return to their parish.

33. Yet these figures are not defended by the existing church leaders. It is not easy to obtain reliable figures for the complete period; the church archives are quite messy, and large periods are missing. In the *Handbook of*

Member Churches of the WCC (Van der Bent 1982), the MIP is reported to
have twenty thousand members, but this figure should also be accepted
with some reserve. The current president of the MIP does confirm that this
must be an exaggeration, although he states that during the 1960s there
were between thirty and forty member churches. A possible reason for the
overstatement of the MIP's membership could be that the Argentine
churches came to be taken into account as belonging to the MIP, when two
IEP congregations from southern Chile (1964, 1968) with extended trans-
Andean missionary work decided to join in with the smaller MIP.

  34. This MIP central building, called *Pedro Monnt*, was for some at stake
in the process of schism that followed the incident. When finally it was
rescued by the MIP, it was no longer used as the main church building. Later,
SEPADE used it as a store for the relief goods it distributed. A few years ago
a small annex of the Ochagavía congregation—now considered the central
congregation—started to function in the former central congregation,
Pedro Monnt.

4

Pentecostals in a Working-Class Neighborhood of Santiago: The MIP Congregation in La Victoria

La Victoria is a legendary place, both within and outside of Chile. The neighborhood, a relatively small and densely built up working-class area just to the south of the municipality (*comuna*) of Santiago, belonging to the municipality of Pedro Aguirre Cerda[1] is famous and notorious for its cohesiveness and combativeness but also for inaccessibility to, and even hostility toward, strangers (be they Chilean or foreigner). My plan, then, to study a Pentecostal church in that particular location met with surprise from more than a few people. This surprise was articulated with reference to scientific criteria ("why are you going to such an atypical, nonrepresentative, place?") or to the lack of safety for a Western anthropologist. The latter factor, La Victoria's reputation as a violent place, indeed scared me a bit at first, but after my first visit I forgot about the warnings, because the Pentecostal community I got to know was extremely hospitable and proved particularly interesting for my research. I soon grasped that if I were to study the details of Pentecostal politics anywhere, then it could best be done in this particular congregation.

The MIP temple in La Victoria is in a narrow, but paved, street, surrounded by private houses, and close to another Pentecostal church belonging to the IMP denomination (see later section on IMP). Most of the streets of the neighborhood, however, are unpaved and the houses of a very different size and quality (housing projects have never been implemented here). A rough survey of places of worship suggests that at least twenty-eight such places are known in the neighborhood, most of them Pentecostal (Galilea 1987, 83, 84).[2] To the visitor entering La Victoria, it is not the amount of temples that first attracts attention, but the omnipresent wall-paintings, representing heroic events, especially from the Allende past, as well as all kinds of messages to the visitor (slogans calling for peace can be found next to calls for armed struggle). It is obviously a poor neighborhood with high unemployment, where many people live on the proceeds of temporary jobs. The neighborhood is a stronghold of the Communist Party; propaganda slogans are painted everywhere. The neighborhood council (*junta de vecinos*) is under the total control of the Communists. This Communist dominance has been present from the early years of the settlement, although with a long interruption during the period of the military regime, when the council, and in fact the whole municipality, was brought under government control.

La Victoria since the Land Seizure in October 1957

The La Victoria neighborhood dates back to an organized land seizure (*toma*) in 1957. The invasion took place at the end of the Ibañez government (1952–1958), when the problem of the shortage of housing was for the first time presented as a state task (Chateau et al. 1987, 18).[3] However, the efforts of President Ibañez and his successors (Alessandri 1958, Frei 1964, Allende 1970) to improve the housing situation of the capital were limited, if measured against the ever-growing need for houses of the rapidly expanding migrant population of Santiago.[4] Self-reliance therefore became the dominant principle for all those who attempted to settle in the capital during the period between 1940 and 1970. This self-reliance varied from spontaneous squatting to organized land invasions (see Beijaard 1983, 100–109, 113–114). Beijaard suggests that violent state reactions to land seizure were normal, but they became less dramatic toward the end of the Ibañez period, when the housing problem was simply too pressing, and the political weight of the urban masses too great on the eve of the 1958 elections (ibid., 114).

The people who invaded the area that was later called La Victoria took advantage of the relatively permissive demeanor the authorities adopted at this stage. In his *Para una historia de los pobres de la ciudad* (*A History of the Poor of the City*, 1988) Vicente Espinoza, researcher at the Santiago NGO SUR, gives a detailed account of the events that led to the foundation of La Victoria. Espinoza describes how on October 30, 1957, at dawn, hundreds of families from a very precarious, overpopulated, and fire-afflicted settlement called Zanjón de la Aguada (on the fringe of the Santiago municipality) started to occupy the semiagrarian area of La Feria. To avoid alarming the police, they even wrapped up the wheels of the carts on which they had loaded their properties; after some days it became evident that around two thousand families had settled on the spot (Espinoza 1988, 252). The invaders immediately started a process of negotiation with the city authorities over their case for acquiring proper housing. After a short period of uncertainty and fear of evacuation, the land invaders were permitted to stay on the occupied terrain (ibid., 253–54). The squatter settlement was baptized La Victoria by the beginning of November 1957. Although the government could have legally evacuated the place, the intercession of the archbishop to the president induced the latter to tolerate the situation and even permit the church-affiliated Hogar de Cristo (Christ's home) to start a housing project on the site.[5] These negotiations went relatively fast and the result was unexpectedly positive for the invaders. The political pressure exerted by the Communists and Socialists proved particularly effective during the negotiation and construction process (with a focus on legal, medical, and architectural matters), but there was also great solidarity from other sectors, such as students, trade unions, and food-aid providing organizations like CARITAS (see also Lemuñir 1990, 14, 15).

Espinoza emphasizes that the *pobladores'* (working-class neighborhood dwellers) collective demands for sites on which to build their own houses created a strong group identity (1988, 260–261). The frequent use of the plural *we* by the people in their public statements, and the concern for the neighborhood as a whole instead of personal interest in "my house," are viewed by the author as so many indicators of group identity. For Espinoza, the La Victoria people proved that pobladores were more than an amorphous mass. He also takes pains to demonstrate how well organized and planned the land seizure actually was. The instantaneous organization of the neighborhood into several small ad hoc committees is considered by Espinoza to be another indication of the organizing capacities of pobladores, which until then had largely been denied by politicians,

trade union leaders, and social scientists.[6] In the subsequent twenty
years, the La Victoria success story became exemplary and it was
considered proof of the pobladores' increasing strength, combativeness, and organizing capabilities. The process of self-constructed
neighborhood building made the relatively small area famous (ibid.,
266). The thirtieth of October, the neighborhood's birthday, which
was always celebrated exuberantly, became a yearly manifestation of
pobladores' strength, in which outsiders, including social scientists,
leftist politicians, and (foreign) journalists, participated. La Victoria
is often mentioned when the probability of the occurrence of a social movement of pobladores is discussed.

In a recent thesis on this last subject, however, Salman shows himself to be fairly cautious with regard to the movement-like character
of pobladores' organization. He argues that a movement of pobladores was never very likely in Chile until the mid-seventies for several reasons; traditionally, Chileans had high expectations of
negotiating their demands (via the trade unions). Yet, as we have
seen in the preceding chapter, Chile's relatively rapid urbanization
had created a significant informal sector, in which people from the
ever-expanding slums worked for their living. They were practically
unorganized, compared with the industrial workers in their trade
unions (Salman 1993, 143–146, 350). Only for squatting purposes
was temporary organization built up. With the explosion of grassroots (subsistence) organizations in reaction to the deteriorating living conditions of the late 1970s and early 1980s, in which
pobladores came together to discuss and work on practical topics,
the idea of a social movement of pobladores became popular, especially among NGO workers and social scientists. Among the latter,
two divergent views on the probability of a pobladores' movement
can be roughly distinguished. This was a moot point in the sometimes heated debate between *movimentistas* (those who strongly believed in a social movement of pobladores) and *institucionalistas*
(who had severe doubts about the possibilities of such a movement).[7] The movimentistas saw the massive participation in the national protests during 1983 to 1985 by (especially the young)
pobladores as confirming the ideas they had already developed with
respect to the subsistence organizations that had been mushrooming
in the neighborhoods since the late 1970s. The institucionalistas saw
neither of the two events as bringing about any change in the so-
called inorganic state of the urban masses. They maintained that

real social and political change could only occur as the result of (democratic) state intervention; in that process the political parties had the essential role of brokers.

I refer to this debate because the two main events over which the argument was fought out—the national protests and the emergence of subsistence organizations—had a strong impact in the La Victoria neighborhood. The neighborhood organizations,[8] which were often Communist Party dominated, were particularly numerous, and the 1983–1985 protests regularly turned the neighborhood into a battlefield between youngsters and the military police. It became one of the places in Santiago where organized resistance to the military regime—including street battles, barricades, etcetera—was strongest (de Kievid 1993, 151). But it was also one of the places where repression was fiercest. Many inhabitants can tell stories of murder, torture, or disappearance. It was, for example, in La Victoria that a famous Catholic priest, Andrés Jarlán, was shot in a confrontation; he soon became a martyr.

The MIP congregation, and especially its youth, was actively involved in these protests, but that was far from the only way of demonstrating social commitment. Individual church members participated in neighborhood associations and subsistence activities; in addition, the church itself also started a communal kitchen (*olla común*). In the following sections I will try to make clear the role the MIP congregation and its individual members played in this social and political turmoil, how social participation affected church life and church ideology, and how different groups within the church reacted differently to the situation that presented itself. It will appear that widely differing perspectives on the church's position and functioning exist. Some features of the church's history must, however, be looked at first, because they are most revealing of the particular behavior of these Pentecostals during the Pinochet episode.

The Pentecostal Church of La Victoria

I turn my car to the left, from Avenida La Feria into the neighborhood. It is dark and pouring. The church must be in one of the sidestreets. I stop, wind down my window, and ask a passerby, "Where is the Pentecostal church?" He indicates that I take the second street to the right and look for a striking building on my left, close to the next sidestreet.

"It is the only real building in the vicinity," he adds. A little later I park my car in front of the Iglesia Pentecostal, as the nameplate above the front door reads. (Personal report of my first visit to La Victoria)

"He is the pastor of one of the most traditional and sorely tried neighborhoods of Santiago: La Victoria, and contact with its people have marked him profoundly." (From an interview with Erasmo Farfán in Equipo Evangelio y Sociedad 1990a, 6)

As I have mentioned, La Victoria is full of Pentecostal churches, yet on asking a passerby for the Pentecostal church, I arrived safely at the spot where the MIP held its regular services. When I later told the story to some church members, they could only confirm the stranger's opinion: Theirs was *the* Pentecostal church of La Victoria. How has this image taken root among church members? To answer this question, it is useful to shed some light on the historical bonds between church and neighborhood, and how the church later on understood its social and religious tasks with regard to the neighborhood, especially during the Pinochet years. This active social behavior within the neighborhood is precisely why I chose to make an in-depth study of this congregation; in my opinion in this church the clash between active cultural (Pentecostal) politics and the habitus-determined meaning-making by the majority of the believers can be most clearly demonstrated.

My First Church Service in La Victoria, Calle Los Comandos 4551

I enter the room, hesitating a little, but a friendly old man—whom I later come to know as brother Rafael—welcomes me and directs me to a free seat. I happen to arrive in the middle of a small two-day campaign. That I hear from the pastor, Erasmo Farfán, whom I had got to know as the director of SEPADE during one of my first visits to it, and who became MIP president in January 1992. I understand from what he tells me that this is the first campaign of the year. I am surprised, since my Peruvian experience had taught me that Pentecostals move from campaign to campaign to win new converts. But this pastor explains that his Misión Iglesia Pentecostal does not consider the act of campaigning of very much use. "Everybody knows where our church is; people have heard our message so often, we have other priorities than trying to expand by street preaching." I wonder what kind of a Pentecostal church I have landed in. When Farfán soon returns to his seat, he greets me and explains that others are in charge of the service; "thus, they learn," he explains, when he notices my puzzlement.

Erasmo's wife, Ana, is conducting the meeting. She has the people sing a series of hymns (I try to find them in the booklet I have). Several people recall an important event that has happened to them lately, or they witness to God's treatment of them. Suddenly, Ana invites me to present myself. I know what I am going to say, I have done it before (and will do it again). I explain my work as a Christian anthropologist, as someone who is interested in what people feel about their culture, their belief. I intend to inform Dutch Christians and anthropologists, I continue, about what it means to run a Pentecostal church in a Santiago neighborhood like La Victoria. I add that such knowledge is embarrassingly lacking, and that the experience of Pentecostal communality is most instructive to our Dutch churches as well as filling a serious gap in our knowledge of Pentecostalism. When I finish my presentation, I hear some people adding an approving "amen."

When I sit back, I realize that I am part of the program. After another hymn, a father and his two sons come to the front. They belong to the IMP, and I wonder what they are doing here. Later the father tells me that they play music on invitation everywhere "to encourage sad people who have problems." After their performance, Ana summarizes their message by stressing that "the freedom Christ brings is for everybody in our problem-afflicted neighborhood." Then we sing two more songs, put some coins on the collection plate and listen to Ana reading from Isaiah 53, the prophecy on man's redemption by God's son Jesus. This is at the same time the introduction to the sermon of the night, made by brother Juan, whom I later come to know much better. He starts with a spiritual "God is present here." He then says that he is particularly satisfied tonight, because it is the first time he is preaching during an evangelistic campaign. The text for his sermon is John 12: 31, 32, on the judgement of this world, and how to be lifted up from the earth with Jesus. I feel somewhat disappointed, as I had hoped for a more socially committed, liberationist theme. After all, I came to the MIP church in La Victoria to catch something different from the traditional Pentecostal message. I suggest to myself that maybe today is different, because this is a campaign with an evangelistic purpose. Juan impresses the following message upon his audience: "Someone has paid our debts. For the poor and those who lack self-esteem, we have good news. We have no debt any longer. We are free. We do not have to pay for our debts ourselves, but Jesus did. Whatever your problems, Jesus loves you this evening." This is what I later recall from his sermon, which actually took half an hour. Juan finished with the invitation to come to the front, to the altar, to be converted, to ask for healing, to renew one's covenant with God or to reaffirm one's conversion. Those who do not dare to come out may lift their hands. "We will pray for you," Juan assures. The reaction is disappointing, only a few elderly women move toward the platform. It is definitely not the climax of the evening. There are no new converts. We finish by singing a few more songs, after which the pastor says the final prayer of farewell.

After ample handshaking, I see a family home and drive to the pastor's house. A few other brothers and sisters have been invited; one of them will preach the following evening. The singing by the IMP guests is discussed; Erasmo observes that one of their songs was remarkable, because in it God was portrayed as He who lives in our fellow man. He found it a profound and accurate image, and one that goes against the message that is communicated in most rival Pentecostal churches. That observation I notice with pleasure. Erasmo's church apparently considers itself a deviant Pentecostal community. I feel satisfied when I drive home through the late evening.

After this first occasion, I paid more than forty other visits to the church, and I regularly visited church members in their homes. During the one year of my acquaintance with its inhabitants I learned much about the church's peculiarities, its exertions in the neighborhood, and the various intrachurch tendencies. It was only later that I understood the importance of some of my observations during this first visit, which in fact proved to be the only service with a clear evangelistic goal I ever witnessed in La Victoria; this feature continued to amaze me throughout my stay in Chile.

Although the MIP building in La Victoria is indeed the only Pentecostal church building with an appealing facade, as my guide had told me, it is not (any longer) the biggest church numerically speaking; others, notably the IMP church next door, clearly outnumber it. Yet the La Victoria congregation is still today one of the bigger churches of the MIP[9]; the reports of the 1992 general assembly give the following figures: 72 full members, 24 on probation, and 108 children.[10] Like most other MIP congregations, the La Victoria church is experiencing a noticeable decline in its membership, resulting in growing difficulty in performing its tasks and meeting its obligations.[11] In practice, it means that a relatively small number of active members are in charge of current church affairs. Church growth as a result of active evangelization—the common pattern in Pentecostal churches—is absent in La Victoria. In my opinion, the decline of the attractiveness of the church has a direct link to the policy of the leadership that followed the course shaped by the MIP's national executive committee. Both friends and enemies agreed on this point. In several of my interviews, MIP leaders stressed that they never abandoned the goal of church growth, but that they are well aware that their social, political, and religious choices have caused numerical stagnation or even a decline. For them, joining (and staying with) MIP Pentecostalism demanded the courage to break with religious tradition and speak out for a commitment that was certainly not a guarantee of smooth-running church life. The official MIP line—focusing on ecumenism, social action, and community—was given form at various times during the congregation's history, especially during the past twenty years; how this church line was explicitly taught I was able to witness directly during the services and Sunday school (see section entitled Production and Reproduction of Discourse during Sunday School and Services).[12]

Let me, however, start with the early years of the congregation. There are no written sources on the church's formative years, so I have to rely on the eyewitnesses I was able to track down. One of these was sister Helena who told me the following story:

> We held the first meeting in a place next door to the actual church. When these lands were seized, we, several brothers belonging to the *Pedro Monnt* church, also moved in. I would say that I am the only one left from those days. We came to take this land and when they finally started to partition the pieces of land, brother José Gamba asked for one for the church. . . . He went to the governors [of the neighborhood association] and asked a part for the church. In fact, we got together before he went, in order to pray that his request would be conceded. We knew that the land was to be inhabited and was not destined to build a church on. But when he went, they gave it to him. Only because God touched their hearts. And because he explained to them that we needed a place to worship, since we were all brothers from another church. José offered not only to hold Pentecostal services, but also to run a community center. (Helena, July 26, 1992)

Sister Helena and her fellow believers thus came to La Victoria with the land seizure, bringing with them the idea of establishing a church of their own. They already belonged to the MIP's central congregation of Pedro Monnt, but they saw the new settlement as a perfect place to build their own church. So church and neighborhood were closely linked to each other in the minds of these MIP pioneers. This commitment to the place only becomes more evident from Helena's account of the early period when the brothers and sisters worked on the location. She describes the desolate state of the area on which La Victoria was being built and the complete lack of any basic services. She confirms that the idea of running a community center was shared by all and born out of necessity. Children and elderly people were dying for lack of attention, she assured me. After they had established the "medical post," with primitive first aid equipment, they went to the MIP leaders to tell them that, with the place already in their possession, they were going to hold services and run a community center.

Whatever the impact of this center may have been in practice, it certainly showed an attitude of great commitment to the neighborhood. Helena told the story with some pride, emphasizing that the initiative was theirs and that the first "fruits" were the outcome of their—the brothers' and sisters'—own evangelistic efforts (she mentioned two families who have remained in the church until the present day). To Helena, these formative years were the most beautiful, because so many "wonderful" things happened, such as miraculous cases of healing (which were confirmed to me by other sisters). In those early years, the church was growing fast, and when the first pastor, Eliseo Palma, was appointed, he found an already prospering community. The present pastor of the congregation, Erasmo Farfán, started to visit La Victoria and the new MIP congregation only a few days after the land seizure, although he had never lived in the neighborhood (even after he became the congregation's pastor he never went to live there). He confirmed that there was no direct MIP involvement in the process of establishing a temple in La Victoria, but that the initiative, including the running of a community center, was entirely local. As Farfán himself related, he visited the neighborhood because he assisted Narciso Sepúlveda, one of the MIP founders and a prominent leader, who worked for the Protestant NGO ACE (see Chapter 3) in La Victoria. Farfán also told me that the first head of the congregation, before a pastor was assigned to it, was a man with leftist (Communist) political inclinations. Most probably he refers to the same brother Gamba whom sister Helena mentioned. Farfán praised the man's combination of religious and sociopolitical commitment. According to the pastor, it must have been this man who organized his MIP brothers and sisters during the land seizure but who was passed over when the congregation's first pastor was appointed.

The testimonies I have been using so far to reconstruct the early years of the La Victoria church history were made by women. Although it is certainly true that women outnumber men in Pentecostal churches in general, the MIP case—and La Victoria in particular—is something of a variant on the average pattern. In the early 1960s a first crisis in the young MIP church occurred, when it was decided that women were allowed to preach during the regular services. There were serious repercussions at the congregational level. Sister Helena relates the following.

> The division came, because at that time the sisters could not preach yet; only the men were allowed to do so. By then, there were many male members, there was no need to. . . . But at that time there were some Bible studies in the MIP which led to the conclusion that women could preach as well as men, as long as they had a really convincing testimony. That was the motive for the separation. They—the men— left to found another church, which is why we do not have the number of brothers we used to have. After that, the church continued growing, but never as it did in the beginning. Now we are getting old in this church. (Helena, July 26, 1992)

This last issue of women's participation in church life deserves special attention, because it demonstrates the toughness of gender images under Pentecostal rule. Since the MIP's treatment of the subject is part of its progressive image, I dedicate a special (the next) section to how this subject was dealt with in La Victoria.

Resuming the story of the early years of the La Victoria MIP congregation, there is a clear tendency among church members to present a close parallel between church and neighborhood. Pastor Erasmo Farfán and several leaders in the church council cherish this commitment to the neighborhood. Sister Helena's story of the first years in the neighborhood is, albeit somewhat romanticized, an illustration of the symbiosis of church and people (her view was shared by several of the older church members).[13] Local historian Lemuñir occasionally affirms the Protestant efforts at crucial moments in La Victoria's history (1990, 29, 45), but this commitment is relativized by a SEPADE employee who worked in La Victoria for several years and with the MIP congregation there in particular. For her, the MIP efforts in the neighborhood have been fairly ephemeral, compared with those that the pobladores themselves displayed. I find it hard to evaluate the precise contribution of the church to social and political neighborhood activities, and I even doubt whether such an evaluation would be at all useful. In the following sections I will simply describe what the efforts by the church consisted of, and in particular, how—that is, by which discourse—church members were encouraged to take part in them. Material proof of the social commitment of the church for the years before the military dictatorship is scant. As sister Helena states,

> At the beginning we had this community center, but then a medical post arrived in the neighborhood. People no longer had to come to the church. But there is one thing, this church is still today considered the neighborhood church. . . . We also had communal kitchens. You see, Brother Gamba was an active man, and there was much hunger in the beginning . . . but later the necessity ceased, only to reappear during the military regime, when Erasmo Farfán became our pastor. (Helena, July 27, 1992)

It seems, then, that much of the reputation for being a church devoted to the social well-being of the neighborhood goes back to the formative period of La Victoria. Afterward, individual church members participated in neighborhood organizations, but there were no further church-initiated activities until the mid-1970s, despite the fact that the MIP adopted its own social doctrine in the early 1960s (see Chapter 3). The Pinochet regime marked a turning point in the La Victoria MIP congregation in this respect. Its discourse as well as its practice with regard to social and political issues became much more pronounced, which, as I will show, also brought to light fundamental contradictions within the congregation. For this reason I concentrate on this particular period.

Different Opinions of the Believers: Pastor, Youth, Men, and Women

Opinions about the merits of the Allende presidency (1970–1973) differ widely according to class and political preference. At any rate, Allende's electoral support was strong in working-class neighborhoods. La Victoria must have been voting for him in large numbers (there are no exact figures, because the neighborhood is not a proper constituency). Lemuñir, in his chronicle of La Victoria, describes how on the day of Allende's *Unidad Popular* victory "everything was a big feast, people were embracing each other, and there were only a few houses in which feelings of joy and hope were absent" (1990, 18). Since Pentecostal pobladores did not behave very differently from their non-Pentecostal neighbors in the polling booths (Tennekes 1985, 51), the majority of the Pentecostal inhabitants of La Victoria must have been equally satisfied with the electoral outcome. This was certainly the case in the MIP church. Sister Susana, who is a member of the *junta de oficiales* (church council), told me the following:

> We [she means her own church] are convinced that the church has always been on the side of those who suffer, with the poor. . . . Jesus said 'blessed are the poor.' Here in Chile there are many interpretations; some say the poor in spirit, that is the humble, the meek, but Jesus also refers to the poor, the materially marginalized. We gave it that interpretation, and we have always done so. . . . Always, and that is why we have been Allende supporters, 90 percent of us were pro-Allende. Maybe the only one who was not, was the pastor. (Susana, March 25, 1992)

She then continues to describe the three years of Allende as a feast, just as Lemuñir does. The military coup that followed meant a huge disappointment, but also the motive for social action. By action we should not, however, understand an organized, political resistance at the neighborhood level. Repression by the Pinochet regime was hard; political parties were forbidden, as was any other type of mass meeting. Struggle meant rather the struggle for survival through participation in all kinds of subsistence organizations.[14] Lemuñir confirms that in 1975 several workshops were created in La Victoria (carpenters' workshops, small bakeries, shoe-repair shops) and also an unemployed fund (*bolsa de cesantes*; 1990, 23, 24). There were also soup kitchens (*ollas comunes*). Lemuñir, who has lived in La Victoria his entire life, characterizes the early years of military rule as a period dominated by feelings of powerlessness and fear. The shortage of work was extreme; young people had no work and they had no access to education. They were frustrated and had no safety valve for their discontent, because political organization was impossible. While terror reigned in the neighborhood, the former (political) leaders lost their jobs, grew old, were killed or intimidated, or simply got tired of the situation (ibid., 25). This is

exactly what Salman is referring to when he describes the common
male identity in the neighborhoods of Santiago. The attitude of
searching for political solutions to specific interests by delegating
them to parties and trade unions was an essential part of their habitus (1993, 295). Because this "political road" was blocked by the
regime, men lost their perspective on the future, which could only
with difficulty be replaced by a concern for ways of organizing daily
survival, for example, through subsistence organizations. These became the domain of women, whose habitus, says Salman, includes a
gender-specific direct responsibility for their families that makes
them less sensitive to prejudice of whatever kind against the means
of giving form to this responsibility (ibid., 315, 316). Women therefore had much less hesitation about subsistence groups, in which
they became heavily overrepresented (Razeto et al. 1990).

Salman's distinction of three more or less separate identities
among the Santiago pobladores during the Pinochet years (1993,
290ff) can also be made with respect to the La Victoria congregation. I therefore treat women, men, and young people separately.
This tripartition is also made by the MIP church itself. Women and
youth are viewed as belonging to a separate category and therefore
have their own committee (recorded in the church rules); men do
not have this privilege (yet), but nevertheless their (religious) conduct is believed to be different from both other categories. It is interesting to note that other Pentecostal churches sometimes share
the same classification, but in the La Victoria case the behavior of
the various groups largely coincides with how they are presented in
Salman's book: Women and youth showed more concern for neighborhood matters than men.

The La Victoria Sisters[15]

The La Victoria MIP church started its own subsistence organization, a *comedor popular*[16] (a communal kitchen, in which meals were
prepared for the children) in 1976. Church members had hardly ever
participated in non-church related groups of this kind before.

> In the same Pentecostal temple where the souls were fed, a tremendous
> gesture of solidarity took shape . . . a communal kitchen was started
> with an enormous cooking pan. It was 1976, and hunger was affecting
> people. A hundred mothers got together to prepare food for their little
> ones. (Equipo Evangelio y Sociedad 1990a, 6)

Pastor Farfán, whose quotation this is, strongly emphasizes the solidarity aspect of the communal cooking in the same way as some older church members do when they talk about the same olla practice during the first years of the church's existence. The pastor, as well as most of the women who participated in the kitchen, consider it to have been an act of solidarity beyond the confines of the proper Pentecostal community, a service to the La Victorian community, especially because there was close cooperation with the Catholic church and its priests. Farfán and the women who were involved indicate that the cooking was for all the children in the surrounding neighborhood, but it remained difficult for me to find out the real number of beneficiaries. I was told different stories on the magnitude of the phenomenon. Critics from outside the church pointed out the olla's limited scope to me, declaring that it was mainly church members and their families who benefited from it. Several of the active participants of that time emphasized that, to the contrary, the olla proved that the church was an integral part of the community. But within the church congregation itself the olla did not go uncontested either.

> It even produced a scandal causing several people to leave the church, mainly older people. They believed we were introducing sin into the church, that we were staining the temple by cooking in it. . . . They simply went to other churches, but we felt obliged to continue, although we lacked the means. We went to the market, begging for vegetables and other things. Sometimes people brought a potato, an onion. The temple was scorched completely by the smoke. Later we moved the olla to another place, which was a very poor location, until we could build a community center, in Galo González [a street], when SEPADE started to get better organized, with support from outside, from Holland and Germany. Only then could we paint the church again and use it for its proper purpose. I am mentioning all this to illustrate the difficulties we had in introducing the social dimension of the Gospel, the care for those who are in need, who suffer from hunger. (Erasmo Farfán, October 14, 1991)

As has already been said, women ran the olla. Although some of the older sisters were opposed to such activity within the church, their resistance was quite moderate. After all, the cooking fit well into the widely accepted female responsibility of taking care of the family. Moreover, because women far outnumbered men in the church after the male exodus in the 1960s, nobody besides the women could have performed the task of running the olla. It was also a task that could easily be considered to belong to the duties of the Women's Department. The same happened with the food distribution project (PROAL) and the purchase cooperative (CAP, Centro de Abastecimiento Popular), which SEPADE later delegated to the church women. The first project organized the communal buying of food products at lower prices by poor women's groups; the second consisted of the small-scale distribution of food products, combined with information on nutrition and eating habits. All of the activities within these projects required the acquisition of basic technical knowledge and organizational skills.

Women in La Victoria are dominant among the rank and file of the congregation, as in most other Pentecostal churches, but in contrast to the majority of these churches, in La Victoria they are also well represented in the church council and within the preachers' group. The role of women as preachers is not as questioned within the congregation as it is in other MIP congregations. One of the women I interviewed told me that during a specific period in the 1960s, the pastor was the only male person preaching. Nowadays the MIP La Victoria church takes more seriously the equal rights of men and women in both spiritual and material matters. What does this mean if we take into account how the connection between Pentecostalism and the position of women is viewed in the literature on the subject?

Most Pentecostal women I spoke with would probably agree with the theses by Brusco (1986b) and Butler Flora (1978) that Pentecostalism tends to mitigate the worst effects of *machismo*. In the view of these authors, women's conversion contains a strong element of strategic interest: the hope of transforming their husbands' conduct, especially with respect to family life. Sharing responsibility with regard to this last issue, then, would be the hope many women begin to cherish when they come into contact with a Pentecostal community. Changes in household relations as the result of complete families turning Pentecostal may certainly occur. Yet many of the MIP women I asked about it complained that the fundamental changes they expected to occur had not always taken place. The same holds for the organization of church life along gender lines. Just as Pentecostal women experience a higher esteem for their work within the household, they value the appreciation by male believers for their participation in church life. Yet when we take a closer look at the organization of Pentecostal church life with regard to gender, we see the same pattern as within the households: Women have specific, assigned roles, which generally put them in positions subordinate to men, although they may not always experience this as such.

Although in most Pentecostal churches men and women are considered equals in matters of salvation and grace, their participation in church management is by no means in accordance with that discourse. Women's authority in church matters is often solely derived from the so-called gifts of the (Holy) Spirit, such as the gifts of evangelism, prophecy, or healing. And although it is certainly true that the possession of such gifts provides substantial prestige within the community, which may even be the source of considerable power for women, formal positions are generally taken by men (for concrete examples see Cucchiari 1990 and also Kamsteeg 1991). The argument for this division of power is taken from certain Bible texts, usually from the Letters of the Apostle Paul (for example I Corinthians 14, I Timothy 2).

Thus, in practice, it has proven difficult to make substantial changes in prevailing gender relations. Procedures in the La Victoria congregation, which, together with those of *Ochagavía*, cause La Victoria to be considered by far the most "advanced" of all the MIP churches in this matter, only confirm the toughness of Pentecostal habitus and tradition. As in practically all Pentecostal churches, women in the La Victoria congregation have their own Women's Department (*Departamento de la mujer*), which has its own administration. Such women's groups (often called *grupo de mujeres*, or *Dorcas*) generally constitute the place where women meet separately from the men for a proper service of their own. Often, the presence and direction of the pastor or one of his male representatives is required, but in La Victoria, women are totally responsible for what goes on.[17] The tasks and activities of the Women's Department reveal the traditional gender division of labor in church. The principal task of the department is responsibility for a special female service (*culto de señoras*). Another duty is to visit fellow sisters whenever they have fallen ill or when flaws in their behavior are suspected. Visiting hospitals and evangelizing in prisons are among the traditional women's group tasks.

Additionally, the sisters perform a wide variety of activities that have no clear relation to the tasks of the department as mentioned

in the MIP church statutes (MIP 1977, 27), but which are all related
to service and support. For example, at any church meeting women
are asked to provide food and drink; the department is responsible
for the cleaning of the church building; when there are visitors, the
women are requested to come and take care of their physical well-
being (food, drink, shelter). At a more institutional level, it is the
Women's Department that is related to two SEPADE projects, PROAL
and CAP,[18] as it was also the women who were responsible for the
former olla. No men are involved in these projects.

Despite the continuation of much of the traditional gender division of church labor, there are some noticeable changes, which are
considered improvements by some but deterioration by others.
These changes concern preaching, teaching in Sunday school, and
church administration. Apart, obviously, from the preaching during
the weekly women's service on Monday, women in the La Victoria
church have a preponderant share in the principal sermonizing on
Sunday. The pastor makes a monthly rota of preachers, which includes practically all male adults but also a considerable number of
women. Because women largely outnumber men, the sermon is in
fact delivered more often by women than by men.[19] As with the
preaching, women also outnumber men in the teaching. Most of the
age groups on Sunday morning are headed by a woman; the group
of adult men was in fact the only exception to this rule.[20] Only in
the church council do women not have the upper hand (three out of
five lay members in 1992). Except for the formal positions, then,
women dominate the principal church activities, which is exceptional within Pentecostalism but in line with the fact that the majority of the membership is female. It is true that women are
disproportionately represented in the church council, but the mere
fact that they manage to get there is significant: In most Pentecostal
churches this is out of the question.

When considering women's roles and the discourse on women
that is prevalent in La Victoria, I think various factors influencing
both should be mentioned. The identity of women in the *poblaciones* is generally constituted by their role as mothers and guardians
of the family. If they do paid work—and the vast majority do—it is
preferably work that can be done at home or that at least does not
disrupt their family responsibilities. As Salman emphasizes (1993,
315), women's motives participating in neighborhood associations
are closely related to their family responsibilities. In Moser's terms,

women's productive and community-managing work is aimed at the survival of the family (Moser 1993, 27, 28).[21] Pentecostal habitus, although including men in family responsibility, is probably even strengthening this core identity of women. This is perhaps best expressed by the usual name of Pentecostal women's groups, *Dorcas*, which literally means "a woman who does good works and acts of charity" (Acts 9: 36).

In La Victoria I witnessed various attempts to broaden this woman-and-the-family horizon, notably in the youth group and in a course on the issue of the "Christian family" by the women's program of SEPADE. On one occasion, the youngsters held a discussion on machismo. The women in the youth group all rejected church rules with respect to their behavior. They felt these rules to be unfair treatment (e.g., the request not to wear long pants in church). In the meantime one of the men was constantly quoting notoriously misogynistic statements from a book. The man clearly meant to tease, but the constant repeating of the "woman-is-mother" theme noticeably annoyed the women and girls. They saw it as the essence of machismo, a lack of respect for what they felt to be their primordial calling, care of their families. The SEPADE course also aimed at discussing machismo in the church (the content of the course was in fact part of a hidden agenda; the official theme was Christian family life). Two women from the congregation had been instructed how to give the course, but they met with considerable resistance: Most of the elder women silently listened to what they were told, whereas the men took the opportunity to object, quoting some passages from the Apostle Paul to illuminate their position.

Although it should be stressed that discussing gender topics (the term *gender* itself was never used) can in itself be considered a novelty in Pentecostal churches, which demonstrates a relatively permissive climate in La Victoria, it was a combination of conscious feminist intervention (by the women from SEPADE) and the urge of the MIP's Department of Women to deepen the discussion on Christian family life. The firsthand integral SEPADE initiative, which was not unquestioned within the institute either—has wider importance. It can be seen as an attempt to introduce the feminist world of thought into the world of working-class neighborhood women. As Salman has observed (1993, 325ff), women had not been ready to accept this "new world. This holds even more for Pentecostal women, even within the La Victoria MIP congregation. The La

Victoria Women's Department assumed various tasks outside the
directly spiritual realm, especially in rendering services, but its principal duty was what the church rules call "unity in the maintenance
of spiritual life" (MIP 1977, 27). The same woman who defended the
church's option for the poor, and who had been closely involved in
several projects of social action herself, told me that

> Women are the guardians of spirituality, for example, during the sis-
> ters' service on Mondays; these are much more beautiful than those
> during the week . . . there is much more revival, we pray and pray for
> prolonged periods, and we cry before the Lord. That is much more
> beautiful. That is because among women there is more communion.
> On Sundays, it is totally different. On Monday, we may even witness
> manifestations of the [Holy] Spirit, with similar tumult as in other
> churches. During the prayers we experience the presence of the Lord.
> (Susana, March 25, 1992)

This testimony presents women as keepers of the Pentecostal charisma, which tends to disappear when in the course of time new
generations pass through the church. This tacit religious division of
labor, in which men bear responsibility for the organizational matters of the church whereas women guard the Pentecostal inheritance,
is expressed by the more informal religious leadership of women in
La Victoria. They predominate in the preaching and teaching,
whereas in matters of church rule, their role is less prominent.

The Absent Brothers

Adult men in the La Victoria church can easily be counted on two
hands, even if the pastor is included. There are several younger men
in the youth group, but theirs is another story (see Chapter 2). As I
mentioned earlier, two major episodes disrupted men's participation
in the congregation. When in the early 1960s the pastor, following
the recommendations of the national church board, admitted
women to the pulpit, a large share of the adult men left to join other
churches and even to constitute a new one. The second event to
produce difference of opinion was the growing social and political
commitment the MIP demonstrated, especially during the days of the
military regime. Resistance against political statements by the
church leadership, often directed from the SEPADE desks, was shared
by men and women, but women had participation in a subsistence

group as an alternative (the olla in particular), which in a sense still remained close to the "less harmful" work the Dorcas traditionally performed. As I explained previously, inclusion in this type of social work was not likely to be pursued by men. On the other hand, defending one's interest by political means—which was a central part in men's self-understanding in Chile, as I noted before— collides with the traditional Pentecostal distrust of all worldly affairs. As a result, many adult men in the La Victoria church simply disappeared from the church for many years, when under the leadership of its pastor the church was incited to take sides in neighborhood matters; they simply could not live with such a double identity. Yet, some individual men responded to the social and political teachings that were transmitted within the MIP circles. What some MIP leaders called raising a prophetic voice against social injustice, was in a way put into practice by several of its lay members. I want to treat the case of one of them extensively, since it is a well-documented one and most illustrative for all the dilemmas and contradictions that putting into practice one's social and political commitment involves for a Pentecostal.[22]

The Story of Juan

"When Colo Colo[23] scores a goal, I scream; because I feel like doing so and I just do it."

At the end of a lengthy interview I had with Juan, he made the above comparison between himself as a football supporter and as a Pentecostal believer. Very much like the real football supporter, the true believer is unable to control himself and contain his urge to express his feelings, Juan thinks. Pentecostal fervor is precisely what Juan thinks his Misión Iglesia Pentecostal, and particularly his La Victoria congregation, is missing. In the conversation preceding this final assessment, as well as in a previous interview, he tried to explain to me how it had come to this.

"I started in the church like most of us who are born into it. I went to Sunday school first, and later regularly attended the services. During one period I withdrew from the church, but I later returned, although to another church, in San Bernardo, the Iglesia del Señor (Church of the Lord). I was the leader of the youth group there, but after a while I returned to La Victoria. All that time I had been following biblical courses wherever I could, for I was not satisfied with merely attending the services. In La Victoria I soon became a preacher and teacher in the Sunday school, and I was even a teacher in the annex of Lo Espejo [an extremely poor municipality just to the South of La Victoria]."

At that time Juan was still very much a traditional Pentecostal, as he himself declares on looking back to this period. Now that he and his La Victoria church have gone through the turbulent years of struggle against the military regime, Juan tries to reconstruct how it was that he, out of a traditionalist conviction evolved into a socially committed person. As a member of the present church council, he feels responsible for the current decline of his church; he wants to evaluate what the efforts to replace traditional Pentecostalism by a much less spiritualist religious practice have meant for his church.

"My ideas of how to be a good Christian were purely spiritual; social work did not fit in. Slowly, through the use of the Sunday school textbooks, I learned, first as a pupil and then as a teacher, that the work of a Christian was not limited to the church alone, but went far beyond the walls of the temple. In fact, I understood that there the real work was to be done. But it was not easy, it took an effort to acquire this way of thinking. I had to learn a lot, ask a lot of questions until I finally was able to think otherwise and reach my own conclusions, which meant that I could let go of the traditional views on those people who are said to be of the world, that is, not of my kind. Very slowly I learned to consider them as my equals, although they had indeed not known Jesus, but for that very reason deserved that I mixed with them. Thus my inquisitiveness was born, and I tried to learn more about this through passionately throwing myself into the church Bible courses on Friday. Every Friday evening I was the first to arrive. In the neighborhood I began to take part in a housing committee (*comité sin casa*), of which I soon became the representative. I was the only evangélico among the participants; the rest were Catholics."

It seems that through his cooperation with non-Pentecostals in this neighborhood committee Juan learned practical ecumenism. He explicitly refers to conversations about this interconfessional collaboration in which he and his conversation partners reached the conclusion that they shared the belief in the same God, which enabled them to work together in the struggle for those who needed most. Juan presents his participation in a big land seizure in 1983 as a logical outcome of his growing consciousness (he did not possess a house of his own in La Victoria at that time). In the squatter settlement of Juan Francisco Fresno,[24] as the land seizure was called, Juan became part of the leadership, in which he closely collaborated with several priests who were also involved in the settlement's organization. In an interview with the SEPADE journal *Evangelio y Sociedad*, Juan relates the hardship thousands of families had to endure in their struggle to defend the land they had occupied. The discourse he uses is larded with biblical references which are commonly used in liberationist theologies. The search for "a place of one's own," which the Fresno inhabitants defended, Juan describes as very similar to the Old Testament exodus of the Israelites from Egypt. This liberation, he says, is a legitimate struggle against the oppressor. Describing how the daily tribulations in the encampment[25] (the Pinochet police laid siege to the place immediately) created tensions and even animosities among the people, he emphasizes how understandable this was, if one only thinks of the history of Israel: Like the Israelites of the Bible, the Fresno dwellers tended to forget that "in the end, it will be like reaching the promised land" (Equipo Evangelio y Sociedad 1985, 42).

The formidable task of running the Fresno encampment—numbering some ten thousand people—with only eight people meant that Juan was involved in many conflict situations that produced cracks and flaws in his Pentecostal identity. He realized that he was making concessions to traditional Pentecostal stances (as well as his encampment loyalty): "For me as a Christian leader it was not easy to understand that it is impossible to reach all goals without fighting for them" (ibid., 44). He then describes how he was reproached for his political conduct by Pentecostal pastors visiting the encampment to attend to their church members. He took much comfort from the practice of the Catholic priests who shared the humble life of the settlers. For "being an authentic Christian means participating in the daily activities of the common people, being in their organizations . . . , fighting for the demands of the people, because we are the people" (ibid., 45). "The Christian has to be where his brothers are, in order that they consider him an equal and free themselves of the idea that all Pentecostals are opposed to all the demands the people make" (ibid., 46). "Jesus said that the Kingdom of heaven is among us, and that the Kingdom of the Lord should start here . . . I want to hear them saying: This Pentecostal preaches, but he also puts into practice what he says when he speaks of a better world" (ibid.). Inspired by these words, Juan spent almost two years of hard work in the Fresno encampment. His commitment to the Fresno settlement ended in a personal tragedy. In 1985, Juan, who was president of the encampment at that time, almost got killed during a police reprisal against the neighborhood leadership. His wife was raped, his son beaten, and all of them were threatened with being killed. As a result of this and other threats Juan fled into exile in Argentina, only to return several years later.

Once when I had a conversation with Juan over his neighborhood activism, he started to reflect on what this experience had done to his Pentecostal identity. After emphasizing the positive aspects of the process, he mentioned the loss of identity as a result of the constant ecumenical intermingling. During the whole period in the Fresno encampment he had never felt at ease religiously, but it had taken him years to realize what caused this uneasiness. He had finally come to the conclusion that he had given up part of his religious practice out of respect for the convictions of others. He realized that such is the cost of ecumenism and asked himself if it would not have been better to stick to his own habits. He attributed this behavior—that is, giving in—to the feeling of inferiority many Pentecostals still have despite their apparently strong convictions. Undoubtedly, the long tradition of Pentecostals being disdained by the Catholic majority (see Chapter 3) was haunting him. Looking back and evaluating the advantages of becoming familiar with ecumenism, Juan has become increasingly critical. According to him, Pentecostalism has hardly benefited from this encounter with ecumenism, except in social matters. He even thinks that ecumenism strikes at the roots of Pentecostalism. Those churches that have been touched by the ecumenical world of thought—and he specially refers to his own Misión Iglesia Pentecostal—have adopted what he calls a Methodist-style practice, in which a really Pentecostal spirit is increasingly lacking. He gave the example of what happened when he returned from exile in Argentina and for the first time participated in his La Victoria church. When he showed his enthusiasm aloud, shouting hallelujahs and amens at any moment, he felt his fellow brothers and sisters starting to look at him as if he were the exception. In fact, Juan now is concentrating his energy on this very issue: to bring back Pentecostal fervor into his church. For he himself, despite his long experience in ecumenical encounters and social and political action, says he has not lost his "first love," his authentic spirituality.

It is obvious that Juan's position is ambiguous. He wants a Pentecostal church that is ecumenical, that stimulates social action, but that at the same time remains faithful to its identity, to the old-time Pentecostalism he knows, and which he still perceives in other churches. When he realizes that those other churches do not share his preoccupation for what is going on around them, he cannot do other than, in a desperate plea for equilibrium, stubbornly repeat that social commitment and ecumenism should never mean the loss of a proper Pentecostal identity. But then he seems to realize that this is exactly the tragedy of Pentecostals: According to Juan, Pentecostals tend to be extremists, it has to be either the one or the other. This essential ambiguity is not only limited to the level of individual meaning-making, it directly affects the feasibility of prophetic Pentecostalism in general (see more in the conclusion).

Paradoxically enough, Juan's crusade for the "repentecostalization" of his congregation has resulted in him being viewed by not a few among the La Victoria church members as a representative of traditional Pentecostalism, despite his long-lasting social commitment and ecumenical activities. At the national MIP level, Juan is struggling to establish a lay movement.[26] This effort is directed against the ever-growing dominance of an inner circle of more or less well-educated pastors in the MIP (and in SEPADE), who have—and this is Juan's strongest objection—neglected the lay people's Pentecostal—that is, spiritual—identity in favor of the development of ecumenical ties and social (and political) action. Although Juan knows that he is himself a product of conscious Pentecostal politics (see the last quotation), his present resistance to its consequences and his attempts to revert the process show that it is hard to change an identity that is so closely rooted in Pentecostal tradition. Despite his experience in other fields, Juan feels that he cannot—and should not—leave behind the spirituality that is like a sediment in his heart. Classical Pentecostal spirituality appears to be resilient and able to neutralize or retard very effectively the outcomes of attempts at changing identities.

The fact that the reaction of most church members to the introduction of changes in doctrine and practice was quite extreme is another "proof" of the problematic assimilation of a new—in this case liberationist—discourse into people's thinking and acting. In a way, women accepted the social gospel that was offered to them, but they only executed it insofar as it fit into their specific Pentecostal gender identity. Men were more categorical, both in their rejection and in their embracement. Juan notices that in his congregation hardly any adult men are left.

"We who have stayed are longing for growth in our church," he says. "As an organization our MIP has grown, but we need to expand again; that is what we are missing. I recall what the goals of our founders were; at this year's assembly, I saw a globe on the church banner with the South American map, showing four flags: the Argentinean, the Peruvian, the Ecuadorean, and the Chilean, plus an open space for the Venezuelan. Those were the aims of our founders, which was the vision of a really evangelistic mission. I stood up during the assembly's meeting to denounce the fact that we had been stuck with pure intentions and that I see the faces of the same pastors I have seen ever since I can remember, but that we depend on our leaders. If they do nothing,

nothing will happen. We will just be left alone with our vision, which we consider is a gift of God. We see that our MIP has not grown, which makes us feel uneasy, because that is not Pentecostal; a Pentecostal church is growing, or at least makes an effort to grow. We should not throw overboard all we learned, but we should bring back the Pentecostal fervor and mentality. If we do not, it is as if one is born in the church and grows in it, without ever witnessing or taking part in its growth. And I see the next generations; what do we transmit to them? We do not have very much to give them, because we are a bunch of Pentecostals who have stayed static. We have been busy with inter-nal—administrative, organizational—growth, but we have to dedicate ourselves to the other type of growth, to the great commandment to 'Go into all the world and preach the gospel.' "

In his preaching Juan principally directed himself at the La Victoria young people. What he is particularly taking offense at is that they live their lives without ever preaching the gospel. He does not consider them Pentecostal any longer, because "they have not experienced the presence of the Holy Spirit." They lack any familiarity with the Bible, according to him. "They hardly know how to pray," he concluded from the visits he has paid to their regular Sunday afternoon meetings, "while they are the future of our congregation."

Let us turn to this future of La Victoria and hear how those young people have experienced life in the congregation and beyond it during the last twenty years. What did they do with the discourse of their leaders, and what practice did they work out in the harsh reality of the La Victoria neighborhood? We leave the few men who are left in the church, and particularly Juan with his preoccupations and sorrows, only to come back to them when dealing with the church's exertion with the youth.

The most prominent of all men in the La Victoria congregation, pastor Farfán, was in a way an atypical, absentee pastor, because he did not live in the neighborhood and hardly checked the behavior of his church membership. He preferred to view his believers as responsible people who did not deserve the paternalism that is so typical of other Pentecostal churches. Besides, his busy work in SEP ADE and for the WCC did not permit him to exert such strict control either. He will turn up, however, in the later section on discourse (re)production, in which he was an influential agent of Pentecostal politics.

The Rebellious Youth

When I intermingled with the youth of the La Victoria congregation, they were a strange blend of teenagers, bachelors, and married couples between fourteen and thirty-five years of age.[27] All of them had lived the greater part of their lives under the Pinochet regime, yet, there was a clear generational conflict going on among them. Several of the older men/boys had fought with the police in the streets during the years of protests, 1983–1985, whereas the youngest ones had only vague reminiscences of that period. In their meetings on Sunday afternoons, these experiences of the past were never a topic of discussion, but the older participants felt that their behavior during the protests had marked a dramatic change in their participation in church life. In fact, during a large part of the 1980s the youth group ceased to function properly.[28] The group was only recently recovering from the setback of that period.

Like most Pentecostal churches, the MIP has youth groups functioning in practically all its congregations. The usual activities of such groups range from Bible study, singing, and going out to visit sister groups, to street preaching and testifying. An interesting phenomenon in Chile was the cyclist groups (*ciclistas*) who went out to preach in isolated spots, often in the rural areas around Santiago, carrying their Bibles under their arms on their bicycle tours. This was definitely a youth activity, which according to some of the older MIP members must have been a pleasant and meaningful task. The MIP La Victoria congregation used to send its young people to attend the annexes in Lo Espejo and José María Caro, both of which have since become independent congregations.

In the 1970s, however, after the military coup, the traditional pattern of behavior of the youth group in La Victoria was challenged by the rapidly deteriorating circumstances in the neighborhood. As Salman shows, in general the young people in the poblaciones most directly felt the impact of the regime's economic policies (1993, 334ff). They were also denied a public space to be young, and political activity was extremely dangerous. As Lemuñir—still almost a boy at that time—observes, in the población La Victoria "the days passed almost without hope, without any motivation from outside" (1990, 25). Feelings of great impotence reigned among the youth. The Catholic parish seems to have been one of the very few places where young people could come together and share their frustration (ibid., 24). But in the MIP congregation, opportunities to do something were not totally absent. As we have seen, in 1976 a soup kitchen was set up and run by the Pentecostal sisters. But as a now-adult member of the church council told me, the young people went out in search of food, urged by the pastor.

> The youth group helped in the search for food; we went on a cart together with other young people to the nearby neighborhoods, asking for food, which we brought to a store in the church . . . we realized that the gospel was to be understood through service, that is by giving food to our fellowman. That is why we did this without feelings of shame. (Patricio, April 14, 1992)

In this activity, a "proof of social responsibility," as one of the boys confirmed, the church youth mixed with non-Pentecostal youngsters. A similar collaboration with nonbelievers took place during the organization of the so-called summer camps for children, which were initiated by SEPADE.

> In 1980–1981, they started those *colonias urbanas*—the summer camps—a week of organized recreation for the children within the *población* itself. They also asked if the church youth could help; the reaction was overwhelming. It was there that we started to commit ourselves to the community, because we, the assistants at the camp, were a group that was recruited from the church and from the neighborhood. That mixed group of camp helpers started to establish friendly relations, since we participated without being a separate group; we intermingled and made friends everywhere. But I remember that we received a preparatory course and also that in the church sermons we were urged to participate in social action. At that time the discourse was changing; the pastor, and his son Daniel in particular, summoned us to assume our social responsibility. (Pedro, March 12, 1992)

Other youth members also talk with enthusiasm about this period in which they worked together closely with people from outside the closed community of Pentecostal believers. The turn to community work provided a meaningful alternative for these Pentecostal youngsters who were no longer focused on their own religious (Pentecostal) group.[29]

Yet this change of meaning-giving in the youth group did not happen quietly. Within the group itself as well as between subgroups and the church council there were prolonged conflicts, which in a way continue to the present day. The central issue in these debates is the participation in the national protests from 1983 onward and the profound impact of these events on the behavior and identity of the congregation's youth. Pedro, whom I quoted in the foregoing, relates how in 1982 a group of around twenty people started to undertake a variety of activities in a neighboring settlement. There they began to help in an olla and carry out several other community tasks, together with the settlement's inhabitants.

> At the beginning we did beautiful things; the moment we arrived at the camp, we distributed food, and then we sat down around the olla and we sang hymns, in order to display our Christian identity. These were rich moments; it was like revising the classical evangelization techniques and practicing what we called 'bring not only the Word, but also the bread.' We were obsessed by this idea. Yes, we preached, at least if what we said can be called a sermon. At any rate, we made it clear that we were Protestants. [He does not say Pentecostals] (Pedro, March 12, 1992)

Although the La Victoria sisters were opposed to the youth participating in an olla other than the one run by their own church, the youth had no major problems with the church council at that time. That changed after the first day of national protest, May 11, 1983. As Pedro recalls, many of the youngsters working in the neighboring community became attracted by the strong communist and socialist militancy of the people they were working with. When the protests became the dominant event in La Victoria in the years 1983–1985, the greater part of the church youth became totally dedicated to what was called the "people's struggle" against the dictator. Consequently, they ceased to appear in the church; many even abandoned the church forever after being confronted with the strong criticism of the older church members, who repudiated the violent participation of the youth in street protests.[30]

The participation of the La Victoria people in these protests was massive, especially among the youth. As Lemuñir describes vividly, there were pitched battles with the police, resulting in numerous wounded on both sides; in the three years of strongest protests, at least seven people from La Victoria were killed and many were arrested, tortured, or temporarily banished (1990, 26ff). Protests were strongest in those neighborhoods where leftist parties had most supporters. Among these neighborhoods, often the result of a pre-1973 toma, La Victoria was renowned for its (political) pugnacity; hence, police action was especially grim there. This could not prevent, however, tens of thousands of people marching into the center of the capital in September 1984 to attend the funeral service of the priest Andrés Jarlán, who had been killed in La Victoria (de Kievid 1993, 151; Lemuñir 1990, 37, 38). These turbulent years were also leaving their mark on the La Victoria church youth.

> On the protest days, we all went on the streets as a group, that is to say, not as the youth group of the church. It was by coincidence that we met there. I think this was shocking, particularly to the *hermanas*, but in fact to all the church people, except for our pastor Erasmo, because he was there during the protests, in the church, to help those who got wounded. The whole congregation was upset. The church really fell into a crisis. For several years the youth 'retreated.' No young people went to church any more. (Maria, July 21, 1992)

By 1982, at the annual MIP conference in the southern port Talcahuano, a polarization among the MIP youth had already become noticeable. For Pedro, this was a conflict over social commitment between the radical youth from La Victoria (together with the Ochagavía congregation) and the more outspoken traditional groups of the MIP, although the majority took a "neutral" (silent) position. But even within the La Victoria group, there was no unanimity. Pedro says,

> We started to send representatives from the youth group to all the emerging neighborhood associations, for example, to the La Victoria youth's association. But on one occasion the situation became critical. One of our delegates no longer wanted to represent the youth group, but to go as a party member. Our discussion became vehement; people started to leave. Those who left were people prepared to work for the community, but not to explicitly enter the political game. After their disappearance, the rest soon dedicated themselves to politics. On the eve of the first protest day, nobody had spoken about his or her plans to participate, we just met on the street. We went separately but it appeared that we were all present. As a group we began to participate actively from then on. We were a tight group, with strong mutual relationships, sharing the ideal of fighting against the regime. Several people joined us for that reason, but they left when in 1986–1987 the

whole thing slowly collapsed. These newcomers even went to the services for a while, but just for friendship.

It was a beautiful time. We also organized recreational activities,
apart from the regular building of barricades and participation in
street block committees. We liked it, because we felt the appreciation
of the community because of our participation as Pentecostals. We also
worked with the Catholic church, in a kind of a joint ecumenical effort. At the same time, there were also evangelistic campaigns; they
[the church council] also tried to reactivate street preaching, but we
did not agree, we did not participate of course. We were not in the
mood for those things. (Pedro, March 12, 1992)

The young Protestants were regularly summoned by the church
council to stop their participation in the ever more violent street
protests, but they were never expelled. Although pastor Erasmo
Farfán could not approve of the violence, he continued to defend
the youth. He himself ran a sort of emergency medical post in the
church—with the help of some youngsters—where victims of the
confrontations with the police could receive first aid treatment.
When the fights were over, in 1988 after the national plebiscite, it
turned out that church membership had seriously declined: Very
few young people were still attending church. Only in 1990 did the
youth group start to recover, although very slowly, from the exodus
the mid-1980 events had produced in the La Victoria church.

How could these young La Victoria Pentecostals radicalize so
easily? I think that the main reason for their ability to think and act
differently was their religious socialization (habitus); these youth
were brought up with a different sort of Pentecostal teaching than
their parents had known. From its very start in 1957 the church and
its believers have seen themselves as an integral part of the neighborhood. There have been disputes on the "styling" of this relationship,
but it has never failed to exist, and was always present in the preaching and teaching. The open-door policy that the MIP leadership has
upheld from the beginning was particularly practiced in La Victoria.
Its pastor, whose pastorship roughly coincides with the period of
the military regime, was a particularly convinced supporter of ecumenism, in the double sense of the word: openness toward other
churches as well as to the outside world. He never failed to "prove"
this with the Bible. Hence, an entire generation of Pentecostal youth
grew up under these tolerant conditions. They were never prohib-
ited from starting social action on their own and were even actively

incited to take a clear social stand. We can understand this motivation when we hear the following:

> Even in our MIP there are churches with people for whom the only thing that counts is the spiritual, nothing to do with the outside world, only to save the soul, or something like that; I believe that is not correct, the Lord Himself never withdrew from the world, He never held Himself back from situations which might lead to death, religious and political persecution; He was with prostitutes, with sinners . . . how else could He have brought relief if He had not walked in darkness. If we do not follow that example, we should restudy the biblical lessons and then see what happens. . . . Because if we go to the Old Testament, the prophet of God knew he would be persecuted and killed, but he accused the king and condemned his abuses, he never tapped on the shoulder of his king, but showed him the injustice . . . our church has to play the role of the prophet of the real God. Then the church becomes the voice of those who lack a voice, doing what others do not dare. But there is room for many in God's vineyard. Some say we just have to stay close to the Lord, while others are too much addicted to the world; I think we need to seek for equilibrium: not so close to the Lord that we do not hear our suffering brothers anymore, but neither stuck to the earth so that we are unable to hear God. (Patricio, April 14, 1992)

The spirit my interviewee describes has been the dominant one for at least the last twenty years, but the equilibrium he speaks of has never been achieved. The La Victoria youth came of age in a Pentecostal church where they acquired many notions of a social gospel and relatively less of the spiritual fervor with which their parents had grown up, and which was still found in other Pentecostal churches. The quite extreme situation that reigned in the mid-1980s with the violent protests in the neighborhood only reinforced this tendency, with a massive exodus from the church as a result. Some sought refuge in other churches, but a large group merged into the radical youth groups of the neighborhoods.[31]

When I was in La Victoria during my fieldwork, I was able to closely examine the attempts to win back to the church those young people who had dissociated themselves from it. At first, I did not understand why the church council was so tenacious regarding this issue, for I noticed that the youth group was quite big and, compared with other MIP congregations, even relatively well organized.

Several people had returned from the neighborhood associations to the community of church youth and were trying to reestablish the group and find new activities and forms of behavior. As I slowly started to realize, it was in this changed orientation that the fundamental source of conflict was rooted. As one church council member often remarked, "they have their group in our church, but they are not Pentecostal, they only know the name, but do not have the spiritual experience." I think he was right in *his* way. He, and other senior church members who knew the old spiritual and emotional exuberance by heart, would love to see the youth return to this Pentecostalism, and he was increasingly annoyed by what he called the "nonspiritual things" the youth were engaged in.

The list of themes for the youth's meetings the older church members take offense at reads as follows: Satanic sects, five hundred years after Columbus, machismo, music, groups dynamics, ecumenism, and so on. At the meetings themselves, there was always a short prayer, the reading of a Bible text, and prolonged singing; I hardly ever noticed people referring to the Bible or to religious inspiration, except for one meeting that did have a clear Pentecostal flavor, on "our encounter with God." This session did not have particular appeal to the youth—only a small group participated—and the theme itself did not provoke enthusiasm. Some women confirmed they had had a personal encounter with Jesus, but others—mostly men—confessed they possessed little experience of the kind. One man declared "to have seen Christ in a child prostituting herself, that is, in a person who was suffering."[32]

What was probably even worse in the eyes of part of the church council was that only very few youth participated—and then only occasionally—in the Sunday school. Such participation is seen as particularly relevant, because it is believed that Sunday school is the appropriate place to learn the fundamentals of Pentecostalism. But as my young interviewees told me, they consider the sessions "boring"—as they do most of the regular services. Efforts to bring about a greater commitment to church life by giving the youth a share in the conduct of the services had little effect. They bluntly refused to participate in street preaching.

It seems that most young people are quite confused, because very little of the "old" Pentecostal way of life is still regarded as appealing. It looks as if the MIP Pentecostal youth of La Victoria is suffering the same identity crisis that is affecting the Chilean pobladores youth in general (Salman 1993). They are aware what sort of a meaning-making they no longer accept, but there is no clear alternative as yet.[33] When I asked about their Pentecostal identity, many confessed that they could not give me a clear answer, and some even declared they no longer felt Pentecostal.

> I really do not know exactly . . . maybe we are sticking with the last scheme, in which I knew very well what the role of the group was. That was the social field; for us youth new ground opened up, because we could do a lot helping the people, and through that we grew . . . now there is no space in the church which could channel the youth's energy.
>
> One of our biggest problems is the absence of Pentecostal identity; we put being Pentecostal on a par with being from La Victoria, but personally there is little awareness of our identity . . . for me being Pentecostal has to do with a relationship with God, but I do not consider myself an average Pentecostal . . . it has a very close connection to being in this world, with doing things for the right to life, to contribute to the needs of the world. (Pedro, March 12, 1992)

When I asked about how he differed from, for example, a Methodist, this same Pedro had difficulty explaining himself to me.

> There are only traditional differences. Personally it is difficult to explain, I am starting to mix up things . . . but it is not that identity in which they teach you how to act and how to behave in the church. We don't have that identity of this and that characteristic which makes you a Pentecostal. (Pedro, March 12, 1992)

Pedro still feels that he is a Pentecostal, despite the fact that he is unable to give a clear definition of this identity. For one of my other interviewees, this lack of a positive identity was reason to reject the term *Pentecostal* altogether.

> I don't feel Pentecostal. If we speak of Pentecostals, we speak of people with their heads in the clouds, who do not live the whole gospel. People tell me I don't look like a Pentecostal. Pentecostals have their way of clothing, of living, they are traditional. You are different, they tell me. The Pentecostal church of La Victoria is different, that is why I do not feel Pentecostal. . . . Well, maybe I am contradicting myself, but it is not that I don't feel Pentecostal. It is that we ourselves are realizing that being Pentecostal does not mean being someone with so many

limitations, locked in one's own church, just living along with a number of rules and norms. I identify with that different gospel, caring for our fellowman, about what goes on in the neighborhood . . . I mean, when Jesus walked on this earth, he shared everything." (Maria, July 12, 1992)

It is this different kind of reasoning that dominates the youth's meaning-making and that contrasts in many ways with that of the older generations in the church. Prolonged sermons, long emotional prayers, nightlong vigils, singing slow hymns, street preaching, periods of fasting, all those elements of the traditional Pentecostal pattern of behavior fell out of favor with the youth. "God does not want that much sacrifice," one told me. And Pentecostal gifts are not much sought for, but as one woman, referring to the Pinochet days, said to me, "God was with us, accompanying us in those difficult days." To her this was as clearly a gift from God as any of those other gifts that are traditionally known as Pentecostal.

Earlier in this chapter I mentioned how one of the congregation's leading men, Juan, expressed his desire to restore, or revitalize, his church's Pentecostal stand. With respect to the church youth, his effort is unlikely to produce effect. The young people are quite sure that such a restoration is not what they are waiting for, although it is not absolutely clear what they do want either. The fact that the church was rooted in the combative neighborhood of La Victoria had been taken to its limits by the youth—at least in the eyes of many older church members—and this did not only spring from the fact that they met with military repression. The social gospel was also taught fairly explicitly from the pulpit. Although in a much less authoritarian way than is usual in Pentecostal churches, the La Victoria pastor played a significant part in spreading the discourse. The fact that this same pastor was neither a spiritually fervent nor an authoritarian man made it even more unlikely that restorative efforts would be successful. As many from the La Victoria congregation affirmed (some with approval, others with a feeling of regret), "the church is like its pastor."[34] That means in this case a situation in which authoritarian manner as well as spiritual effervescence have been moderate. Since the ecumenical, social, and prophetic convictions of the pastor are strong, he has put much energy into winning his community for this cause, which for him did not end when the military regime lost power; ecumenism, social action, and

communal solidarity were much-preached values in the Sunday
school meetings as well as in the regular services during my visits
to the La Victoria church. Thus I have been able to observe how
Pentecostal politics took shape. The next section provides some examples of its effects on the meaning-making of the different categories of church members.

Production and Reproduction of Discourse during Sunday School and Services

Outsiders often think that Pentecostals devote all their free time
to the church. Among the believers themselves it is a well-known
secret—and an often-heard complaint that dedication to church
matters is not as complete as people say; total devotion to the church
is part of the official discourse. As a big survey shows, less than half
of all Chilean urban Protestants regularly—that is at least once a
week—attend at a church meeting, which is, for that matter, still
much greater than Catholic observance (Fontaine and Beyer 1991,
82).[35] My experience in La Victoria is that church attendance is noticeably less than the foregoing average indicates—I could even establish a downward tendency during the year of my stay. Calls for
stricter observance were often made, then, but as pastor Farfán once
sighed, "we have taught our people to participate not only in church
matters; now that participation has declined everywhere in the
neighborhoods, our church does not escape this tendency." The call
for repentecostalization that was made by some lay members must
also be viewed against this background.

    The urge for more frequent spiritual participation in church life
and the emphasis on communion and community participation were
the two dominant themes in the Sunday school and Sunday service
meetings. I will now focus mainly on the second issue, which is,
however, intimately related to the first. What this means in practice
is that I will try to summarize the themes of the sermons I heard
and the contents of the discussions in the adult Sunday school
group. The sometimes detailed reproduction of events is necessary
for obtaining a clear insight into the processes of meaning-making.

Sunday School

    Since 1985 the MIP has had its own national Sunday School De-
partment. This teaching department annually lays down, among

other things, the main guidelines for the teaching in the respective MIP churches. At the first national assembly it was determined that Sunday school teaching should "make people think," and that its style should be "comprehending, not authoritarian, imitating Jesus who never bent people to his will" (Sembrando 1985, 5). The material to be used in the classes was obtained from various sources: the committee of the national department itself, the theologians from SEPADE, other MIP theologians, and during one particular period, mainly from the PUEC (Proyecto Unido de Educación Cristiana, United Project of Christian Education[36]). No MIP churches were ever obliged to use the recommended teaching material, however. Consequently, some churches have hardly ever used it, whereas others, including the La Victoria congregation, have leaned heavily on the existing guides. During my fieldwork period, material from at least two sources was used: from the PUEC and the MIP Sunday School Department. My examples refer to texts from these methods of teaching.

The Sunday morning classes in La Victoria were split up into six or seven groups. Apart from those, there was a children's room where the youngest played and also received a simple Christian instruction (and some food and drink).[37] The meetings always offered a service-like part, but the heart of them was the group discussion about the theme of the day. From the beginning, my place was automatically in the adults' group, in which I participated whenever I went to church. Because this group was always joined by the pastor, who also had an important contribution in the discussion, it is by no means representative of the total Sunday school practice in the church, not to mention other MIP churches. What I do maintain is that these group teaching discussions provide a clear example of what I called Pentecostal politics in Chapter 2. Pastor Erasmo was certainly not a dominant figure in the meetings, yet his contribution did have a special meaning for the others. In other words, his meaning-making was taken seriously by all the others. He was able—to a certain extent—to impose his opinion upon the others. His formal position of pastor could only contribute to this, although he never referred to it. His well-rounded views could only strengthen the effect of his message. In order to make clear how I assess this process, I will reproduce two sessions more or less extensively.

Two Sunday School Classes

One month before my departure to Holland (August 1992) I joined
the class of my "brothers and sisters" on a cold Sunday morning.
Recently a course had begun with the central theme "The action of
the Holy Spirit." The course, the subject of which was unmistakably
Pentecostal, had been designed by the seven teachers of the respective
La Victoria Sunday school classes—who, together with the pastor,
constitute the local Sunday school department. The initiative was born
more or less out of necessity: there was no PUEC material available,
and the MIP Sunday school department did not offer anything new at
the time. Each of the teachers had prepared one class. The central Bible
text of the complete course was "It is no longer I who live, but Christ
who lives in me" (Galatians 2:20). The texts for this morning were
from Acts 1 (v. 5) and 10 (vs. 44–48), which are about the baptism
with the Holy Spirit as a gift that is open to everybody. The text for
this session, which had been prepared by sister Helena, was read aloud
by all of us, after which a discussion started under the leadership of
sister Susana. She set the tone by saying "we have to *feel* the presence
of the Holy Spirit, not only *know* about it through texts or teachings."
Then, two young women testified, rather timidly, about the comforting role the Holy Spirit played in their lives. I was asked for my opinion. I referred to the metaphors of wind, fire, and water, which all
point to the fact that the Holy Spirit has to be experienced. Then what
I had been hoping for such a long time happened: Pastor Erasmo,
thanking me for my contribution, explained what Pentecostalism
meant to him. (In my notebook I comment: Never was prophetic Pentecostalism so clearly "explained" to me). Let us hear the pastor:

"The Holy Spirit is God reaching out to man. But God is a figure far
away, Jesus is God becoming human and hence somewhat closer to us.
The Holy Spirit is closest to us. It comes inside us, like an energy. It
produces change, but not a change which is only personal, but a turn
toward the world. The Holy Spirit has such wide scope that we can
hardly understand it. Therefore, we have to open ourselves much more
instead of keeping it for ourselves. We tend to keep salvation, Jesus,
and the Holy Spirit for ourselves, but that is a severe limitation. The
Holy Spirit is action, and it produces changes in society. The prophets
of the Bible are examples of this. We Pentecostals often cling to the
idea of a God whom we can possess. But the images of the Holy
Spirit—water, fire, wind—they tell us that the Spirit cannot be con-
trolled, it is a major force. We are right if we say that the Holy Spirit
is in this church, but that is not all. It is in the denunciations of the
prophets; what else can give us the inspiration to denounce?"

Sister Susana then gives her interpretation, saying that "The Holy Spirit gives us a new identity, makes us be born again, something which has to manifest itself." Farfán says: "The Holy Spirit comforts, pleads, and defends; It is with us when we stand up, and it is never passive." A young man stands up and says: "In people's suffering we better understand the Holy Spirit; the Holy Spirit is unity." Brother Rafael interprets the words of his pastor by confirming that it is indeed the Holy Spirit that gives him the energy to serve in the church. Sister Susana relates a dream in which she heard the angels sing. Is that her experience of the Holy Spirit? She asks if personal growth is possible without the Holy Spirit. The pastor responds that to ascertain growth one should look at the fruits of the Spirit: love, peace, kindness, and so on. The young Jaime repeats that the hope the Holy Spirit provides produces action, not passivity. Then, pastor Erasmo remarks that they need a teaching course on Christian ethics, because "We know how to handle a personalistic and legalistic type of ethics, but the Holy Spirit summons us to a much more encompassing ethics." (Sunday school class, July 26, 1992)

Two months earlier I was in a class where the theme was "You are God's Temple" (I Corinthians 3:16). It was the tenth lesson of a course book on Mark, prepared by the PUEC (1991), which was used as a guide for three months. It was part of a series called "Walking with God's People" (*Caminando con el pueblo de Dios*), which can be characterized as an effort to illuminate the liberating exertion of God on behalf of humanity.[38] As I mentioned earlier, these PUEC materials have been amply used by the MIP, and particularly in La Victoria. There was, however, growing criticism among the users, which was mainly over the political overtones in the books and the small amount of room that was left for spiritual life. In the Mark textbook, every chapter started with a "fact taken from life," which indeed often had a political dimension. The chapter that was discussed in the session I will now discuss, started with a general description of the Te Deum (I have already addressed this discussion in Chapter 2). There were only a few people present in my group of adults, and only four joined in the vehement discussion. Pastor Erasmo had not come that particular morning.

Brother Rafael asks me to say the opening prayer and read the "fact taken from life." The Mark text is on Jesus' cleaning of the Temple (Mark 11:15–19) and the central verse according to the textbook is verse 17: And he taught, and said to them "Is it not written, 'My house shall be called a house of prayer for all the nations'? But you have

made it a den of robbers." The reference to the Te Deum alluded to in
the "fact taken from life" I find rather indirect; the Te Deum is presented as a meaningless ritual of thanksgiving. The yearly meetings
with Pinochet in the IMP cathedral are never directly mentioned, but
the text stresses that Jesus rejects the church's oppressive role toward
the poor by expelling the merchants from the temple.

"The temple in Jesus' times represented a system which oppressed the
people and alienated it ever more from a real encounter with God.
Services were held which did not give a central place to God and his
beloved creatures—the human being. The temple is used instead by
the oppressors, be they religious or political, to exploit and commit
injustice to the weakest and most needy, who, assuming it would
please God, submitted." (PUEC 1991, 57–58)

The complete chapter is a critical comment on the Te Deum event
and the questions for discussion are put in such a manner as to almost
ensure that outcome. It is precisely this paternalistic tone in the PUEC
courses that has produced negative responses among its users. But on
this occasion the conductor of the session, brother Rafael, just ignores
the lesson's message. After my short reading of the text, he gives a
symbolic interpretation of the Mark text on Jesus' cleaning of the Temple: "We need to clean the temple of our hearts." For him the text
does not mean anything for Chilean Pentecostal church politics. The
two young men who are in the group are visibly getting annoyed by
this interpretation. Finally, one of them, Daniel, complains that we
should keep to the text instead of producing long monologues. He
wants to affirm that the Te Deum services are prostituted services; he
becomes highly indignant, to which Rafael reacts immediately with a
rhetorical question: What is the use of always criticizing? Then sister
Susana supports Daniel's position: "We have to raise our voices without restraint if we see churches or people act in favor of their own
interests instead of those of the powerless." The other young man,
Jaime, agrees and adds that a government that is not recognized by the
people is not acceptable to God either. For him the Jotabeche church
is exactly the temple that needs a radical cleaning. "The Te Deums
shame us Pentecostals," Susana sighs, "and reminds us of the big contrast with the brave actions by the Catholic Church." She then describes the anti-Pinochet efforts by the Catholic Church and the
ecumenical Protestants. She explains how this resulted in the birth of
the CCI and the Consejo de Pastores. The three—Daniel, Jaime, and
Susana—start a passionate discussion on church democracy. The Consejo churches are accused of being highly authoritarian and not having

an eye for the common believers. Susana asks Rafael if he knows about the free discussions and democratic procedures at the MIP assemblies. He does not, but Daniel then observes that there is no reason to exaggerate about these either. He makes a casual remark about the youth and the authoritarian behavior of the MIP government toward it.

During almost the whole discussion Rafael has kept silent, but when the bell rings he takes the lead again. He rereads verse 17 of the Mark text and says a short prayer. When after that the respective groups report on the discussion, I hear no references to the Pentecostal Te Deum at all; Rafael himself, giving an account of our discussion, repeats part of his personal comments. The young men of our group are sulking, because Rafael is giving only his part of the story. They also complain in my presence over the halfhearted treatment of the PUEC material, but they agree when I suggest that the teachings are not particularly open-ended. They can see that it is difficult for many Pentecostals to go along with the PUEC interpretations and suggestions,[39] but at the same time they feel that no justice is done—by people like Rafael—to their legitimate interest in themes like today's.

In Chapter 2 I emphasized that examples like these demonstrate the need for a practice approach that considers the actor's meaning-making in relation to a structural context. Here I stress that it is not only the mere fact of the Pentecostal Te Deum that influences people's behavior and opinion; the treatment of this subject in a Sunday school class reveals that different actors (re)produce different meanings and that the teaching material employed plays a crucial role in promoting a clearly defined meaning of the word *prophetic*, which gives prominence to the duty of Pentecostals to denounce. At the local church level, then, this case shows the effort common to all the Protestant institutions of the ecumenical tendency, to strike at the roots of the regime by trying to affect its credibility and legitimacy among Protestant (Pentecostal) church people in order to contribute to its overthrow and the restoration of democracy. In the next chapter I will elaborate on this theme when I look at the leading role of the SEPADE agency; in the following section I give some more examples—taken from the preaching—of how in the La Victoria church efforts were made—especially by the pastor—to direct the religious meaning-making of the believers from a person-centered toward a world or community-centered vision and practice.

It is difficult to measure the results of the efforts made to promote community thinking in Sunday school. Although I realize that it is

only one example, I want to make mention of a case in which one
of the brothers—Rafael again—declares he has finally learned the
meaning of a certain concept. During my last visit to the La Victoria
Sunday school we had a discussion on the "unity of the Spirit." We
spoke about community as the opposite of individualism. At one
point I summarized the discussion by asking, "do we consider, then,
that our relation to God passes through our fellowman?" Rafael
immediately translated the latter part of my question into "the acceptance of my neighbor in the neighborhood." "This comm*unity*,"
pastor Erasmo stressed, "does not mean uniformity: It means har-
mony in diversity, the complementarity of the many gifts of the
Spirit." Rafael seemed relieved by the discussion; he claims to have
learned a lot, especially the idea that unity does not mean uniformity, as he had first wrongly interpreted my words. He was pleased
to realize that there is no need to have all the gifts in order to be a
good Pentecostal: "the Holy Spirit manifests itself as She chooses,"
he affirmed. After the closure of the meeting we stood back and
discussed how fruitful these discussions were. Rafael was enchanted.
I asked myself at that moment if I had witnessed an instance of that
complex process of religious change.

Preaching

The sermon is the central part of every Pentecostal service, and
the reactions to it are supposed to indicate its quality. In many
churches preaching is the exclusive right of a select group of respected male church members; in a few cases, the pastor is the only
person entitled to sermonize. In the MIP La Victoria church a rota is
used, which draws from a lengthy list of brothers and sisters, including the pastor. The church council decides who is fit to preach. Since
the MIP has admitted women to the preaching, and the majority of
the congregation of La Victoria is female, the average La Victoria
service differs considerably from what happens in other Pentecostal
congregations; a woman stands in front of the congregation fairly
often. Pastor Erasmo Farfán usually preaches only once a month.

Most sermons in La Victoria were very much like the first one I
heard, which was described at the beginning of this chapter: They
predominantly focused on the relationship between God (Jesus) and
the individual believer and only rarely touched upon the wider implications for the church community and the world outside that

"narrow circle" (these were the words the pastor once used). Yet, pastor Erasmo regularly tried to broaden his congregation's perspective. Community and ecumenism were the themes Erasmo often spoke about. I will summarize two of his sermons and illustrate their message.[40]

Two Sermons by the Pastor

The annual conference of the MIP in January 1992 had established that the MIP should try to regain the ground it had lost; that is, try to change the tendency to decrease and reflect on the "inspiration of the church" (*espíritu de la Misión*). A month later pastor Farfán touched upon this theme in a service and said we have to win persons, souls, and bodies, complete, not purely spiritual people. And we should do so from the perspective of community with other churches. In his sermon, on I Peter 2:1–10, he explained how a church should be built. The Bible text on "living stones" well expresses the combination of dynamism and solidity the church ought to be, Erasmo taught. "You are those living, dynamic members constituting a church, whose foundation is Jesus, the cornerstone," he told his listeners. "Together the stones are a house and in order to build that house, all the stones are necessary. That house we see in this Bible text," Erasmo said, "is the symbol of a new community, where none of the stones is left over. Nowadays," he continued, "there are many partitions between and even within church communities. We have to set aside that individualism and accept each other. That is what the term *ecumenism* really means: an open house for this world." He then emphasized that this text of Peter calls for action: "being a 'living stone' means that we church people should suit the action to the word."

It appeared, then, that Erasmo Farfán did not aim to win souls. In one of the interviews I had with him, he explained that it was indeed part of his world of thought that growth should never become a goal in itself. "What we in the MIP want," he told me, "are people who live their faith openmindedly." This vision was certainly not commonly shared by the ordinary MIP Pentecostal.

The meaning of what a Pentecostal should ideally be like, Farfán made clear in a sermon on "the new heaven and the new earth" (Revelation 21). He started by emphasizing that after the creation, God declared that it was good. He then strongly rejected those opinions that focus on the wickedness of man and the lost state of the world. "We now live in the time between God's creation—which was good—and the apocalypse, in which all things will become good again," he maintained. "The world is only 'groaning,' as if in labor. That means that the pain is a pain of hope; everything will become new. We see pollution all around us, we see people suffering, but we are also certain that all that will come to an end. But that is not a process that takes place independently from us human beings. We have a role to play in this."

His fundamental question was "what can we, as a Pentecostal church and as individual believers, contribute to the process which will finally end with the new earth and the new heaven?" In Erasmo's view human beings—including Pentecostals—have a role to play in the struggle for a better world. This postmillenarian concept of history, is not widely shared by Pentecostals. Yet, it is profoundly biblical according to Farfán, "since God sent Jesus to support us in the struggle for the new earth. Jesus came to us in the middle of the process which leads from the good creation to the new earth (and heaven). He gives us new life, which enables us to continue working for this better world instead of shutting ourselves off from it. That is the meaning of 'knowing Jesus personally.' " That is also the meaning of the song Erasmo had sung before the start of his sermon: "I've Got New Life (*Tengo Vida Nueva*)."[41] He emphasized that we have to ask ourselves what we can do for humanity that suffers from egoism. "There is no reason to ask desperately what to do, since we have Christ at our side. We should not get paralyzed by the complexity of the problems which confront us. We should look for things which are within our reach." He then gave a few examples and rhetorically asked, "are we a community?" Lots of "amens" are heard, but Erasmo immediately asked why there are so many frictions in the church then. Silence was the answer. He went on to stress that "it is time to think, to open ourselves, to really apply Christian ethics." He referred to the discussion we had had that morning in the Sunday school class and ended his sermon by explaining what the base should be for an ethics that aims to construct a society reigned by solidarity: "the acceptance of one another which follows from God's first commandment of love. That will give coherence to the community we need whenever we want to work in this world."

What this "working in this world" means was interpreted from another angle in a sermon by one of the lay brothers, Patricio. He gave his sermon after the afternoon meeting of the church council, in which the stagnant nature of the congregation was a hot topic. It is another example of the dilemma of the La Victoria MIP members: Should they return to the old-time Pentecostalism or continue doing it their own, prophetic, way?

A Layman's Sermon

In preparation for the sermon we sing an often-heard song: "Christ Needs You to Love" (*Cristo Te Necesito Para Amar*).[42] I sit next to Maria who has not brought her Bible with her. "I'm not a Pentecostal," she says for fun. We read Ephesians 2:1–10. It is about God's grace by which we are saved. It ends in verse 10 as follows: "For we are His workmanship, created in Jesus Christ for good works, which God prepared beforehand, that we should walk in them." Brother Patricio first notices that a small revival is taking place in the church. He then refers to a call to reassume the prophetic role of the MIP he had heard during the last "fraternal" conference of MIP churches in the Ochagavía congregation. What does he mean by that? Is *prophetic* the same as *missionary* to Patricio? It seems so, because he continues to stress that "what is needed is a translation of 'spirit into works'. We are doing that in the teaching, in our social action work, but it also has to appear in proclamation. There we often stop at good intentions. First, we did street preaching, then we did it from door-to-door, but finally we also dropped that last approach."[43] He says he has had this sermon in mind for a long time and that "the Lord has repeatedly confirmed that he should deliver it. The spiritual revival we are witnessing now, must be translated into a new evangelism. None of us can shirk his/her responsibility in this matter." He then passes into prayer, asking God "to give us the courage, to take away our 'coldness' and draw us out of our inertia." In my notebook I write: "attempt at restoration of evangelism? Very little approval from the audience; no Pentecostal sparkling. Church is like its pastor. Pentecostalism is indeed a confusing phenomenon."

By Way of Comparison: The Neighbors from the Iglesia Metodista Pentecostal (IMP)

Visiting the IMP congregation Los Comandos after a discussion with the MIP youth on the theme of machismo, as I once did, was a remarkable experience. Whereas the MIP congregation is a largely independent church, the IMP congregation is in fact only one of the many annexes (*clases*) of the IMP Jotabeche in the center of Santiago. If the MIP building is becoming too big for its decreasing population, the IMP temple—a fairly exact copy on a smaller scale of the Jotabeche cathedral—can hardly contain its more than two hundred members. Both church communities, although meeting at a distance of no more than fifty meters, are separated by an enormous gap, which neither of the two tries to bridge. The respective members just ignore each other and hardly even salute when passing in the street.

The close yet seemingly unbridgeable distance between the two churches is highly symbolic: They are both Pentecostal, but from totally opposing traditions. In the preceding sections I described the vicissitudes of a Pentecostal community in which ecumenism, social commitment, and lay participation were important, although, contentious topics. I did so on the basis of extended observations and interviewing. However, I never studied the IMP congregation as closely as I did the MIP one. Obviously the results are more stereotypical in the former case than in the latter. I believe, however, that I formed a clear impression of the meaning-making process in the Los Comandos IMP church.[44] The hierarchical organizational structure of the IMP has produced an authority structure in which control of the religious meaning-making of church members is of central importance. The result is that the IMP, despite the far larger scale on which it operates, is a much more uniform church, both in the aspect of formal organization and in the content of the Pentecostal message that is propagated. I will pay attention to both aspects, focusing of course on the La Victoria congregation.

The IMP annex in La Victoria was opened just after the foundation of the neighborhood, although not in its present location. It has led a rather wandering existence and has never been involved in community events in the neighborhood. Some older men told me that particularly during the time of the Pinochet government the church kept its distance from public life in the neighborhood and even reduced the normal street preaching for a while. Lemuñir (1990) takes a negative stance toward those evangélicos who, he thinks, consider themselves better than their neighbors and refused to join the community in the resistance against Pinochet. About fifteen years ago the present location of the temple was acquired, but the present façade is from a recent date. Since the annex is not an established IMP church, its leader is not an ordained pastor, but an *encargado* or *guía de clase* (deputy). The man does not live in the neighborhood; he is only appointed temporarily, in direct representation of the pastor of the Jotabeche church, Bishop Javier Vásquez. The vast majority of the IMP churches in Santiago are in fact no more than Jotabeche annexes, under the leadership of an encargado.[45] In practice, this means that the encargado, like the choir leader, is regularly transferred and replaced by another. The congregation has to provide reports of its activities regularly; incomes from the tith-ing—from all annexes—flow directly to Jotabeche, although only part of it comes back to its origin. The IMP church can be considered an immense pyramid, headed and directed by the bishop and a small group of pastors from the executive committee (for a complete dia-gram of the IMP organization, see Zenteno 1990, 53–55).

When I first visited the annex, the encargado had only been in charge two months, and the new choir leader was presented to the congregation that very morning. This occurred during a Sunday school meeting, in which a talk was given by a group of teachers who had received their lesson the previous day in the Jotabeche church from the bishop himself. Last, but not least, that very day there was to be no regular evening service in La Victoria, because it was the congregation's turn to attend the Sunday evening service in Jotabeche—with the rest of the annexes from southern Santiago. All of these events, although appearing to me to be coincidental, are so many "proofs" of the firm hold Jotabeche keeps on the IMP church, particularly within the Santiago region.

I had been warned beforehand by MIP leaders that I would only hear a gospel of fear on my visits to IMP churches. One of them even told me indignantly that in the IMP the source of Bible texts is often not even mentioned to the listeners, supposedly because that would only divert the attention of the audience. That same man accused IMP bishop Vásquez of paternalism because the bishop once said that he did not want to bother his believers with difficult Bible texts. It may be that I was biased by these MIP informants, but in La Victoria as well as in the Jotabeche mother church I did indeed only hear severe sermons and teachings that emphasized the imminent return of Jesus and the risks of missing salvation. The tenor of most preach-ing in Jotabeche is clear from the following account of a weekday service (May 28, 1992):

> I sit in the half-filled and cold building on Alameda, Santiago's main avenue. A church elder and bishop Vásquez sit on the immense stage. Fifteen children are rapidly baptized. Then the elder preaches without first reading the Bible. During his short sermon I find out that he is talking about Hebrews 3:7–8: "Today, when you hear his voice, do not harden your hearts as in the rebellion." His message is "to be converted now" (today), because "tomorrow may be too late." Subse-quently bishop Vásquez delivers another sermon from Luke 16:19–30

(about the rich man and poor Lazarus). His message is that the gap between heaven and hell is real and unbridgeable. On my way back I conclude that I have been confronted with a clear and dichotomous worldview, in which good and evil were clearly defined and the saved lived separately from the lost.

A similar theme, which had never been treated in my presence in any of the MIP churches, was alluded to in practically all of the five services I witnessed in the IMP Los Comandos congregation. I will give a description of one of them.

An IMP Sermon from La Victoria

I enter the church after my regular visit to the MIP youth (afterward the encargado makes a casual remark about the difference between the two churches). A huge painting of a flowing river hanging above the pulpit immediately attracts my attention. The service has started already; the choir is singing, but I cannot find the hymn in my hymnal. The brother-in-charge then reads from Matthew 24:1–13. I feel we are going to hear a sermon on the approaching end of time, a classic topic of Pentecostal preaching. The man gives a colorful picture of all the signs of Jesus' imminent coming. "Although we do not know the exact time, it can be any moment," he maintains. "Our present-day suffering in this world is unescapable, but stems from our wicked nature." He quotes from Romans 7: "For I know that nothing good dwells within me" (v. 18). This message is repeated in many variations, with examples from daily life, and is rounded off with the affirmation from Luke (v. 13): "But he who endures to the end will be saved." The speaker stresses that this perseverance means faithfulness to the IMP, to Jotabeche, to Los Comandos, to the present-day bishop, and to the late bishop Umaña. "We should never go to other churches or preachers, who are often false prophets."

The church members confirm the sermon with lots of amens and hallelujahs. The musicians start playing and money is collected. Finally, we sing hymn number 397: *Yo Sólo Espero Ese Día* (I'm Just Waiting for the Day when Christ Will Come). In the second stanza of the song is, "I'm no longer of this world; I belong to the kingdom of heaven." It is the only time during my research I am reminded of Lalive d'Epinay's characterization of Pentecostals as people who have withdrawn from this world. After the service, I stand next to some brothers. They all shake hands with the encargado. They tell me not to go to that other church (the MIP) where women are allowed to preach (they know about this, I notice). Half-jokingly, one man summons me to visit bishop Vásquez, who "will teach me how to shave" [I had grown my beard during the fieldwork]. I do not really feel at ease; I wonder if I am spoiled by the intercourse with the MIP Pentecostals? (July 12, 1992)

This Los Comandos congregation has a stable, and even increasing, membership. It practices street preaching, and its members are proud of belonging to the big Jotabeche cathedral. They are taught to obey orders from above (from the same Jotabeche and the bishop) and to cling to a rather eschatological worldview. I am unable to decide whether all these Pentecostals really share this worldview. I did not establish as close relations with them as I did with the MIP believers next door; the details of their meaning-making and the possible variations in it simply escaped my observation. I know, for example, that there is growing opposition to the hierarchical regime of the IMP by more ecumenically oriented young people from various IMP churches in Santiago. They resist the authoritarian church rule and triumphant discourse upheld by its leaders. Ossa (1991) counts these latter people among the "progressive" Pentecostals; yet, I really doubt whether in the Los Comandos congregation in La Victoria there were any followers of this tendency. MIP leaders in La Victoria would have known if any people with deviant opinions existed among their IMP neighbors. Significantly, people have never moved from the IMP to the MIP, while the opposite has happened, albeit occasionally.

Miscellaneous News from La Victoria Pentecostalism

At the end of this chapter it is useful to ask what all the different voices we have heard were telling us. Some voices referred especially to the formative years of La Victoria, others, to the past period of military dictatorship. Still others commented on the present situation and pointed to future developments. As for the MIP congregation, these different phases might be characterized as follows: In the first phase, spiritualism and community-building went hand in hand. The MIP pioneers in the neighborhood seem to have been able to combine a strong commitment to community issues and a high degree of spirituality. In the second phase, political polarization predominated, and the third shows an incipient tendency toward restoration of the emphasis on spiritual life and evangelizing.

All the interviewing and observations underlying this rough peri-
odization were done in the context of the postdictatorship political
situation, when the prophetic Pentecostal voice was increasingly losing credit and giving in to voices that preached going "back to normal." Those who had never sympathized very much with the MIP,
SEPADE, or the CCI now tend to perceive these three—and the people
in them—as obsolete and simultaneously scorn their past role. In
my view, the La Victoria case shows how closely MIP Pentecostalism
and politics have always been linked to each other, and to a large
degree still are. As much as the extreme political situation under
Pinochet provided the right context for raising a prophetic voice,
the "normalization" after 1989 reduced the urgency to make political stands. Moreover, the emphasis on political prophesying and its
supposed irrelevance in the present situation overlooks the many
other issues that the MIP church has broached. Ecumenism, social
commitment, lay involvement, women's participation, and liturgical
renewal are matters that are still in discussion within the MIP, its
congregations, and a group of CCI-affiliated churches. This became
clear during a national meeting (called "Pentecostal Dialogue") in
1991, organized by SEPADE and attended by some seventy people
from different Pentecostal churches. It was intended to keep the discussion going among Pentecostals on issues such as the state-church
relationship, ecumenism, women's participation, and social participation (Sepúlveda 1992b). At that event, voices calling for a "return
to our Pentecostal task of proclamation" were heard alongside of
strong pleas from people who defended the benefits of an "open"
Pentecostalism. This meeting was followed in 1992 by a meeting of
similar character but then only for Pentecostal women. Both encounters did have a positive response from a number of Pentecostal
churches, which proves that the prophetic spirit had not been totally
extinguished.

That prophetic Pentecostalism has nevertheless not come out of
the struggle as a flourishing movement but instead is facing decline
does not exactly prove that it was wrong from a (liberation) theological perspective. Looking at it from a scientific viewpoint, such an
observation completely misses the point. What it does prove, is that
the protagonists of prophetic Pentecostal politics on the one hand
overestimated their capacity to radically and rapidly change beliefs
and practices of church members who had been soaked in Pentecostal tradition. In theoretical terms, they neglected the impact of

Pentecostal habitus.[46] On the other hand, insofar as they had managed to involve people more in socially and politically participatory behavior, they paid the price for this success after the 1989 elections, when the rapid and general decline of interest in such behavior among Chileans (see de Kievid 1993; Salman 1993) made no exception for prophetic Pentecostals.

There were, however, other factors that at least diminished (and in fact have always limited) the attraction of the MIP La Victoria when compared, for example with its IMP neighbors. Many initiatives by MIP leaders simply required a mental switch, which for many church members was difficult to achieve. Thus, for example, it was unthinkable for many that Catholics can be regarded as fellow Christians and not as potential converts, or that working together with Socialists could wield any positive result, and so on. The older church members in particular had appropriated these positions to such a point that abandoning them was experienced by them as giving up a central part of their Pentecostal identity. According to Ortner and Bourdieu, in socially turbulent situations, habitus may be challenged and often even changes. The years of dictatorship in the neighborhood may safely be called tumultuous. And indeed, the Pentecostal habitus was challenged and even bound to change, yet this only had profound consequences for the youth. They learned a more open and less polarizing Pentecostalism, which could only very laboriously be wiped from the minds and bodies of the older church members, who in most cases openly refused to have "their Pentecostalism" recast.

Another important factor concerning the MIP's (lack of) popularity was lack of time (I have already referred to this in Chapter 3). Time invested in (supposedly) nonchurch matters not only meant that these were done less thoroughly but also that the "real church work" devolved onto a reduced group of people, while others spent their time on neighborhood and community work. Again, this is especially true for the youth, but the example of Juan also provides a case in point. Another element affecting the MIP's popularity was the fact that for the MIP the advantages of belonging to a regime-friendly church like the IMP applied in reverse. The material and physical risks were far from imaginary in the "culture of fear" that reigned in the neighborhoods (Lemuñir 1990; Salman 1993, 193). These risks were higher for men than for women, which explains the stronger social participation of the latter, especially in practices that in their view most suited their gender roles. But at the same time, the relatively privileged position women enjoyed in the MIP was seen by more than a few men as striking at the roots of Pentecostal authority structure. The penetration of feminist ideas through SEPADE only reinforced men's criticism but also provoked doubts among women. The strong influence of SEPADE over the MIP, which manifested itself in various other ways, caused disapproval too. Somehow, pastor Erasmo's efforts were also experienced as belonging to this interference from outside.

It is important to emphasize here again the different measure of attraction the prophetic discourse and practice had on men, women, and youth—the categories I distinguished. In very general terms, men were either very much pro or contra. I met some who were reveling in the liberation theologian discourse, whereas others abhorred even listening to it. The majority of women warmed easily to the idea of suiting the action to the word (as in the olla for instance). The youth, on the other hand, would like to have led the church into far more radical stances and actions. For that reason, many left the church out of frustration, and became involved in neighborhood activities that were either initiated by the Catholic Church or by the Communist Party. For the youth, the relatively strong power positions of certain church members and their families caused a lot of resentment, especially since the prevailing discourse (and the church rules) so strongly stressed church democracy, in contrast with other Pentecostal churches, like the IMP.

The neighboring IMP church, however, provided some attractions that the MIP was clearly missing. I have already mentioned the fact that the IMP and its huge temple in Santiago were a symbol of success. Access to power, symbolized in the Te Deums, also played a role for the humble IMP believers in the neighborhoods, who for decades had had to cope with discrimination and had been the laughingstock of their neighbors. Although the La Victoria congregation still seems to be a largely poor community, several members proudly mentioned the economic progress made by fellow IMP people (and expressed in the number of cars parked in front of the temple) from the nearby church in Lo Valledor Sur and Jotabeche. For them the IMP church was the mirror of success (in this life), although for most poor La Victoria people the certainties of the IMP eschatological message and its otherworldly benefits awaiting them continued to have more weight. The straightforward but unquestionable truths of the IMP sermons I heard breathed some clear rules against dialogue and ecumenism. Living in such a spiritual backwater does have a clear appeal to people, for the self-imposed prohibition not to "look over the fence" provides a measure of cohesiveness and strength to a church. This is even recognized by some of the strongest defenders of the prophetic position in the MIP La Victoria congregation.

If it comes to calculating numbers, then, the winner of the Los Comandos "street derby" is obviously the IMP. MIP leaders, like their IMP colleagues, refuse to be content with numbers. The difference is that IMP leaders maintain that it is the high quality of their message that attracts people, whereas their MIP rivals accept that their message may produce disappointing results, despite its high(er) quality.[47] It is exactly this last viewpoint that some congregations within the MIP have always rebelled against, and which has recently been put forward again by MIP lay member Juan (see above). Whether the desire to bring the MIP back into mainstream Pentecostalism is likely to bear fruit, I will discuss this in the conclusion of this book, when I deal with the plausibility structures of this peculiar branch of Pentecostalism.

Notes

1. Pinochet's military government changed Chile's administrative structure in 1974/1975. Before that, there were 25 *provincias*. The new division has introduced 13 regions, subdivided into 51 provinces and 335 municipalities (comunas). Nowadays, the province of Santiago contains 32 comunas. Pedro Aguirre Cerda has 130,441 inhabitants, according to the 1992 census. According to this same census, the total number of inhabitants of Santiago is just over 5 million.

2. This number, although certainly not an exact figure, is disproportionately high when compared with the rest of the municipality of Pedro Aguirre Cerda. I have no suitable explanation for this fact, and neither does the author of the survey. According to the last census, the percentage of Protestants in the comuna is 14.1 percent (11.1 percent for the province of Santiago, 13.2 percent for the whole of Chile; these figures refer to the population over fourteen years old).

3. Under Ibañez's government (1952–1958) the CORVI (Corporación de la Vivienda, Housing Department) was founded and relations with private building companies were reinforced.

4. The urbanization rate in Chile rose from 49 percent in 1930 to more

than 70 percent by the 1970s (Drake 1993, 89). This process resulted in a spectacular increase of the population density, which was particularly pressing in Santiago. The amount of inhabited land grew mainly as a result of land invasions and the use of former agricultural land for urbanizing purposes (Espinoza 1988, 245). Between 1952 and 1959 the number of families living on squatted ground rose from 16,502 to 32,307, i.e., between 5 and 8 percent of Santiago's population (ibid., 247).

5. SEPADE possesses a short video film, showing the heroic efforts made by the church and by students assisting the people with the construction of their houses. From the 1940s onward, the Catholic Church demonstrated a growing preoccupation with the poor. It not only criticized the government's housing policy openly but also delivered prefabricated houses through the Hogar de Cristo.

6. Lemuñir points to the existence of political frictions among the people from the very beginning. Socialists and Communists struggled over the neighborhood's leadership for three years (1990, 17). Internal political friction has been endemic in La Victoria up to the present day; communal interest and political interests have often intermingled.

7. Salman's book attempts to reconcile both tendencies, stressing the merits of both (1993, 4). He does not pay attention to the role of Pentecostals in the events he focuses on: the numerous subsistence organizations and the wave of protests during the early 1980s.

8. These included the so-called organizaciones económicas popular (OEP's people's economic organizations), such as *ollas comunes* (communal kitchens). Mothers' clubs (CEMA's, *Centros de Madres*) and neighborhood councils were largely co-opted by the regime and can henceforth not be labeled as belonging to a proper social movement (Razeto et al. 1990).

9. Only one of the sixteen other MIP churches, the one in San Gregorio, has a bigger membership, according to the 1992 general assembly report.

10. All people over twelve years old can become church members. Fully fledged members (*en plena comunión*) have to meet certain conditions (principally the public expression of their disposition to participate in church life), after which the local pastor proposes to the church council that their petition for approval is accepted (see the church statutes, MIP 1977, 13–15). It seems that the procedure is not very clear to many people, because I often came across church members who were not really sure about their status. In other Pentecostal churches the demands of full membership are more strict (often the pastor admits only a select group into this category).

11. In 1980, there were still 91 full members. The limited attractiveness of the type of prophetic Pentecostal church the MIP wants to be creates serious organizational problems, which in turn contribute to its scant popularity. See also the conclusion on the probability structure of this kind of Pentecostalism.

12. Which direction the MIP should follow, is also a topic of special interest at the annual assemblies, where the future of the church is always amply discussed. The fortieth anniversary of the MIP in February 1992, which was celebrated during the assembly in Buin, was particularly dedicated to opening a new perspective that could lead the MIP into the next century. Resuming the church's evangelization task was a recurrent theme in the meetings as well as in the lobbies.

13. A similar tendency to romanticism and idealization of La Victoria history can be found in the stories of Lemuñir (1990) and Espinoza (1988), although the first author does pay attention to the numerous political quarrels.

14. Lehman calls them *organizaciones de sobrevivencia* (survival organizations, OEPs; 1990, 179). The more common term in Chile is *organizaciones económicas populares* (Razeto et al. 1990). They include small workshops, groups of unemployed, consumer groups, housing groups, health groups, education groups, cultural groups, women's groups, youth groups, pensioners' groups, and so on.

15. Although all female church members address each other with the term *sister*, the plural *sisters* is supposed to mean the *elder* women. Therefore, the primary identification of female youth is with the youth, not with the women; the transition from one category to the other is, however, quite fluid. The actors themselves do not have clear answers as to the criteria for this changeover.

16. In ordinary language *comedor* and *olla* mean more or less the same. Historically in Chile ollas aim at the complete food supply of whole families, often in periods of crisis (e.g., strikes), whereas comedores provide extra food for children only.

17. It is worthwhile, although not surprising to see that no parallel men's department exists (although it was in preparation after the approval at the 1992 general assembly). The sum of all church activities is assumed to be men's domain, whereas women have a separate room of their own.

18. Lately, project activities have diminished sharply. In 1992 they were reduced to the distribution of milk powder (from Europe, through SEPADE) among a selected number of families (from within and outside the congregation).

19. Pastor Farfán complained to me that this system of rotation enhanced the tendency of people to attend only those services in which they expected to hear a sermon to their taste. As far as I can see, sermons preached by women were no less appreciated than those by men.

20. Halfway through the year of my stay, teaching groups for men and women separated. Before that, they functioned according to the same rotation system that is applied for preaching.

21. It should be stressed that women's identity as constituted by their

"domestic responsibility and welfare provision" (Moser 1993, 29) is a stereotype, which is often contradicted in Chilean practice, where women do have a tradition of working outdoors and activism. Nevertheless, it cannot be denied either that women's habitus—through socialization—predisposes them to identify with this cultural standard (which is often labeled as *marianismo*).

22. This case is based on an interview published in the first issue of *Evangelio y Sociedad* (1985), in combination with two lengthy interviews I had with the person concerned and what I heard him saying during sermons and informal meetings. I do not include this case because of its representativeness, but this Pentecostal man does display the capacity to explain his constant struggle with the relation between Pentecostal tradition, the social circumstances demanding a reaction, and the input of a new Pentecostal discourse plus the ensuing practices. It also shows how this man's meaning-making, and his corresponding behavior, changed when new opportunities offered themselves in the context of the surrounding conditions.

23. One of the best soccer teams in Chile, which is especially popular among working-class people.

24. The other settlement resulting from a toma was called *Raúl Silva Henríquez*, which was also in Santiago's southern municipality of San Bernardo. These were the only major tomas during the Pinochet period. They are named for the Catholic cardinal of that time and his predecessor.

25. In Chile *campamento* (encampment) is the word that is often used for a squatter settlement in its early stage (see Beijaard 1983).

26. During the 1992 MIP general assembly, Juan was trying to win supporters for this movement among lay people from other congregations. It seems he was having some success and even found a ready ear among some of the pastors.

27. Because the Women's Department is considered by the youth to be for older women and there is no specific men's department, people may stay in the youth group for many years after they have established a family.

28. "We were busy with other things" (*estuvimos en otra*), as the boys used to tell me often.

29. Lemuñir describes how for the non-Pentecostal youth the Catholic parish offered the same chance to give meaning to an otherwise seemingly senseless world: "our only task [in the Liturgy group] was to . . . show solidarity with those who had fallen victim [to the regime] (1990, 24)."

30. This rejection of violence was common to most adults in the Santiago neighborhoods and definitely was not restricted to Pentecostals (see Salman 1993, 329ff). Yet in the La Victoria congregation the issue caused a conflict with serious consequences.

31. During the fieldwork I did not do any interviews outside the church realm. I met some of the ex-MIP youth through those who had stayed in the

church, but how they fared, I know principally by way of the declarations of church people.

32. At that occasion I was also asked about my experience. I talked about my former experiences in the Youth-for-Christ movement, but my story must have sounded as "disengaged" (I had difficulty verbalizing the measure of involvement this had meant to me) as most of their stories appeared to me.

33. Only the theme of music (and singing) raised enthusiasm among most youth members. They planned to start a course on guitar playing, to compose a new songbook, and some mentioned that music could be the evangelistic instrument of the future. Some were inspired by experiences with Assemblies of God services (especially the way of "praising the Lord" in the music and the singing). Efforts to enlarge the role of instrumental accompaniment and the use of new songs only caused ambiguous reactions. One reason for that is that an important part of the Chilean Pentecostal churches, unlike the North American ones, have developed almost without the use of musical instruments (even clapping is still rather uncommon).

34. The prominent (power) position of the Pentecostal pastor is often emphasized, both in the literature on Pentecostalism (e.g., Lalive d'Epinay 1969) and among adherents themselves. To many believers, their pastors and bishops are like small gods (see for example the section on the La Victoria IMP church).

35. Ideally, a Pentecostal should devote at least the whole of Sunday to his or her church. In the morning, participation in Sunday school is obligatory; in the afternoon, there is the youth group and the evangelistic campaign, and in the evening, everybody should reassemble in the principal worship service of the week. As an interested researcher, I sometimes carried out the whole program; few brothers or sisters ever joined me in this "sacrifice."

36. The PUEC was an ecumenical project, which started in 1984, and was supported by several Protestant churches—IPCH, MIP, Methodist Church, Presbyterians, Protestant Church of Vitacura—and financed by external donors, including the Reformed Churches in the Netherlands. Its goal was to produce teaching materials for Protestant Sunday school classes as well as to organize teaching courses for Sunday school teachers. The PUEC was finally dissolved in 1993 after prolonged internal quarreling.

37. The children's classes are the best attended of all; apparently many parents, without belonging to the church, send their children to receive some attention and food, and to play freely. I was told repeatedly that literally hundreds of children from the neighborhood have known the MIP Sunday classes without ever becoming a church member; they are said to retain good memories of the church. Sunday school as a service to the surrounding community was a goal that was pursued by various other MIP pastors,

too. In general, Pentecostals believe they create more room for the children in their churches than the Catholics do; hence, they also believe they have more children within the church walls. Some even think that, by not counting children under fourteen years of age, the last census (1992) presents too low a percentage of Protestants (Godoy 1993, 40).

38. Other PUEC series consist of leaflets that are adaptations of materials written by the Brazilian hermeneutic theologian Carlos Mesters, who has dedicated himself principally to offering base communities new ways of reading the Bible from a liberationist perspective (de Wit 1991, 113ff).

39. An evaluation of the complete PUEC project made in 1993 precisely pointed out, among other things, the scant information on the reception and practical treatment of the PUEC material in the Sunday school classes. It was noticed that PUEC employees showed only limited interest in the reception of their products (oral information by Hans de Wit).

40. Preaching in Pentecostal churches is often called *traer el mensaje* (to bring the message). Very often there is no message in particular, other than the gospel itself. I think pastor Erasmo's sermons were carefully designed to promote new messages—and meanings—among Pentecostals.

41. "In my life something very special has happened. I've known the Lord. I have learned what the Lord says. He says 'if you open your heart for Him, He will give you new life. I've got new life' (repeat three times). In this world there are things that attack our souls, and which we sometimes cannot overcome. But Christ will give you abundant life, so that you can win and have new life." This song refers to a personal new life, but Farfán gave it a much wider meaning by explaining its implications for action in the world.

42. "Christ needs you to love. Neither race nor the color of your skin matter. Love all as your brothers and do well. To those who suffer and are sad, give them love; to the modest and the poor, give them love. To those who speak other languages, give them love; to those who *think differently* [my italics], give them love. To your best friend give them love; to those who do not greet you, give them love." The tenor of the text is that of an almost equal alliance between Jesus and the believer. This message, taken together with the unconditional love for mankind propagated in the song, makes it rather atypical for use in Pentecostal churches. I think it expresses well the influence of the prophetic discourse in this particular congregation.

43. See the opening quotation of Chapter 1.

44. I spoke with several IMP church leaders, but I did not tape any interviews with them. The Los Comandos leader refused repeated contacts, with reference to the absence of permission for this from his superiors. Lay people used the same argument, assuring me that they had nothing to say either. I realize that such a reaction belongs to any introductory phase in a research environment, but it is also a clear indication of the hierarchical organization of the IMP church.

45. Several of the Santiago annexes are indeed large churches, but they are still under the direct control of the Jotabeche pastor and his church council. Centralism is very strong within the Santiago IMP, and only a few churches on the outskirts of the city have their own pastor. In the rest of the country the power of the central IMP church is much smaller.

46. I did not pay attention to it, but the same overestimation of the impact of leadership decisions on ordinary believers characterized the bearing of the Consejo de Pastores.

47. It is not only among the leaders that this argument is defended; I once heard a leading old woman in the congregation defending the church youth, who despite possessing some obvious vices, did not play tricks secretly. "I'd rather see my boys smoking on the streetcorner than fooling around with a knife at night," she asserted.

5

The Nongovernmental Organization (NGO) SEPADE: Shaping Pentecostal Meaning-Making

In the previous chapter we observed how pastor Erasmo Farfán tried to spread a Pentecostal message of community and social commitment among the congregation members in La Victoria through his sermons and Sunday school classes. This was not just a matter of personal idiosyncrasies; we have seen that the MIP church leaders made a conscious choice to adopt a social and ecumenical stance almost from the start in 1952. Pastor Farfán, although not involved in the earliest skirmishes within the IEP mother church and the subsequent schism, has been a prominent lay member in the MIP from the early 1960s onward. He started to perform pastoral work in La Victoria in 1975 (one year after the foundation of the MIP development bureau SEPADE [(CTA by then)].[1] We have seen how Farfán's congregation became involved in neighborhood issues, especially after the military coup in 1973. The congregation also became a source of support for SEPADE's neighborhood activities, particularly after 1978 when Farfán became SEPADE's second director. Pastor Farfán, then, is the link between Pentecostal church politics and NGO politics, not least because through him most members of the La Victoria church community have in some way or other been involved in the SEPADE work.

In this chapter, I want to show how and under what conditions SEPADE was constituted as an instrument of Pentecostal development

politics and how this NGO evolved, particularly during the years of
the military regime in Chile. It started in 1974 on a limited scale
with only a few people, but in the extreme political context of a
military dictatorship, which to a large degree determined the institution's focus. SEPADE's history is also directly linked to the international political and ecumenical effort in Chile during the Pinochet
period, but its roots as well as its impact cannot be examined without looking at the local level on which it worked. Although the
majority of SEPADE's development activities had nothing to do with,
or were only indirectly related to, (Pentecostal) churches, I nevertheless emphasize its role as an agency of Pentecostal politics, that
is, as a bureau explicitly aiming at changing Protestant, and in particular Pentecostal, meaning-making. I realize that this is one-sided,
but I do this because I want to demonstrate the peculiarities of religious change through this particular case. In this chapter, I aim to
demonstrate that it was not only the MIP church itself that propagated a prophetic message in and through its congregations but that
the responsibility for the expansion of these notions was furthermore delegated to a separate, and semi-independent church organism, the NGO SEPADE. The role of international development
cooperation in Chile will receive attention, especially SEPADE's relation to the Dutch cofinancing agency ICCO, because without foreign
sponsors, no such a thing as SEPADE could have functioned. This
chapter can therefore also be read as an effort to provide feedback,
although on a limited and clearly defined scale, on the effects (impact) of this type of international cooperation. This was also a major
issue during the consultations with ICCO in preparation of the
fieldwork, yet the research was never designed with a view to producing the sort of evaluation that is commonly made in the field of
development cooperation.

Departure from Tradition: The Genesis of a Pentecostal NGO

Even in our church a strong effort was needed to assume the social
dimension of the gospel. Social work was very much resisted and only
accepted for inner church goals, or in biblical terms: for faith purposes
only. Attending the sick and the poor, as long as they were church
members, caused no problem, but the opening to the outside world is
something very new in the church, and in fact it only emerged visibly
from 1974 onwards, that is after the military coup. After 1973 the

situation was so serious that nobody could escape from poverty in the
poblaciones. The very children of church members were begging in
the streets. One could say "necessity knows no law." I think that a
situation was reached which permitted the brothers and sisters to rethink their limited conceptions of the gospel. (Erasmo Farfán, October 14, 1991)

From the early 1960s, the MIP had stimulated the formation of
social service committees in its local congregations as a result of the
biblical discourse on social action that had been established at the
annual assembly of 1963. As the foregoing quotation reveals, the MIP
leaders, including president Erasmo Farfán (member of the church
committee for almost fifteen years now), have always been confronted with the difficulty of promoting a "social gospel" that
crossed the church boundaries. Ironically, the radical changes in
Chile after 1973 produced the circumstances that favored the opportunity to intensify efforts at the social awakening of Pentecostals. In
Chapter 3 we have seen that a substantial part of the Pentecostal
leadership took the side of the Pinochet regime (the Consejo de
Pastores), whereas a minority opted to struggle in defense of the
"oppressed social sectors" for "participatory democracy and social
change" (SEPADE 1988, 3, 5). For the latter group, the Pinochet regime and the effects of its socioeconomic policy meant a challenge
to organize their churches in an effort to leave behind what was
called "the historical tendency to exclusiveness and sociopolitical
marginalization" by Pentecostals (ibid., 27). SEPADE, being one of
the main institutions working on this "challenge," thus saw as its
principal task "the promotion of social participation in working-
class sectors," although in the course of its existence its focus on
the specific Protestant (Pentecostal) target group became ever more
noticeable.

The formulations of the 1988 SEPADE policy document I have just
quoted are parts of the discourse that had become fashionable in the
communication between NGOs and Western donor agencies. Neither
the former nor the latter had made any significant contribution in
Chile before the military coup of 1973. NGOs hardly existed in Chile
before then and Western development cooperation had shown little
interest in the country because of its relatively stable political and
economic situation (Schuurman 1991, 44–47). The NGOs that
emerged after 1973 and the foreign donors shared a common goal,

which was the redemocratization of Chile. For SEPADE to make a contribution to the achievement of this goal meant an effort of socioeconomically consciousness-raising among Protestant—mainly Pentecostal—groups and churches among which its staff and officers worked. It was a long way, however, from the first improvised attempts at organization to the final result, a fairly smoothly functioning development agency. I will first highlight the organization-building, because it reveals much about the NGO staff's way of thinking and organizing, which has not essentially changed over time.

In 1992, a Chilean organization consultant, a friend of one of the SEPADE leaders, noticed that the way people worked at SEPADE was characterized by familiarity, friendship, solidarity, informality, and goodwill, which worked fairly well given the fact that SEPADE's primary aim was helping people with problems (SEPADE 1992, 7). As we will see later, the document this consultant produced rightly maintains that this working atmosphere had been dominant, without much alteration, from the very start until the early 1990s, when, in the opinion of the expert, it became obsolete. But "informality was everywhere" in the Chilean NGO sector of the 1970s and 1980s, as is also maintained by Hojman, whose judgments are based on field observations and lengthy surveys (1993, 10, 21). The same author affirms, however, that this informality does not mean that there was no accountability or that NGO work was haphazard, although it has certainly proven difficult to assess and evaluate the wide variety of social development projects executed by NGOs (ibid., 10).

During my fieldwork, people from other Protestant churches than the MIP regularly charged me of working with people—that is with SEPADE—who had set up this NGO with only one purpose: providing work for MIP members, particularly its university- trained people, whose professional careers had been frustrated by the military regime. Ironically, this cynical view could be applied to most other NGOs as well. In this point of view external—foreign—donors meant a lifeline for all those skilled professionals, especially those from the social sciences, who were doomed to unemployment or unskilled labor by the regime's politics.[2] Again, this aspect is certainly part of the truth, but it is too easy an argument to discard NGO work as irrelevant and view the institutions only as organisms of self-service. NGOs did more; they trained, for example, numerous qualified professionals for working at the grassroots level. The so-called OEPs (see Chapter 3), to name only one important category, benefited greatly from their support (Hardy 1989; Salman 1993), but detailed accounts of NGO (daily) politics and relations with target groups are scarce.[3] I think studies like the present one reveal (part of) the impact of NGOs that have worked, and are often still working, in Chile over the past twenty years. When it comes to gaining insight into the meaning-making impact of the manifold NGO-performed work, I think we cannot dispense with such detailed case studies. A time- and money-consuming impact study of the cofinancing program of the Dutch donor agencies did not get any further than concluding that NGOs working under repressive regimes had a considerable, although hardly measurable, impact, particularly in the area of "social edification" and "organizing and defending the opposition" (Stuurgroep 1991, 45). In the case of Chile, the impact study is unable to reach any further conclusions than that NGOs played a significant role in the redemocratization process, which cannot be further assessed, among other reasons, because of the limited monitoring qualities of the donor agencies themselves (Schuurman 1991, 58).

To achieve this, I turn to the group of people that started the SEPADE organization in 1975. For this reconstruction I heavily rely on the views of Gabriel Guerrero, an economist who was with SEPADE from the very start until 1994, and who was most willing to provide his account in graphic detail. Guerrero, the son of a recalcitrant IMP member, was one of the four people who in 1974 made a proposal for the MIP committee to establish a Comisión Técnica Asesora (CTA) that would be able to handle foreign aid for solidarity projects, like soup kitchens, scholarships, and others. As an economist, he might have found a proper job quite easily (economists were in the regime's good books), but that was far from sure. The labor market prospects of the other SEPADE founders were even less certain. Marta Palma had finished a study on social work, Francisco had lost his job as a professor of theology at the CTE, and Samuel Palma (who had taken refuge in Argentina and joined CTA only later) had not even finished his sociology studies. Apparently it was Francisco, a declared socialist, who took the initiative and drew in the three young students from the Concepción University: Gabriel Guerrero, Samuel Palma, and his sister Marta. These youngsters had demonstrated clear social commitment and leftist political sympathies.[4] Samuel Palma and Marta Palma were MIP members, Gabriel

Guerrero became a church member only later. In later years, members of two other leading MIP families, the Sepúlvedas and the Farfáns, joined the SEPADE team. The most prominent one of these was Erasmo Farfán, the La Victoria MIP pastor, who gave up his relatively secure job as an accountant to become the CTA director in 1978. This was a significant step, because for him there was no economic incentive to join the initiative—as for the others—even though he ran the same risks of (political) repercussions as the others. In 1981, Juan Sepúlveda joined in to reinforce the NGO's relation to the churches.

The fact that in the course of its history members of the three families mentioned have increasingly put their stamp on SEPADE, until the present day, has given rise to many rumors and accusations. For instance, SEPADE's enemies—of whom there are more than a few—mockingly call it SEPAFA, after the first letters of the family names. It should be noted, however, that it was in no way exceptional for NGOs to grow out of the informal activities of a group of close friends, or even relatives. The degree of family involvement in SEPADE may have looked striking from the early 1980s onward (as it did to me), but characterizing the NGO as a "family affair" from the start is too heavy a charge.

It should, however, be clear that the SEPADE founders did not represent a crosssection of the MIP membership. They were well-educated and all belonged to the families that led the church. Marta and Samuel Palma were children of the MIP chairman of that day. Erasmo Farfán—who had succeeded his father-in-law in the La Victoria church—was the brother-in-law of Francisco, whose father had belonged to the founders of the MIP in 1952. Economist Gabriel Guerrero became closely tied to the Sepúlveda family, headed by the architect Narciso Sepúlveda, who was the church's secretary for long periods of time.[5] In Chapter 3 I stated that the originators of the MIP had a noticeably higher educational level than the average person in the IEP they left. This holds to an even greater extent for the people who took charge of the SEPADE initiative. Their academic experience and foreign contacts (especially in WCC circles) increasingly struck at the roots of their Pentecostal habitus. In the conclusion I will come back to this important point, because these same people had the power and opportunity to attack traditional Pentecostalism, using SEPADE as the vehicle for this attempt.

Francisco, from whom the principal impetus for the foundation of a church relief agency came, won over the MIP to his initiative by making a fervent plea before the church committee, in which he stressed that the stark reality of the early years of the Pinochet regime compelled the church to put into practice the social commitment the MIP as a Pentecostal church had been confessing since the early 1960s. But Francisco was not just guided by his religious convictions. He had a strong political motivation and was also the only MIP member with experience in the ecumenical world. The history of the CTA project, at least in its early phase, depended to a large extent on Francisco's personal ecumenical relations.

Francisco was ordained as a pastor in 1958 and sent to Uruguay to start a church there.[6] He soon became involved in the Montevideo Association of Pastors, the then chairman of which was Emilio Castro, who was later to become WCC general secretary. As Francisco told me, this participation meant as much as the transition from an intellectual backwater to a level of lively theological discussion and ecumenical disposition. Soon afterward—at the 1961 New Delhi general assembly—the MIP, together with the IPCH of Bishop Chávez, became a member of the WCC. It is unclear to me what role Francisco performed in this process of WCC affiliation; afterward he obtained a WCC scholarship to study theology in Buenos Aires (Argentina), with the help of the liberation theologian Míguez Bonino. When in 1966 Francisco returned to Santiago to become a professor at the recently founded CTE (where he stayed until 1973), there was considerable opposition to his return, particularly from MIP president Víctor Pavez. As Francisco points out, there was a struggle going on within the Pedro Monnt mother church between those who wanted to renew and strengthen the open character of the MIP and those who wanted it to become a second IEP (the mother church from which the MIP had separated in 1952). For Francisco and others, Pavez had developed into a kind of "shepherd that feeds himself instead of caring for his sheep" (a reference to Ezekiel 34). Those in Pedro Monnt who felt themselves victims of the growing autocracy of Pavez—who ignored the basic democratic principles of the MIP—turned to Francisco, who had decided to start working in La Victoria, where his father was pastor. Two years later, Pavez was expelled from the MIP after a big (sex) scandal, but he took a substantial part of the Pedro Monnt congregation with him when he founded his own new church.[7] After Pavez had left, however, other MIP leaders had more breathing space to express their social commitment and political preferences, to which Pavez had apparently been an obstacle. Francisco, whose pastoral credentials had been taken away from him—most probably through Pavez—managed to gain financial support from the WCC for a project with Uruguayan, Argentinean, and Brazilian exiles. This all happened against the background of the political regimes of Frei and Allende, which succeeded in mobilizing Chilean lower-class people, including the Pentecostals, to a higher degree of (social and political) participation than had ever happened before.

As I explained in Chapter 3, these social and political changes during the 1964–1973 period encouraged a minority of Pentecostal leaders to join in attempts to propagate new, participatory, forms of local government and social work. Francisco was one of them, and above all the one with the most contacts at the WCC level. By the early 1970s he had become a member of the WCC Faith and Order Commission, the task of which was to reflect on the character of church unity and ecumenism. He was also part of the CICARWS department (Commission on Inter-Church Aid, Refugees and World Service). This permitted him, in his own words, "to slowly learn about the tremendous potential for support from abroad and about donor agencies." In 1973, after the military overthrow, Francisco was at a CICARWS meeting in Sofia, at which it was suggested he looked for organizations in Chile that could receive foreign help. A first attempt to work through ACE (see Chapter 3) turned out to be a failure,[8] which finally caused Francisco to decide not to continue with ACE but to propose the establishment of a separate organization, under MIP responsibility, that could handle some externally financed projects.

According to Francisco himself, he had to invent a discourse that mentioned a social commitment going beyond the scope of the church's terms of reference in order to satisfy possible foreign donors. Thus, in the proposal he made, no money was asked for church-building, furniture, or for pastoral relief funds; the first initiative consisted of church-related soup kitchens. All in all, the preamble to SEPADE's start was characterized by a combination of good intentions and a high degree of improvisation.

Yet, when CTA took shape in 1975, the founders did not have to start from scratch. The ecumenical ties the MIP had established since it first became a member of the WCC could easily be activated once the decision was taken by the church committee to engage in social work. International indignation about the military coup was general and the readiness to finance initiatives aiming at the relief of the grossest injustices of the military repression was great. The consequences of the economic policy and political repression of the regime—increasing poverty and a state of collective tutelage—were exactly the wrongs the fight against which northern and western agencies of development cooperation were ready to spend their money on. The result was a boom in Chilean NGOs concerned with children's welfare, nutrition and malnutrition, "popular education," health care, cheap housing, human rights, cooperatives, and so on. As Hojman (and many others, see Schuurman 1991) maintains, it was relatively easy for NGOs to obtain funds from abroad, and "the conditions attached were minimal, *at least in the case of social development NGOs*" (1993, 9, 10; my italics).

In the case of CTA, the story was the same. The WCC, which had publicly condemned the military regime soon after the coup and praised church leaders who raised their voices, was willing to emphasize its feelings by financial means. In 1979 the WCC cofinanced, with more than 100,000 Swiss francs, CTA social service and community development projects among the poor victims of the regime (see CCPD/CICARWS project overview 1979, 170). By that time, there were several other big Western donors providing funds for CTA projects, among which was the Dutch ICCO, which held out great hopes of financial support to the young bearers of the CTA initiative. As Gabriel Guerrero says:

> The triennial social service program the WCC approved really gave us a future perspective, which was very important in a time when long-term planning was utterly precarious. And then we met the representative of ICCO, whose attention had been drawn to our work by his WCC contact persons during a visit to Chile. When he surveyed our activities, he typified it as an integral community development program, much to our surprise. He estimated that such a program fitted ICCO's possibilities well and valued ICCO's possible contribution at 100,000 to 150,000 dollars. When we started elaborating the program, we became aware that such an amount of money would allow us to move into a different place from the church building, so that we would also be free to develop activities, which according to church tradition could only be performed outside the church. Since we had no previous experience in dealing with foreign sponsors, we had drafted an ambitious program with an equally extensive budget. Again much to our own sur-

prise, we were granted the money we had asked for. That in fact meant that we could establish ourselves as an institution, but I really had never thought of SEPADE as a place to work at, I simply could not imagine it would come to that. (Gabriel Guerrero, November 29, 1991)

Guerrero would probably never have continued to work in such an organization as CTA if it had remained the group of semivolunteers who started the initiative, because working in an NGO against the regime was risky. His suggestion was that it was precisely the generous offer from abroad that persuaded people like him to stay with their own creation.[9] It was indeed a general phenomenon that international donors spent money on civil groups (NGO) that tried to render assistance in the numerous emergency situations, and organize political resistance to the regime. However, in concrete cases—like the CTA/SEPADE one—a wide range of specific goals and expectations influenced the disposition of ICCO to establish and subsequently enhance the relation with its Chilean recipient.

In order to expound ICCO's interest in CTA, the account of its Latin America desk officer, Cees Oskam, is fairly revealing. His opinions must be viewed against the background of important shifts within the pattern of ICCO's expenditures. ICCO started its development aid activities in 1964 and was soon involved in the Dutch cofinancing program after a positive decision from the Dutch government. ICCO's specific task was to be the channel for projects initiated by churches and organizations with a Protestant background (mainly in Africa and Asia, especially Indonesia). The sharpest growth in expenditure took place between 1974 and 1979 (ICCO 1985, 15). Annual reports show that funds allocated in Latin America started increasing rapidly from 1975 onward; in that very year the first regional secretary was appointed. Four years later 40 percent of the funds disbursed went to Latin American projects (ICCO 1979, 5). The motivation for this growth was mainly political: "to stimulate processes of social awakening that might contribute to the liberation of the oppressed, suffering from repressive regimes" (ibid., 11). The growing attention to human rights problems in Latin America on the part of the WCC and the South American Bishops' conferences of Medellín (1968) and Puebla (1979), in which the theology of liberation came prominently to the fore, provided the circumstances that favored ICCO's work in the continent. ICCO's hesitation—nourished by the institution's Protestant character—to work on this predominantly Catholic continent were rapidly overcome during these years. So the second half of the 1970s showed a major shift of attention toward Latin America, accompanied by a boom in the available funds. At that time, then, the willingness to support any promising initiative was great. From the report of ICCO officer Cees Oskam's first visit to Chile, in September 1976, we can read that the CTA was such a promising initiative.[10]

> This is a group on the left wing of the Pentecostal community. Contrary to most Pentecostals these people are very ecumenical (they became a WCC member in 1961). Its executive organism is CTA, headed by Francisco, pastor and formerly active in CICARWS. This organization is also politically clearly leftist. Most CTA people belong to the MAPU, a leftist split off from the Christian Democrats. They are keenly against the Pentecostal "flirting" with the regime, and much more politically engaged than ACE. They work on behalf of political prisoners for example. Consequently, Francisco has been visited by the secret police four times.
>
> We have met this group by way of the WCC, which has already been supporting them for a while. The work is similar to that of the Vicaría and ACE, but that is no problem: this happens to be the work that has to be done. Here again we see projects of human development, arising from strong feelings of solidarity and a certain amount of charity. The MIP, however, has one other very important objective, which is to raise consciousness among the evangelical [his words] Pentecostals, and to induce them to leave their religious verticalism. In a country like Chile, where Protestants have not particularly shown their best side, this endeavor therefore certainly deserves ample support.

ICCO's Cees Oskam further indicated that he had visited the CTA work on the ground ("I now know how they work"). He mentioned among other things the soup kitchens and made a plea to put this activity on the project list. He considered these kitchens to be the core of the CTA project, although he admitted feeling some hesitation regarding the financial accountability of this particular activity (with reference to earlier experiences). Contrary to the normal procedure, he proposed not to consult an impartial opinion on the project. This, he estimated, would be impossible to obtain; "since Chile finds itself in a state of civil war, we should accept that necessity knows no law."

At the time of the second visit to CTA by ICCO's Cees Oskam, in November 1979, CTA had already become a stable counterpart of ICCO. The report of the visit showed that ICCO, that is, its representative, had great confidence in CTA. As the "social wing" of the MIP, which is said in the document to be one of Chile's biggest Pentecostal churches, which is obviously a clear mistake, CTA is praised for its ecumenical dedication (WCC membership, participation in WCC commissions and Latin American ecumenical institutions). The new director, Erasmo Farfán, was characterized as a prudent and open man, "who will probably be able to avoid an unbridgeable gap between the church and its social organization, a situation in which both sides would no longer be able to acknowledge each other's work."[11]

In his travel report Oskam showed that he was aware of the potential problems CTA might have to face as a result of its explicit church ties, its use of the legal personality of the MIP, and the recruitment of its staff from among MIP church members. It was expected that ICCO would have to invest much time in coaching CTA, as an ecclesiastical organization that was so closely watched by a potentially rebellious rank and file. But the complication was thought a challenging one, because "it is really one of the few Protestant organizations in Chile that is consciously working on the real liberation." This quotation may suffice to indicate the extraordinary importance that was attached to CTA as an ICCO partner, especially since CTA was believed to be moving toward the establishment of a broader support among other Protestant churches. The fact that several people from churches belonging to the MIP tendency sat on a CTA consultative council (*consejo consultivo de iglesias*), raised high expectations regarding "the possibility that in the future the support of CTA may by widened." Oskam's serious overrating of the MIP's numerical strength (see previous paragraph) can only be understood given the great confidence he had in the whole project.

In 1981, on the occasion of his last journey to Chile and his departure as ICCO desk officer for Chile, Cees Oskam described his Chilean portfolio as a good, but in no way unproblematic, "package." The biggest organizations supported by ICCO were ACE, SEPADE, and the Vicaría, which were characterized as organizations working with the grass roots and aiming at organization building. It was regretted that only these three ICCO-sponsored organizations were directly church-related,[12] but the hope was expressed that through them others could gain access to ICCO. The positive aspects of the Chilean counterparts mentioned were depicted: Their political preference was diverse, like the nature of their work; the (financial) administration and mutual collaboration were sufficient; and they were flexible and inclined to invest in human resources. Most ICCO-related NGOs shared the following three objectives: organizational self-reliance, the lifting of the isolation of marginalized groups, and the preparation of leaders and cadre-training through the method of "popular education." At the end of his last evaluation, Cees Oskam listed the prospects for the near future and maintained that only small alterations in ICCO's Chile program were to be expected. New organizations were only to be considered worth supporting if they were suggested by ACE and SEPADE. Church projects, when related to SEPADE, should be treated with benevolence, even if the quality was dubious, because *"they may always play an important formative role within these churches"* (my italics).

The above account reveals that the ICCO-CTA/SEPADE relation was built on trust, and from the side of ICCO, on strong hopes of awaking consciousness among Protestants (Pentecostals) and engaging them in social action. As Juan Sepúlveda maintains, there was some discrepancy between both parties on the latter aspect. It seems that CTA/SEPADE was not aware of the fact that it was so highly valued by ICCO because of its potential role among Pentecostals. On the other hand, at least part of the SEPADE staff had increasing doubts about the feasibility of the whole consciousness-raising effort among Pentecostals.[13] Moreover, the relation of mutual confidence was in fact one among a limited number of people. At ICCO, until 1981 only one man could be addressed by the Chilean (and in fact all Latin American) counterparts.[14] During the time of my fieldwork in 1991 and 1992, two of the original founders of SEPADE were still there (Gabriel Guerrero, Samuel Palma), and Erasmo Farfán had been its director since 1978. Pioneer Francisco had been removed from the team in 1978 (see footnote 11); Marta Palma had in October 1986 become desk officer for Latin America at the WCC in Geneva. Meanwhile, several other leading MIP people acquired a position in the SEPADE team. Among them were members of all three previously mentioned leading MIP families.

In 1978 ICCO's Cees Oskam had already come up with questions about the strong family presence of the Palma brothers and sister (their father was MIP president at the time). The reaction by the CTA team was one of indignation; who was trying to discredit them? The critique was in part denied—there was indeed a confusion over one particular surname; not all Palma's belonged to the same family— but was also warded off with reference to the prevailing circumstances in which no qualified Pentecostals could be interested in the kind of work CTA did, because Pentecostals preferred pastorship to social work. This supposed lack of qualified and enthusiastic people to join the Pentecostal development agency, SEPADE, had two consequences. First, the initiators of the project felt that their control over the agency was legitimate from the point of view of the quality of their input and disposition. On the other hand, they felt a strong urge to proclaim the need for, and consequences of, a socially committed Pentecostalism. This desire is poignantly manifested in the conclusion of the 1979 CTA evaluation: "It is necessary to develop a socio-ecclesiastical analysis producing new biblio-theological ideas. This is indispensable to guarantee the institutional support the team actually enjoys" (Carrasco et al. 1979, 96; ICCO 1980).

Thus far, I have presented the SEPADE organization as a tightly knit family network, which, under the brutal military regime of Pinochet, got together with the intention of giving concrete shape to the social commitment that had always been latently present in their MIP church. From the beginning, support from abroad (WCC, ICCO, the English NGO, Christian Aid, etc.) had been generous and almost unconditional. This support, in combination with the tremendous challenge posed by the presence of a cruel military regime, meant that the SEPADE team set to work resolutely on the task of constructing and implementing "socioevangelical" ethics, as the editorial of the first edition of *Evangelio y Sociedad* announced (SEPADE 1985, 1). How this was done is described in the following section, in which I propose to unravel the range of activities that were undertaken from the CTA/SEPADE office and its staff.

Efforts at Community Development

The first CTA project sponsored by external funds was called "Social Service at the Neighborhood and Rural Level" (1976). Financial contributions were made by several agencies (among them ICCO), on the request of the WCC (CICARWS program). The document presenting the program starts by briefly mentioning CTA's starting points: ecumenism, pluralism, a holistic approach, participation, and creativity. The specific activities should all be understood as efforts aimed at the achievement of a new society, or "a new heaven and a new earth." Parting from this postmillennialist vision, the promise is made to stop working only when they hear "that loud voice from the throne saying . . . and death shall be no more, neither shall there be mourning nor crying nor pain anymore, for the former things have passed away" (Revelation 21:3–4). Concrete actions are said to be inspired by Bible texts like Isaiah 58:7 ("Is it not to share your bread with the hungry"), James 2:15ff, and Mark 1:1ff.

The *comedores infantiles* (soup kitchens for children) constituted the nucleus of CTA's early work; these kitchens were indeed about "sharing bread." Meals were prepared for children, most often by women from the Protestant (Pentecostal) churches where these comedores were situated. Although most comedores were linked to a local church (often a MIP one), its beneficiaries were not merely church members. Household incomes were used as the criterion for participation, in a similar way to the scholarship program. The latter supplied children from poor households with educational aids. Apart from these more or less structural relief programs, several sorts of temporary help were applied. Urgent cases of health and housing problems and a wide variety of other emergency cases were attended to. The youth from the Ochagavía and La Victoria MIP churches, for example, once worked on a roofing project in their neighborhoods. Dramatic individual cases of emergency were also served. On these last occasions, which were frequent, church women's groups played an essential part. The preconceived goal was to bring people who were in hopeless situations into one of the neighborhood organizations (comedores, unemployed funds, ecumenical centers, artisan workshops, youth groups, and other OEPs, see Chapter 3). Given the fact that most of the work devolved onto church people (women), it was obviously the church-related initiatives like the comedores that "benefited" most, that is, received new customers. It should not be surprising either that Sunday school attendance, for example, in La Victoria, increased notably because of the simple fact that a cup of milk and a roll were given to all children attending the classes. I was told by several women from MIP congregations that it had always been possible to keep some milk powder separate from the comedores' stocks for use in Sunday school meetings. Women from the Dorcas groups complained that this particular windfall was fading away since SEPADE had started to cut down its food-rationing program. This process started in the early 1990s, when international development cooperation with Chile was reconsidered. SEPADE functionaries in their turn, had difficulty explaining the logic of international food-aid policies to the former beneficiaries in the churches. The reduction of food aid notably contributed to the loss of credit SEPADE enjoyed among its "customers" in the churches.

The second project designed by CTA was called "Integral Urban and Rural Community Development." As I have demonstrated, this program came about at the suggestion of ICCO's Latin America desk officer of that time, Cees Oskam. This suggestion, fitting well into the community development wave that dominated international cooperation in the 1970s (Moser 1993, 194), was quickly and enthusiastically picked up by the CTA officers. This program had a broader scope than the previous, at least on paper, because it dealt with health problems, the organization of agricultural communities, social service, education, food distribution, and community centers. As was required in a community development plan, participation of the local communities received due attention. Pivotal in the project were the community centers, from where most of the activities of the remaining parts of the project were coordinated. Two of these centers were especially built for this purpose: one in La Victoria, the other in the south Chilean city of Los Angeles.

When I started my research in La Victoria in 1991, the La Victoria community center had recently been closed. In the postdictatorship era, it was presumed that neighborhood activities should be performed through the local organizations, making use of the available infrastructure, in an attempt to contribute to the democratization process at the local level. Under democratic rule, courses for leaders of neighborhood councils (*juntas de vecinos*), for example, were taught in a municipal building instead of using the SEPADE-owned center. Yet during the previous decade, the center had accommodated a wide range of activities. The building site was bought in 1976, but it was not until 1980 that it became fully operational. Most activities resulted from the children's programs, of which a day nursery was the main element. Parents of children assisting at the day nursery received some elementary educational coaching. On Saturdays preinstructed monitors organized a recreational program for neighborhood children (Centro de Recreación Infantil, CRI). Besides these regular, often weekly, activities, the community center housed several workshops, for example, sewing classes and one on social and Christian consciousness-raising aimed at Protestant women. Several youth's clubs—from the church, the university—and a theater group were also allowed to make use of the center.

The range of activities I refer to were selected from the 1980 report by CTA to its sponsor ICCO, but the type of work has not changed radically since then. What certainly did change was the scale on which the organization worked. The financial means grew proportionately with the expansion of the program, and, as we have seen, especially in the beginning, even faster.[15] The increase of the SEPADE personnel kept pace with the expansion of the financial means and the addition of new working areas. Health care, agricultural support, social service, education, food aid,[16] youth training, child care, workshops for underprivileged groups, and trade union support are all on the long list of activities performed by SEPADE/CTA. Its field of action, then, was largely comparable to that of many other Chilean NGOs during the time of Pinochet's regime.

What made this NGO different from the rest, however, is that it had its origin in a Pentecostal church and that one of its important goals was to change the socioreligious attitudes of Chilean Pentecostals. Instead of treating the whole of SEPADE's projects, I prefer to treat only those projects in which the specific application of the concept of community development[17] is most visible, particularly with a view to the specific Pentecostal target group. I realize that I am doing injustice to the SEPADE work as a whole, by focusing on its church-related efforts only. The scope of this book, however, accounts for this choice. The positive side, then, is that it enables me to work out in detail the Christian (Pentecostal) development cooperation enterprise. I will start with what became one of SEPADE's central objectives, to make the churches subservient to the community. In the course of time, this aim was institutionalized in a project called "Protestant Social Participation" (*participación social evangélica*). A major concern of this project was to design a new social ethic and teach it to church people. The youth/children's program was another concretization of this effort toward subserviency. In the nutrition program the ambiguous outcomes of the central objective are most clearly visible.

Teaching Social Participation to the Churches

In an internal evaluation document from 1986, SEPADE describes it-self as primarily an educational organization. "SEPADE understands its contribution to the working-class world (*evangélico* and non-*evangélico*) through what in our country and in Latin America in general is called 'popular education', which is the social practice working-class sectors display toward the formulation and execution of an alternative socio-political project" (SEPADE 1986, 48). Participation by the target groups in the discovery of their rights and the design of a project to defend them are key concepts of this development strategy, which, in Chile, became popular after the overthrow of what is called the "people's government" of Allende (ibid.).

SEPADE from the beginning had the Protestant segment of this working-class world as an important target group. In CTA's first community development program (1977) two important claims regarding its possible impact were made. First, CTA claimed to have a profound contact with "the base," particularly the Protestant congregations, distinguishing itself at this point from ACE and, to, a lesser extent, the Vicaría. Second, it maintained it was able to integrate Protestants into works of Christian commitment. The latter was presented as extremely important, because Protestants "have played a far too passive role in the social, political and economic process of its own people." With a clear hint to the conclusions of sociologist Lalive d'Epinay (1969), CTA declared that it was concerned with breaking the "social strike" Protestants were conducting. Logically, a major effort was made to involve as many churches as possible in the organization's work. In 1979, the already mentioned "consultative council of churches" was founded to facilitate CTA's entrance into the respective Protestant (Pentecostal) churches. Apart from the MIP, the Iglesia Wesleyana, and Iglesia Cristiana Universal (Universal Christian Church) supplied two people for this council. Six other, mostly Pentecostal churches are said to be involved in CTA's practical work (among them the IPCH). This involvement consisted of participation in one of the CTA projects, like the comedores or the recreational activities for children (CRI), but also in occasional workshops on Chile's actual situation and the role of the churches. Parallel to this concrete work with the churches a line of research was started. This research had two focuses: The first was a sociological one, aiming at mapping out the behavior of the

Protestant segment in Chilean society, the second was a theological inquiry in order to establish the biblical foundation for social action.[18] The sociological study took a long time to produce results. In 1987 a working document was produced (Canales et al. 1987) and finally resulted in a book called *En tierra extraña II* (Canales et al. 1991). The latter work provides an excellent view on "Pentecostal politics" in practice. I will therefore discuss the case study, presented in Canales's book under the name "Cordillera: Pentecostalism and Social Change" (Canales et al. 1991, 117–170), and contrast it with my own fieldwork observations. From an analysis of the SEPADE documents and its periodical *Evangelio y Sociedad* (1985–1994) I will comment on the theological project on Protestant social ethics in the next section.

The Cordillera Case

The authors of this case of action research take as the central characteristic of Pentecostalism the notion of leaving "the world" (= salvation) through conversion (Canales et al. 1991, 118). For the authors, this implies that Pentecostals have lost the identification with their social groups of origin. Once converted, Pentecostals no longer identify themselves with the people from the poor sector to which, in fact, they themselves continue to belong. Recovery of this poor identity—the reconciliation of Pentecostals with their poor fellowmen—is of crucial importance, and the book is written with the intention of making a contribution to the realization of this objective. The target groups for this operation were Pentecostals from a number of peasant communities in the southern province of Bío-Bío near the city of Los Angeles, for which SEPADE chose to use the term *Cordillera*. In these communities SEPADE, in close collaboration with the MIP, started an emergency program in the late 1970s. Soup kitchens for the children were the first activities, soon followed by the so-called CAPs (Centro de Abastecimiento Popular, communal purchasing center). In 1991, some eight hundred families are said to have participated in this expenditure-saving project. Besides the communal purchasing, SEPADE provided each participating family with an additional quantity of milk powder. Moreover, the beneficiaries themselves effectively took part in the running of the project. Therefore—because it implied organization of the people—this CAP project is called the biggest and most active social organization (OEP) in the area (ibid., 120).

The CAP program was not limited to Pentecostals, but its use of the MIP churches' infrastructure attracted a significant number of them.

For those, the project offered additional Bible courses (through the MIP churches), as an instrument to raise consciousness about their belonging to a socially deprived class. It was thought that working together with non-Pentecostals would help Pentecostals to break out of church boundaries and to attenuate their stereotypical rejection of any action in "the world." The research aimed to find out what meaning Pentecostals gave to their participation and, what is more important, whether or not a shift of the Pentecostal identity occurred. The results of the interviews conducted for the research are presented on a continuum that ranges from a simple reproduction of the traditional Pentecostal attitude ("this is no business of the church"), through assimilation ("I did it to show the Catholics that being a Pentecostal is not bad") and extension of it ("blimey, I say to myself, I've nothing to eat tomorrow"), to a final transformation of the Pentecostal identity ("God loves the poor man, this is the real gospel"). The crucial switch is made when people realize that the world is not a sinful place, but that *the world* is only a synonym for sin (ibid., 140).

It is a pity that from the description in the text it is impossible to deduce how this new Christian ethic was taught. Apparently, the interviewees are particularly asked to reflect on what has been changed in their attitude toward society. We do not hear how this process, with its successes and setbacks, took place over time; what can be read in the accounts is that people take different positions on the road to reaching the desired new ethic.[19] We hear about the different positions but not how people got from one position to the other, whereas the role of intervening actors, such as SEPADE, remains unclear. A serious omission in the text is a final appraisal of the total endeavor. It is only on the last page of the book that we get a glimpse of the less positive face of Pentecostalism. The caveat presented there says that mutual comprehension among Pentecostals often leaves much to be desired and that conflicts, rivalries, and schisms are of daily occurrence. The actual possibility of changing Pentecostal identity, which implies a profound cultural change (of meaning-making), is not for the most part questioned. I realize that an accurate appraisal of such an attempt at cultural change is indeed no easy job; the present book is, among other things, meant to demonstrate the difficulty of both the attempt and its assessment. Yet I maintain that the authors of *En tierra extraña II* pass over the slowness of cultural processes too hastily in their enthusiasm for the supposed results of the project they themselves initiated.

What we have seen in the foregoing Cordillera case is that a community development project (CAP), started out of sheer economic necessity and, with clear charitable properties, became a means to further efforts to construct a new Pentecostal social ethic. Unfortunately, we are not given the details of the process, and we do not obtain a clear insight into the impact on the Pentecostals involved. What the authors of the case do tell us is that the rejection of participation in the SEPADE program was only a temporary reaction by a small number of people. This could very well be the case. During my fieldwork, which mainly took place in Santiago, I hardly ever met Pentecostals from MIP and other SEPADE-related churches who disapproved of SEPADE's socioeconomic projects. Of course there were many complaints regarding the distribution of food, the criteria for admittance in a project, and so on. This kind of criticism from the beneficiaries can to a large extent be explained by the fact that it happened to be a limited good that had to be divided among a large number of potential clients. However, I never heard of people refusing to participate in one of the distribution projects.

A more serious criticism was directed against SEPADE's consciousness-building effort, which lay at the roots of the organization's reason for existence.[20] I interviewed various of the fiercest opponents to SEPADE from within the MIP. They always told stories about the worldly behavior of SEPADE officers, about the anti-Christian teachings they propagated, but these comments were never very much to the point. They told me, for example, how they abhorred ecumenism talks, but they could scarcely explain what it was that sent them into a fit. Maybe the following account reveals part of the discomfort experienced by anti-SEPADE people:

It was in a preparation course for Sunday school teachers (a SEPADE extension course). The theme was how to prevent young people from becoming drug addicts. Several people, under the guidance of a youngster, gave their opinion, but nobody even mentioned God's name, nor Jesus'. They had not even started with a prayer. So, it was only man that spoke. You know, in order to start a Bible study, you have to begin as God commands, with a prayer imploring the guidance of the Holy Spirit. Then I raised my hand and declared: "Here you have an alcoholic." And I immediately started to teach as it should be done, how God in his infinite compassion had saved me and taught me how to live. After all, we were in a Christian class, and not anywhere else where just medical prescriptions are distributed. I said "no, here the recipe is handed out by God." (Andrés, April 6, 1992)

The almost physical repugnance to SEPADE and its course, which can be deduced from this example, illustrates how deeply the Pentecostal habitus is incorporated. My interviewee's Pentecostal identity was an experiential (corporal) one, which was diametrically opposed to the "intellectualist" verbal discourse he felt exposed to in the SEPADE course. His reaction, then, was very appropriate: He resigned. A deeper understanding of what it was that was most alarming to this interviewee, we may get by listening to an opposing story by one of his "adversaries," who demonstrated a clear enthusiasm for SEPADE and its courses.

> Well, now I accompany the pastor to the SEPADE course, but before, he [the pastor] had invited others to come with him. They had gone with him, but only once. They said they did not like it at all. For example, the brother with whom we had this confrontation the other day . . . , he has been trained in a Bible institute run by the Assemblies of God; he has his own theology. When SEPADE people came to our church to teach some courses, for example on how the Bible was composed, or on ecumenism, the people only came to the first meeting and stayed away thereafter. I myself like this pastoral course I'm doing now [the base course on pastoral coaching]. To give an example, in the course we had to do a sort of role-playing, in which we had to imagine all kinds of problems about which people might want to consult us. We were taught how to react as human beings, not as superior pastors, who normally only refer to God, Jesus and heaven awaiting. We were taught to be different, to be a different kind of counselor. But they [those who only went once] complained to the pastor and told him that they did not agree with SEPADE's line. Hence our pastor does not invite people anymore, and he even does not announce SEPADE courses from the pulpit. He does not dare any more.
>
> There are people who have no idea about our church [the MIP], who don't know about its objectives, its meaning. In one meeting in La Victoria I heard a man complaining that the MIP had betrayed the principles of its founders, since it no longer behaved like a *Misión* (mission), that is by preaching the gospel. And many people who were present uttered consenting hallelujahs and amens. Really, only very few people know what the MIP is. Take for example the PUEC Sunday school material [the PUEC was to a great extent a SEPADE initiative], we do not use that any more, since they consider its contents politically inflammatory stuff. Yes, in La Victoria, in Ochagavía they do use that material, *but there the pastors have a far higher cultural level.* (my italics, Jorge, December 6, 1991 and April 21, 1992)

What seemed to give the most trouble in the SEPADE officers' teachings, then, was that an image of man was communicated that emphasized self-reliance and responsibility, which goes far beyond the total surrender to God. The classic Pentecostal relationship between man and God is affected, which for the traditional believers opens the floodgates of worldly influences. What was suggested in the SEPADE courses, is characterized by them as ephemeral and useless, containing only partial solutions.

The SEPADE program for 1987 for the first time mentioned the organization of such workshops as the proper ways to contribute to the realization of the central goal, the construction of a Christian social ethic. By that time, it was more or less clear to the SEPADE people what that meant, but it seemed equally clear that it would not be an easy task to spread it among the main—Pentecostal—target group. The strategy employed consisted of first winning over church leaders and pastors to the new ethic, with the future perspective that activities (including workshops) could be opened to a Pentecostal lay public (SEPADE 1987, 24). When I did my fieldwork, this top-down strategy was still in vogue. As the 1991–1993 triennial program reveals, the target group of the "Protestant social participation program," as it was then called, consisted of Pentecostal pastors and lay people who held leadership positions. The trickle-down effect appeared to be still very limited. I will now give a lengthy example of a SEPADE course/workshop, the "advanced course for Protestant community leaders." I was allowed to participate in this course, which was a core element of the SEPADE church program, and which explicitly touched upon the trickling-down of new ideas and practices, by means of "responsible leadership." I was allowed to participate on the condition that I would not be a mere observer but instead do my best to support both teachers and participants during the training sessions.[21]

A SEPADE Course

The pastoral teaching course I participated in consisted of eight afternoon sessions (twice weekly) and was held at the SEPADE office in Santiago. It aimed to improve the leaders' capabilities in detecting community problems and starting initiatives in collaboration with other neighborhood organisms (SEPADE 1991, 31–32). This objective, so nice on paper, was to be attained by acquiring and subsequently applying the "active listening" or feedback method (following the North American psychologist Carl Rogers). This technique was explained and practiced under the leadership of two SEPADE-employed pastors and an external consultant, a North American psychologist. When I joined the group at the third session, I heard that the first two meetings had been moderately attended. This time, there were thirteen people, and I was surprised to see that they were almost without exception pastors, the majority of them belonging to the "old-boys (and girls)-network" of SEPADE. Moreover, this session appeared to be the best attended of all, although the course was originally scheduled for a maximum of thirty participants.

I was surprised by this scant interest in participation, because of what SEPADE's director had once told me about the many people that were reached by his organization. If SEPADE had indeed such great appeal, why then was the interest for this particular course so limited? I also began asking myself how many Pentecostals were among these people and how many of them had become acquainted with SEPADE's Christian social ethics discourse? What was the impact of this Pentecostal politics of consciousness-raising? What was the reason that so very few people could be interested in it? Was it the general loss of interest in social action and community development that all Chilean NGOs in the post-Pinochet era were complaining about, or did it also have to do with the quality of the NGO offer? These and other awkward questions came to mind during my involvement in the SEPADE program.

With these considerations in mind I continued with the pastoral course about active listening. As the principal argument for such a course the point was made that pastors and other experienced church members are preeminently counselors of the congregation's membership; hence their principal quality should be the ability to really listen. People are said to approach their pastor mainly when they have problems, with high expectations regarding his/her problem-solving qualities. Most of the pastors present very strongly agreed, but much to their surprise they were told that they were not such good listeners at all. It was stated that in the pastor-client relation it is the pastor who dominates the conversation and puts forward his (her) views, which more often than not do not match with the believers' expectations. At the end of the session, the pastors were sent home with the instruction to attend to their clients in as unbiased a way as possible during the weeks preceding the next meeting and not to apply standard Pentecostal answers, like "pray more, sister" or "maybe it is God's will." At the next meeting, some of them appeared to have given it a try, but they reported serious difficulties. The active-listening method was therefore amply practiced among the course participants themselves.

The teachers of the course presented it as the only way in which people could feel they had been taken seriously and the real problems of believers could be grasped; therefore, they promised to take as much time as necessary to master the technique and get rid of the classical, hierarchical relationship between pastor and client. The exercises proved to be difficult and amusing at the same time, but at the next session people began questioning the usefulness of the method. What should be done if people want clear and rapid answers? Was it not the task of the pastor to provide answers to those who asked for help? Were they not obliged to answer according to the Pentecostal norms? At what moment could the pastor begin to answer, and even contradict, the client? What about the constant time pressure in this job?

When I heard these questions, I realized that what was happening in this course was a total reversal of the classical role of the pastor in the church community.[22] The answers to the questions posed were often very straightforward, especially if the psychologist in the team gave them. What it boiled down to was that pastors could not claim to have a monopoly of wisdom. But the participants were only partly satisfied with that message. Was there really no room for action, then? In the answer to that question, I for the first time heard a reference to the Bible: You will know them by their fruits; in other words, only the results will decide whether the method works or not. The rest of the course remained focused on the deconstruction of the classical pastoral problem-solving methods. With the assurance that promising results were to be expected from the application of the new method, the course ended.

Most of the participants in the case discussed had prolonged experience with SEPADE activities, but from their comments I infer that this course struck at the roots of their Pentecostal identity. Off the record, most of them told me they felt great hesitation regarding the practical use of this course. Although the people who took part were all church leaders, who had most often participated in several other SEPADE activities and might be expected to be susceptible to new discourses, the course message seemed too revolutionary. What then, could be the reason that there was so little enthusiasm for the course's central message, and more generally, why did this kind of course have such a small power of attraction anyway?

First of all, it should be taken into account that the vast majority of Pentecostal leaders are self-made people. When they become pastors, they do so as a result of prolonged practical experience. Their pastoral role, then, is shaped by the patron-client model that is commonly accepted in Pentecostal churches, as Lalive d'Epinay (1969) rightly postulates. Within the churches belonging to the non-classical, prophetic tendency in Chilean Pentecostalism, this behavior has so far not been eradicated either. Even the MIP, with its strong emphasis on church democracy and lay participation, suffers from it. The new pastoral attitude taught in this course cannot be expected to simply replace a practice that is rooted in Pentecostal habitus. At a more conscious level, the pastors and other church leaders notice very clearly that the adoption of this method directly affects their power position.

Secondly, there is another aspect at play rooted in Pentecostal habitus, namely the vast gap between Pentecostal practice and NGO activities. For most Pentecostals it is simply unthinkable to undertake any action without a religious—biblical—motivation. I especially allude to the religious discourse Pentecostals employ. Since the Bible is for most Pentecostals the outstanding authority in all matters, they prefer to have it at hand at all times. Any activity that neglects this central place of the Bible, then, is likely to produce limited results. I discussed this with SEPADE officers, who then explained to me what their fundamental dilemma was: If you do not use Bible texts, you have no real entrance with people; if you do use them, you need a lot of theological explanation to avoid a fundamentalist reading. But theology is not trusted either. Both options, then, have their own weaknesses. In the course I participated in, theology hardly played any role. Each session started with singing and praying, but the "active-listening method" was not recommended from a biblical perspective. The psychologist present turned out to be a supporter of the psychologist Carl Rogers, but this scientific claim could hardly cause much enthusiasm on the side of the participants. This lack of specific religious backing as experienced by the Pentecostals was a source of uneasiness, which I met not only at this particular course but also in most other SEPADE projects.[23]

A third argument for the moderate interest in SEPADE courses like the one just presented has its roots in the past. During the 1970s and 1980s, participation in SEPADE courses required a good deal of courage, for it was common knowledge that NGO activities were regarded with suspicion by the military regime, which, through an extended network of informers, managed to establish a culture of fear. Therefore, participation was a conscious act of resistance, a step that not many people were prepared to make. In the present situation, after the transition to democracy, this element of fear has ceased to exist, but nevertheless, a general decline in NGO and grass-roots organizations' activities has arisen. SEPADE has noticed this most clearly in its community development program, but its church-directed program has also suffered from this growing lack of interest.

In another area of the SEPADE work, belonging to the women's program, interest in the SEPADE contribution was also quite small. One of the program's aims was to train a group of female Protestant (Pentecostal) leaders in matters of gender, social organization, and the implementation of projects. Although the women's division at SEPADE had a feminist theologian in its midst (the others were not Protestants), the women who received this training apparently did not receive a religious discourse that they could sufficiently appropriate and apply in their teaching during Sunday school classes.[24] On one occasion, two of the women who had received the SEPADE training introduced the subject of machismo in a local MIP church. Most of the women present were eager to discuss this theme, but some of the men were able to dismiss its relevance easily by quoting a few famous Bible texts from the letters of the Apostle Paul. Here, the point is not whether these men were well informed or not but that the women in question could not assert in their defense any coherent vision that was rooted in a biblical discourse, an omission similar to the one I observed in the pastoral course.[25]

We have seen in this section that SEPADE, as the development agency of the Misión Iglesia Pentecostal, assumed a clear educational function with regard to the Protestant/Pentecostal churches to which it had access. This teaching role comprised the promotion of social participation by churches, by urging them to join in SEPADE's community development program, but also the offer of a varied training program, of which I have given some examples. The central objective of the latter was to bring about a change in the traditional Pentecostal identity. The recovery of the "identity of the poor" pursued by the SEPADE team, is viewed as a necessary step leading beyond commitment and service, to a more active stance, which entails making legitimate demands and defending collective rights (Canales et al. 1991, 168). The SEPADE staff felt obliged to assume a pioneer role with respect to the latter. In the next section, I will look at the role SEPADE played in the political field. This role was understood as a prophetic one, denouncing the abuses of the military regime, as well as inciting the Protestant churches and their members to adhere to that message and actively raise their voice against oppression.

Prophetic Outcries in the Wilderness: Attempts at Political Mobilization

During the nineteenth century, mainstream Protestantism in Chile maintained close relations to politics and political parties, especially the Partido Radical and to a lesser extent the Partido Liberal (see Ortiz 1993). Representatives of the historical Protestant churches engaged in the political struggle, even in Parliament, in defense of democracy and the separation of church and state (ibid.). Yet Chilean Pentecostals, who entered the scene from 1909 onward, did not follow the example of their Protestant ancestors. For them, participating in politics was the equivalent of delivering themselves to the world; they saw evangelizing as the primary task of every convert, which, as a consequence left little time for anything else except work. A recent survey on the position of Chilean Protestants paid ample attention to this topic, and the results made clear that in this respect, very little has changed since the early days of Pentecostalism (Fontaine and Beyer 1991, 102ff).

If the governments of Frei and Allende had shown an increase in political participation, particularly at the neighborhood level, the military coup broke off this process very effectively. Until 1983, the year of the first protests, any political activity was forbidden, and opposition groups operated secretly and without much conviction. The efforts of the Catholic Church, the NGOs, and the many grass-roots organizations that arose during the first half of the Pinochet regime were principally directed at relief work and hardly spoke out publicly against the rulers. In Chapter 3 we have seen that some of the Protestant church leaders seized the opportunity to ingratiate themselves with the regime; they founded the Consejo de Pastores as their representative. Until the early 1980s the Consejo had no public rival within the Protestant field.

Like the Vicaría, SEPADE initially focused on relieving the victims of the regime's policies and only gradually developed a more explicit and political critique of the regime itself. As can be read from

SEPADE's 1986 internal evaluation, the "critical Protestant segment," among which SEPADE reckoned itself, could only make itself heard from 1983 onward. Before that, solidarity work prevailed over public manifestations of criticism, for reasons of severe censorship and autocensorship (SEPADE 1986, 12). When we look at the SEPADE programs, we can indeed see that in the course of time, effectively from 1981 onward, consciousness-raising within befriended Protestant and Pentecostal churches became a topic of growing importance. Yet the projects in which this took place scrupulously avoided the use of political terms and topics. In the 1984–1986 "community development" program, there was a theological-pastoral subprogram; in the 1981–1983 version, this was simply called "support to the churches." Yet in the previous triennial program no projects of that kind figured. This autocensorship, which resulted in the cautious formulation of its programs, served a double purpose: to avoid trouble with the authorities as well as with the Pentecostal audience. For the first, political pronouncements could easily be seized upon as a pretext for withdrawing the legal personality of the MIP that SEPADE has always used. For the latter, any reference to political motives could discourage people from participating in the programs. From 1987 onward, the intentions of this church program became more clearly stated; first it was renamed "the construction of a Protestant social ethic," and in 1988 it read "social participation of the churches." The appearance and subsequent evolution of this part of the SEPADE work in the written project documents reflects the ever more visible, political role SEPADE played in the resistance to the military regime. It was most visible in the following areas: public statements, organization/institution-building, and the publication of background articles in its magazine *Evangelio y Sociedad.*

Yet the political messages of SEPADE's activities have always been conveyed by using religious language, such as the reference to "the voice crying in the wilderness" (Isaiah 40:3). An analysis of the first two numbers of the SEPADE journal *Evangelio y Sociedad* may serve to illustrate the wide scope of SEPADE's activities and interests, although at the same time it tried to keep a fairly low profile. The latter aspect of SEPADE's appearance was mentioned to me by its advocates and opponents alike. The present director of the NGO and the president of the CCI confirmed by word of mouth that this reticence was chosen deliberately in order not to discourage other churches from participating. It was thought wise, moreover, not to emphasize the solvency that donations from abroad supplied; this could only stir up the allegations of self-glorification and self-enrichment.

> Much of the work done by the MIP committee is in fact done at the office of SEPADE. The same holds for the CCI and the PUEC. If Juan Sepúlveda, Erasmo Farfán, or I myself speak at a certain occasion, a meeting of the pastoral program or a press-conference, the people view us as church people. (Samuel Palma, Ferbruary 28, 1992)

> The CCI could support itself only with the support of SEPADE. For example, the prayer campaign,[26] was half paid for by SEPADE. Why? Because we had to strengthen the CCI, which was our contribution to the Protestant world. But we provided substantial contributions to any meeting, meditation or publication. We have guided the Protestant world constantly. (Carlos, SEPADE officer and CCI president, June 24, 1992)

Adversaries of SEPADE, however, never missed a chance to mention how well they knew that SEPADE was at the bottom of every initiative on the prophetic side.

> Shall I tell you where they [SEPADE] pull the strings? To start with, they control the access to the WCC (Erasmo Farfán, Marta Palma). Then they have [sic] the CTE (Juan Sepúlveda), CCI (Daniel Godoy, Daniel Farfán), ECLOF (Narciso Sepúlveda). And of course, SEPADE itself is accessible only to those whom they like, and by no means to people from the grassroots. (Eduardo, IMP member from Concepción, December 6, 1991)[27]

Even if we allow for a reasonable measure of exaggeration from both sides, it seems clear that SEPADE has indeed had a strong influence within the ecumenical Protestant field. It is therefore interesting to see what kind of political message was spread. Let us see how the SEPADE spearheads of denunciation, reflection, and organization-building were intertwined in the early issues of its periodical.

The Message of *Evangelio y Sociedad*

The editorial article of the first number of *Evangelio y Sociedad* (1985) points to the crisis Chile has been plunged into by the military regime and to the consequent challenges that the churches have so far not been able to answer, owing to a lack of necessary tools, criteria, and experience. In short, the churches are said to urgently need a Protestant (Pentecostal) social ethic that allows for answers to questions like, "are Christians allowed to join the protests?" or "how is it that some Protestant leaders support the regime, while others demand that democracy is restored?" On page 5 is a public condemnation by the CCI (itself still in the making) of a fivefold murder. Then follows an interview with an Argentinean bishop on the violations of human rights in his country. Next comes a contribution by the liberation theologian Richard Shaull on the biblical bases for democracy. After an article focusing on the hermeneutic reading of the Bible texts concerning women, three testimonies on the role of Protestant churches under authoritarian rule are juxtaposed. This article ends with the reproduction of a public letter by the CCI, demanding the return of democracy, and signed by Gabriel Almazán (Presbyterian, president) and Juan Sepúlveda (MIP/SEPADE, vicepresident). Next comes a profile of the new general-secretary of the WCC, the Uruguayan Emilio Castro, who makes a plea for ecumenism and rejects all accusations of Communist sympathies. After this interview, we get another one, with MIP member Juan (see Chapter 4) on his commitment to neighborhood activism and the price he had to pay for it. The last article is by Juan Sepúlveda, the magazine's general editor. It contains an overview of WCC thinking on social problems. The number ends with a Bible study lesson on "how to live the kingdom of God in this world," which among other texts, treats the famous verse "my kingdom is not of this world" (John 18:36). As an appendix to this first issue, a separate paper, by another liberation theologian, Franz Hinkelammert, is included, in which the economics of capitalism is rejected on the basis of biblical arguments.

The second issue of the magazine is a continuation of the search for (the roots of) a Protestant social ethic. The contributions again leave little room for doubt about the political message. The first article contains an interview with the first CCI president and recently appointed CLAI secretary for the Andes region, Gabriel Almazán, who declares all Chileans guilty for the present disastrous situation of the country: "God's judgement strikes all of us inasmuch we have remained silent and blind toward injustice, but especially those who have the governing power." A connected article, by Juan Sepúlveda, makes a plea to break the silence and speak the truth, using the gospel of John as a startingpoint. He ends his article by stating that "the fruits of a regime of lies are murder, suffering and death. . . . We leave to the readers the task of extracting the actual meaning of this biblical reflection." Next, the Argentinean liberation theologian and ex-WCC president, Míguez Bonino, describes how Protestants in Argentina reacted to the

military rulers. The reaction of the oppression of liberation theology
by the Vatican, in the person of Leonardo Boff, is strongly criticized
in a short notice. Then we switch back to Chile and read a public
notification of adherence to investigation judge Canovas, who had accused the military police of a threefold murder. From the WCC central
committee meeting in Buenos Aires comes an interview with the female MIP member of the committee and SEPADE officer Marta Palma.
Another interview, with bishop Toro of the Wesleyan Church, reveals
the daily struggle for the poor by a small church. It ends with an
expression of thanks to all institutions supporting this struggle, like
the CCI and SEPADE. Toro concludes that the gospel's central message
is justice. This same message, justice and liberation, is considered to
be the central contribution of Wesleyanism to Latin American Protestantism. The defender of this position, Methodist theologian Míguez
again, thus provides the theological-historical endorsement for the political conduct of the Chilean Wesleyan church of bishop Toro. The
magazine ends with a Bible study lesson on "how to live up to Christian hope in the face of fatalism and apathy."

From this short summary of the first two *Evangelio y Sociedad*
issues, it is clear that they contain strong and theologically based
political messages and statements. The next two issues—the last to
appear under the military regime—struck the same note; the fourth
issue had as an appendix the previously mentioned open letter to
Pinochet, the most political document ever delivered by the CCI.[28]
The focal point of the SEPADE churches program (headed by Juan
Sepúlveda) during the 1984–1987 period was a dedication to this
task of directing public opinion and coordinating consultations with
other church-related organizations. This meant frequent talks and
joint action with the Catholic Vicaría, and with the ecumenical fasic
and Diego de Medellín.[29] This period of feverish activity, which
partly coincided with the riots and protests in the working-class
neighborhoods, is considered by the principal actors to be the time
in which the "prophetic voice" sounded most loudly.[30]

The open letter to Pinochet was drafted by a triumvirate and sent
to the churches to be discussed (Sepúlveda in Ossa 1992, 37). Yet we
do not come to know to what extent people from the respective CCI
member churches were involved in this process, and more precisely,
what their contribution was in this discussion and if they finally
agreed with its contents. Because my fieldwork was done within a
totally different political context, it is only in retrospect that people

gave their opinion about the politically turbulent events of the mid-1980s. Juan Sepúlveda quite accurately points out the interpretative difficulties of my fieldwork observations in this respect:

> The fieldwork was done in a situation which was completely different from that to which the leaders [of the CCI] responded. . . . When the letter to Pinochet was published by the CCI (or other similar documents) the degree of tension and violence in society had grown to such an extent that the general feeling was that "something had to be done." *Even* the ordinary members of the Pentecostal churches [at least those referred to in the current study] considered that their pastors and leaders rightly gave their opinion on the matter. Speaking as an actor in that historical event—and therefore possessing a biased view—I still think that when the prophetic action of the CCI reached a climax, the ordinary members of the MIP in Santiago approved of this kind of interventions. Many of them participated actively in the "Prayer Campaigns" [between 1985 and 1990]. (Personal letter Juan Sepúlveda, June 1994)

Even if we assume with Juan Sepúlveda that a significant number of MIP believers supported the actions of their (SEPADE) leaders, the question remains what it was that they were prepared to support. Surely, most MIP members wanted to be freed of Pinochet,[31] and SEPADE and the CCI were accepted as the channels through which this desire could best be manifest. This by no means implied, however, that they embraced the liberation theological discourse, so compactly represented in the *Evangelio y Sociedad* magazine. Its circulation among ordinary church members was limited, and as the SEPADE staff frankly acknowledged, its contents were hardly accessible to them either.[32] The impact of the prophetic discourse among church members, therefore, remains at least an open question. Here, a parallel with the pastoral teaching program described previously suggests itself. In both cases under discussion there is a yawning gulf between the various discourses used by church (and NGO) leaders and the ordinary Pentecostal church members, even if these latter participated in SEPADE activities.

With the return of democracy—or as some say, from the start of a transition period leading to it—SEPADE's role changed from one of an accuser to one of a critical companion. The process of re-democratization of Chilean society was the topic SEPADE, like most other NGOs, embraced. At staff level, friendly relations with

representatives of the leftist political parties in the coalition government of president Aylwin were maintained. As the triennial program (1991–1993) shows, expectations about the possibilities of
joint action with government programs were high; SEPADE took on
the role of guardian of the interests of the poor and their participation in the transformation process (1991, 5). The "neighborhood
organizations" program was therefore continued, in which further
emphasis was laid on local democracy through the reinforcement of
the neighborhood councils. These *juntas de vecinos* were viewed as
the crucial links between the grass roots and the municipalities
(ibid., 8).[33] Three types of activities were designed to reinforce local
democracy: schooling for neighborhood leaders, the provision of
material facilities for these leaders, and a series of projects aimed at
"improving the quality of life." This part of the SEPADE program,
however, met with little enthusiasm among the pobladores it was
aimed at, as I was able to witness on several occasions myself. At
the time of the municipal elections in 1992, SEPADE started a campaign, like other NGOs, to call attention to the importance of these
elections for the people; Protestant candidates were also interviewed
and presented in the SEPADE journal.[34] Yet as a consequence of a
radical internal reorganization of the SEPADE bureau and overall program, the neighborhood project was dismantled. Simultaneously,
there was a growing disposition to cooperate with government programs, such as those advanced by FOSIS (Fondo de Solidaridad e
Inversión Social, Solidarity and Social Inversion Fund). After 1990,
Chilean NGOs in general maintained friendly relations at government level—in part because of declining external funds. These nongovernmental organizations, then, are facing increasing challenges
now that the boundary with government-initiated work has become
diffuse (see, e.g., Wils 1991).

In the next section, we will return to what in the early 1990s came
to be called the failure of popular education—of which this part
of the SEPADE program (along with the pastoral one) was a clear
example—and its repercussions on (international) development policies. Moreover, we will hear voices criticizing the part SEPADE
played. These criticisms, however, are not specific to this particular
NGO; as I hope to show, they belong to a much wider critique on the
impact of development aid channeled through NGOs (see Stuurgroep
1991; Edwards 1989). Much of what is nowadays considered to have
gone wrong was in fact the outcome of a broadly shared series of

presuppositions among a vast range of international development agencies and NGOs. All these presuppositions had to do with the fundamental question of what role target groups were to play in development, how they were to be reached, and to what extent they should (and could) be directed from the outside.

Critical Voices

In the course of its institutional existence, SEPADE's central objective has shown a growing emphasis on its contribution to the development and reinforcement of what was called the active participation of "the people" or "working-class sector" in Chile's "democratic reconstruction" (SEPADE 1986, 28). The first phase of its existence (1975–1980) was largely dominated by actions resulting from a spirit of solidarity. After 1980, when Pinochet's authoritarian constitution came into operation, and particularly with the beginning of the national protests in 1983, SEPADE began to take a more active part in awakening the consciousness of its target groups (the urban and rural poor, and the Protestants in particular) through "popular education" methods. Initially, the goal was for people to participate more actively in community organizations, whereas later the efforts became more concentrated on stimulating local democratization initiatives. *Participation*, then, has been a key word in SEPADE's institutional politics from 1980 onward.

Participation was also the central notion in the development concept handled by SEPADE. Development was defined as "a liberating process aimed at human beings who are conceived as creative subjects of their own future" (SEPADE 1984, 3). Development was viewed as liberation to be achieved through participation. The role of the SEPADE institution was considered one of facilitating and accompanying people in the process of "recovering their voice" (ibid., 4).[35] Such a view corresponded well with those of the external donors. The mere title of the ICCO development policy document, "Development and Participation"—highlighted here because ICCO has been SEPADE's main sponsor over the years—is suggestive in itself. ICCO's development policy, which is strongly influenced by WCC thinking, has chosen the perspective of people's participation as its angle and is defined in the document just mentioned as "economic growth tied together with social justice and self-reliance" (ICCO 1985, 10). Whereas ICCO aims to reach the poorest and the most marginalized through programs that give priority to this central goal, SEPADE claims to promote the capacities of the same working-class sectors. Since the two organizations shared a close identification with the WCC, their cooperation over matters of development was obvious.

In international development politics, from the second half of the 1970s the "participation" discourse succeeded the modernization current, which was largely nonparticipatory. From then on it became the central concept in all major aspects of development intervention (Oakley 1991, 6), to such an extent that it is tempting to speak of "participation rhetoric," especially because so few attempts at evaluation of the impact and depth of this development politics device have been made (at least regarding Dutch development politics; see Frerks 1991 and Hoebink 1988 for the exceptions). The acclaimed pros—higher efficiency and effectiveness, improved self-reliance, coverage, and sustainability—strongly depend on whether the people themselves tangibly benefit from participation in development projects (Oakley 1991, 18). What follows in this section is a contribution to an ongoing and extremely fundamental discussion within the field of (inter)national development cooperation.

As already stated above, SEPADE claims to have (had) broad access to people from the lower classes (SEPADE 1986, 32). Yet the end of the military regime has brought a sound kind of self-criticism. According to the present director, SEPADE had in former years been an inwardly looking group of people with a high degree of commitment and a strong belief in "the people" and "participation." Internal relations had been extremely horizontal, although the same 'mythology' of mutual solidarity was applied to the NGO's target groups: women, pobladores, Protestants, and youth. It had proven possible to win donor support with this stirring discourse, because it was internationally shared by many institutions. For a long time, it had not been necessary to demonstrate the impact of NGO work, because the mere struggle "for the people" and "against the dictator" could ascertain a regular income flow. When, in the changed circumstances after 1989, demands for effectiveness were being increased, this created serious problems. As the SEPADE leaders argued, ICCO had never been very exacting, and the purport of the communication had in fact been rather superficial from the very beginning until the present day. SEPADE's lack of attention to the impact of its own teaching programs (using the popular education method), in combination with feeble demands from the external donor side, makes an inquiry into the matter of the sustained effects of the prophetic message of social ethics among SEPADE's target groups fascinating enterprise.

Once I heard a SEPADE leader, versed in scripture, heaving a sigh that "no prophet is acceptable in his own country." This biblical reference (from Luke 4:24) may well express a common feeling among Chilean ecumenical church leaders. Although they would probably prefer not to describe themselves as prophets, they all experience opposition within their churches, albeit in various degrees and diverging ways. Because I constantly moved between leaders and the rank and file of churches during my research, I was able to grasp—at least partly—what types of uneasiness with the prophetic discourse and practices were circulating.[36]

Only part of the critique was really directed against the contents of this discourse; many reproaches were leveled at SEPADE's institutional politics of distribution, the arbitrariness of its decisions, and its limited accessibility. Of course there were a certain number of people who rejected SEPADE's crucial ideas and practices categorically.

> In fact, SEPADE's discourse is not Pentecostal at all. They have strong ties with the WCC, but in that respect I disagree. SEPADE, and also the pastors of my MIP, know I disagree with them. I can only meet with people who share the same set of principles. Does not the Bible, the prophet Amos, tell us: 'Do two walk together, unless they have made an appointment?' [Amos 3:3]. In that sense I am a fundamentalist and very reticent with regard to ecumenical encounters. I have been there regularly, but I do not find myself at ease there, certainly not if people start smoking. I find that incompatible with being a reborn Christian. I have no problems meeting like-minded Christians, but that is about the limit. (Enrique, January 7, 1992)

Enrique's opinions differed clearly from the official MIP stance, and more particularly from SEPADE practice. In his José María Caro congregation there were other people with similar ideas, although the pastor was not a strong promoter of the ecumenical worldview either. He was not opposed to the SEPADE work, but he had not assimilated its socioreligious discourse of subservience and prophetic action. He saw the SEPADE-financed CRI and CAP programs functioning in his church above all as a service to the church members and not as a community service. Unlike the La Victoria congregation, the José María Caro church had never become strongly involved in political, antiregime activities through SEPADE work.

> Well, under the dictatorship we just continued working. SEPADE helped us as usual, gave us our milk. In fact, it was then that we got the largest quantities of milk. . . . We never had problems; at most, people were a little afraid of what other people might think of those donations of goods. (pastor Roberto, December 2, 1991)

For the José María Caro congregation, SEPADE was foremost a supplier of material goods, not of new and useful religious messages. The traditional Pentecostal worldview was not fundamentally challenged, simply because new messages were only seldom offered in concrete form. Hence, people like Enrique and his self-proclaimed fundamentalism met little opposition there. The vast majority of the congregation members, however, really only knew SEPADE's food help-projects. Just a few were more deeply involved in the core programs of the NGO (e.g., the previously quoted Jorge). The same situation applied to most other MIP congregations. Critics of SEPADE's public manifestations, often making themselves heard during ecumenical meetings, could be found at all echelons of the denomination, but the majority of MIP members were noncommital. Only the La Victoria and Ochagavía congregations had a stronger identification with—and played an active role in—the SEPADE work, although critics could always be found there too.

So, SEPADE's efforts at Pentecostal politics met with opposition by a small group of conservatives/fundamentalists, although the group of enthusiastic supporters was equally small and concentrated mainly in a few congregations. The majority of MIP members were first of all consumers of SEPADE-provided material goods and often indifferent to the sociopolitical—prophetic—message. Because they constituted the largest group in the church that I studied, I will try to have a somewhat closer look at the attitude these people assumed toward SEPADE.

> The material we use in Sunday School classes is from SEPADE; that is what the cover says. Well, it is a good help to prepare a sermon, but there are some things. . . . Well, when you do not like it, you just do not use it, or you take another part. That is, the material can be used

for a class, or a sermon; you can just use it for that purpose and leave it like that. I mean without making the most of it. That is one of the things that you can do. (Marta, La Victoria, May 3, 1992)

This example illustrates that it is perfectly possible for church members to skip the explicit (and implicit) messages in the SEPADE material.[37] Most of the time this was not done out of disagreement but because the material's purpose was not experienced as particularly relevant. This gap between the way of thinking at the churches' grass roots and among the body of specialists (in the church as well as in SEPADE) was a constant source of concern—and not seldom irritation—to both sides. As a pastor from a neighboring church—who himself for a long time had been given SEPADE support—remarked about the José María Caro MIP church:

If a pastor happens to have become aware of the need for social commitment, without possessing the capacity to convey it in front of his church, he will tend to remain silent and avoid problems which might cause people to leave the church. That is the problem SEPADE has with its churches. Pastor Roberto has that problem—he is unable to transmit the message. Moreover, he has some antiecumenical leaders in his church. So, for a pastor to be able to open his church to serving the community surrounding it, his church members have to share his opinions. If not, it is no use for the church to engage in community work. (Manuel, pastor Iglesia Reformada, December 30, 1991)

This same pastor Manuel represents a group of people who through their relation with SEPADE had developed high expectations as to the continuation of material support to their projects. This problem of dependency, which is also common to many development projects outside the ecclesiastical realm, became more strongly felt when the size and character of the international development aid changed after Chile's transition to democracy. Pastor Manuel had been able to enlarge his church building substantially with the construction of a SEPADE-sponsored community center. He himself had been paid as the center's director. During my first meetings with this pastor—in which he told me the story of his struggle for the recognition of the social dimension of Pentecostalism—I received a very favorable picture of SEPADE as the principal promoter of change in the Chilean Protestant world. Yet relations were quickly disturbed, when in the course of 1991, the flow of money appeared to be finite. Pastor Manuel's judgment suddenly turned negative: SEPADE's politics were arbitrary, its officers were out to favor themselves above the people they were supposed to serve, and so on.

The frustration about changes in NGO politics and its consequences is common to much development work. Part of the explanation is that aid—especially if given over a prolonged time span—sets in motion a process of habituation. Development workers know this is to a certain extent inevitable, but the most frustrating aspect for them is that in numerous cases the presumed genuine social commitment of the people they work with turns out to contain a great deal of self-interest. In the case of SEPADE, the spin-off in terms of jobs, favors, and prestige the development program entailed, created a group of people who depended heavily on NGO money and who were therefore to benefit most from a continuation of the program. The following case illustrates this point.

The Case of Pablo

In the early 1980s Pablo had become caretaker of the day nursery SEPADE ran at the La Victoria community center.[38] Until 1992 his job had been secure. As he himself told me, the job had come as a perfect godsend, when at that time he had run out of work. Pablo also told me moving stories about church activities on behalf of the community. Yet there was always a hidden critique on people within the church, whom he supposed were acting self-interestedly. He suggested that he had expressed his opinions repeatedly, but in vain. The image he tried to offer me was one of a man who could not stand injustice and more particularly, who stood up for equal sharing of the cake [SEPADE money and services]. By the end of my fieldwork, Pablo had lost his job. Soon after that, he and his wife withdrew from the church, after some fruitless attempts to talk his objections over with the church council and pastor Erasmo Farfán. I had to say farewell to him at a time when he was returning to a non-Pentecostal mode of life (e.g., he started drinking alcohol again) and with dubious prospects of work.

I talked over Pablo's case with pastor Erasmo Farfán, who sketched me one of the many dilemmas ecclesiastical development agencies have to face: what to do with the high expectations of material benefits arising among church members as a consequence of the existence of a church-owned NGO that does a good deal of business.

"The worst problem we face is dependency and habituation. Take for example the family of Pablo. They stopped going to church. Why?

Because they feel terribly neglected, because their contract [with SEP-ADE] has been terminated. Our day nursery program was not to be continued and we settled the procedure of dismissal correctly. What happened was a terrible commotion in the church. 'What about solidarity, what is the pastor doing now,' was the reproach I had to cope with. Because they [Pablo's family] had spread their view of the matter, they had convinced many people that they had been wronged by SEPADE. So I went to them and told them to tell the complete story. I explained to them again that all things come to an end, that even children have to become independent from their parents and develop separately. We had been warning him for two years, but he always replied that God was not going to leave him to his fate. But when he finally lost his source of income, he started blaming us for that. This is partly the reason why SEPADE does not only engage church people. That would create strong feelings of dependency. Pablo himself used to say that he could not be dismissed, because he was a church member, you see, but an institution like SEPADE cannot function properly when it is constantly confronted with these and similar claims. Just imagine us having solely Protestant employees; then we would have trouble in the church over every case of dismissal, since the people have in their mind that we are an institution based on solidarity, an institution of the church that will therefore never dismiss a person. This and other similar cases have helped us to constitute our identity [as an organization that must go beyond the welfare approach, he means], but we have had to pay the price in our churches. We not only lost entire churches in the past, but now we are also losing individual church members. The milk program is being phased out, and people are losing SEPADE-related jobs, etcetera. All this causes problems in the churches. The church may be a community of believers, where we rejoice in the Spirit, but it is also a community where the things I just described encounter opposition. It contributes to the community's disintegration; people do not understand these things." (Erasmo Farfán, March 30, 1992)

My evaluation of Pablo's case—which was by no means unique—largely coincides with pastor Erasmo Farfán's analysis. It is a clear illustration of the twilight zone between conviction and interest on the part of the NGO beneficiaries. As a matter of fact, the same was true for the staff members of NGOs, particularly when they parted from such a clear worldview as in the case of SEPADE (see also Hojman 1993, 16, 17). The relationship with a particular Pentecostal church, the MIP, made SEPADE even more vulnerable to this kind of critique. SEPADE was very anxious to spread its socioreligious message, but at the same time had to face the problem that people could superficially adhere to these ideas, while primarily having a view to their personal interest. The mix of spiritual and material benefits SEPADE as an NGO provided for people, was the outcome of the NGO's strong hopes of changing people's religious (Pentecostal) worldview and its desire to also provide concrete material aid. Although a man like pastor Erasmo Farfán seemed well aware of the tension this target entailed, there was still substantial disappointment on the SEPADE side over the disposition and the purely materialistic preferences of its target groups, and especially the limited extent to which new religious ideas had sunk into people. Analogously, however, the SEPADE staff people themselves were also often accused of serving their own interests and of reinforcing their power positions under the cloak of high ideals.

A separate—although related—kind of critique had to do with the tendency toward organizational professionalization, at the cost of solidarity and commitment, that was becoming tangible at SEPADE, as in other Chilean NGOs, after 1989. SEPADE and MIP leaders appeared to be disappointed in the behavior of church members and target groups, yet part of the latter group was equally disappointed in what was observed as the growth of a businesslike attitude in the NGO. The different meanings that were attached to the SEPADE work became more clearly visible with the return to democracy. For the SEPADE staff that was the right moment to start phasing out the charity and solidarity approach, which until then had gone together with their self-conceived role of consciousness-raising. SEPADE officers at last felt entitled to strive for the recognition of their professional expertise, an aspiration, which for a long period, had been subordinated to relief work and efforts at Protestant consciousness-raising. Since large parts of the Protestant/Pentecostal target groups had particularly focused on the material benefits, the contrast between the various interests became more clear-cut.

At the MIP general assembly of 1992, for example, the SEPADE position and role were amply discussed; a vehement discussion was held over the substitution of pastor Erasmo Farfán as SEPADE's director by Samuel Palma, who was not an active church member (anymore). Both the fact that, for this appointment, the official church rules (which assigned this task to the assembly) were said to have been ignored and the clear intentions of the new director to reshape SEPADE were profoundly resisted by several pastors and lay representatives. For Narciso Sepúlveda, threefold MIP president and pastor of the Ochagavía congregation, this replacement was highly symbolical; for him, it represented the loss of influence of the MIP over an institution aspiring to the status of a respected, professional consultancy bureau.[39] Behind this discussion, there seems to have been hidden the same old suspicions about political manipulation that have always been present in the background. Erasmo Farfán was considered to be an indispensable stabilizing element and major guarantee that political preferences would not (again) predominate. It was feared this would happen the moment Farfán withdrew.

My point about the effects of institutional professionalization can probably best be illustrated by referring to the food program. As has been observed earlier on, church members saw this program mainly as a chance to alleviate their difficult living conditions. SEPADE officers never denied that this was one of the planned aims, but under the leadership of Miguel, the brother of SEPADE's director, the program was transformed from a food-aid program into a proper nutrition program, very much in agreement with the food policies of international donors, like the Dutch SOH. Miguel once gave me the following perspective:

I see food aid as a disappearing phenomenon. It is superfluous in Chile; what we need are economically productive projects. What remains of the food aid has to be submitted to severe control. No more charity and gifts to the churches. That is the only way to separate chaff from wheat. Formerly we [PROAL, the food program of SEPADE] supported some five hundred cases [he means churches], nowadays only twenty-five, from which ten are MIP churches. But the quantities are rapidly declining. What we need to do now is teaching people how and what to eat; I mean a real nutrition policy. (Miguel, April 2, 1992)

This attitude of the medical doctor, Miguel, sharply contrasts with that of the recipient, Elisa, the wife of MIP José María Caro pastor Roberto:

Where does all that money go now? Before, we received sufficient products. Now we hardly get anything. The CRI and CAP projects of our church are receiving so little that nothing remains for the church. We will go and look for other sponsors. That won't damage our

relations with SEPADE; what we get is little more that nothing anyway.
(Elisa, July 25, 1992)

What was happening in the post-Pinochet period, then, was a profound reorientation of SEPADE's politics. The prophetic role had become less pronounced,[40] and its role as benefactor of the poor could
no longer raise much support from foreign donors, because Chile's
economy contrasted positively with that of other Latin American
countries. It was for this reason that the SEPADE staff, after prolonged and heated internal debates, decided to transform the NGO
into a professional organization that no longer depended on the will
of one single church but could be considered a really ecumenical
organization. As Gabriel Guerrero told me:

> Actually we would like to limit the church influence over SEPADE; the
> church can only hamper our intentions to develop projects that can
> pass professional and technical tests. In the past we worked together
> as a group of friends who joined together in a common set task. But I
> think it is good that all those professionals SEPADE engages are judged
> on the basis of their professional qualities. That is better for their cur-
> riculum, too. In the near future we will have to collaborate with the
> government and the respective ministries on the basis of our expertise,
> for foreign donor support is likely to stop. That is why we need to
> become a respected consultancy bureau. That is what is going on now;
> look at Samuel Palma, how he dresses. He is the boss now. Efficiency
> requires transparent authority structures. We cannot sit together on
> the floor and wear Indian dresses anymore. (Gabriel Guerrero, August
> 10, 1992)[41]

Within the organization itself this change of attitude was not entirely uncontested. There were complaints about the loss of the
"human dimension" and the sharing of ideas, about the growing
gap between SEPADE and its target groups, and the inevitable bureau-
cratization the rapprochement with the Chilean government entailed. One officer even remarked that the present situation meant a
return to the old Chilean bureaucratic traditions. "What we did during military rule, working 200 percent, is now reduced to official-
dom, working from nine to five, which has nothing to do with
commitment. Ordinary people cannot understand this change of
orientation. But what can we do, if organizational consultants are
having it their way?" Consequently, some cooperators sent in their

resignations, others acquiesced in the new situation, and still others defended the new situation, stressing that professionalization should not and does not necessarily lead to a loss of commitment.

It is also interesting to indicate briefly ICCO's role in this process. Until 1991 the work of SEPADE and the size of its budget were not for the most part questioned. In line with the official Dutch development cooperation policy things started to change dramatically from 1992 onward. Two important events provided the context for a change in attitude toward the Dutch development relation with Chile. First, the desirability of a relation of development cooperation was increasingly questioned, when the initial enthusiasm over the recovery of democracy in Chile had diminished. Supporting the new democracy was initially the startingpoint of the Chile policy of the Dutch government (Tweede Kamer 1990, 2),[42] but shortly afterward a comparative look at Chile and other, especially Andean, Latin American countries was seized upon to revoke this privileged position. Additionally, the impact studies of the Dutch Cofinancing Program for Development Cooperation, which followed the public discussion about the effectiveness of development aid in the late 1980s and early 1990s, urged—among other things—a renewal of priorities, based not least upon a cost-benefit analysis (Stuurgroep 1991). At ICCO, the outcome of this impact study produced an organizational evaluation and consequent reorganization in which *efficiency* was one of the key words. Leaving aside whether this operation was successful or not, it certainly also involved a critical look at the respective country policies. Unlike the Dutch minister, ICCO did not immediately remove Chile from its program, but it was decided to phase out the Chile projects slowly.

For fifteen years, ICCO had been a loyal and generous sponsor of SEPADE-designed development projects. The—supposedly—shared interest in the development of a "new," socially committed and prophetic Pentecostalism (Protestantism) had been the basis of the relationship. As I have already described, the MIP was viewed as a church that might be able to set in motion a process in which more Protestant churches would embrace ecumenical positions and take on their social responsibilities. SEPADE was considered to be the proper instrument in this process. The progress of this process was beginning to be questioned by the ICCO officers for Chile in the early 1990s. As a matter of fact, the very feasibility of the project was viewed with scepticism. Supporting an NGO like SEPADE was something that could easily be defended during military rule, by stressing that it was the "prophetic voice of Pentecostalism"; after the defeat of Pinochet more tangible results were expected. "Popular education" methods aimed at teaching people how to become responsible Protestants—which was the essence of the SEPADE Pentecostal politics—were increasingly becoming vulnerable to the same critical arguments raised against this widespread teaching technique among Latin American NGOs in general. I will paraphrase the argument of ICCO's latest officer for Chile, who gives the following "business-like" point of view:

> Times have changed. For such a small Pentecostal church to decide on the large sums of money that are being spent on SEPADE can no longer happen. SEPADE must become an independent NGO; the banner of the church is not indispensable anymore. This demand should have been made to SEPADE on the occasion of the previous [1991–1993] triennial program, but that has unfortunately not occurred. It would have given SEPADE three years to make the MIP accept its separation from SEPADE. I accepted Samuel Palma's guarantee that the MIP would not stand in the way of this. But reality proved to be different. Now, we [ICCO and the other Western donor organizations] have to be harsh. (Personal communication Johannes Solf, April 1994)

After a few months the matter turned even more dramatic:

> There has been a fight between the MIP Committee and the SEPADE leadership. Apparently the Committee has not been convinced by Samuel Palma about the seriousness of the matter. The MIP Committee must now really be persuaded [apparently ICCO's Johannes Solf presumed that the rest of the church would follow the leaders' decision]. For the time being, we approved a kind of exit subsidy. Any new application can only be taken into consideration if the organizational structure has effectively changed. Maybe it is even too late for them now. ICCO may decide to stop working in Chile altogether; my successor, whoever she or he is, is certainly less familiar with the case and probably less prepared to invest time in it. When I look at it now, SEPADE is really a complicated case of a mix of institutional politics and church politics. The combination of these issues, in themselves quite common issues in our work, has proven to be unmanageable for us. We at ICCO have too limited an insight in such a process. We simply ignored these problems in the past, under military rule. (Personal communication Johannes Solf, June 1994)

At the beginning of 1995, Johannes Solf was still responsible for ICCO's Chile projects, including the SEPADE program. In between, SEPADE and the MIP had agreed to change the church-NGO relationship. SEPADE was to become formally independent, which for the time being ended the prolonged struggle between both parties. The SEPADE leaders who appear in this book finally reached their goal of an independent development organization. Apparently, it was a very close-run thing, but it seems that this last-minute decision saved SEPADE from Damocles's sword. ICCO's Johannes Solf proved himself ready to reward the efforts of the SEPADE staff to reach their goal of independence, which was also ICCO's. As he told me,

> It would be too hard to stop now. All our ICCO partners received the message that we will stop financing them by January 1997. Maybe we can make an exception for SEPADE and go on until mid 1998. (Personal communication, January 1995)

As this last episode shows, it was the leaders—of SEPADE and ICCO—who talked and negotiated. I was not in Chile while this all happened, and I was not involved in the process, but I do wonder what the Pentecostal believers of the MIP have thought of it. It looks as if they have had only very little participation in the decisionmaking, as most commonly happens in the field of development politics.

The critique of SEPADE from ICCO's side was in fact the first time that the NGO had been confronted with critical remarks from its donors. It is time now to evaluate the meaning of this and all the other sorts of criticism SEPADE has had to endure in its twenty years of existence.

Prospects

In the foregoing survey of critical accounts of SEPADE's work it should be taken into consideration that I registered this critique during a period in which the major reason for the existence of SEPADE—the military regime and its Protestant supporters—had ceased to exist.[43] In Chile it is nowadays generally felt that in the post-Pinochet era, people, including Protestants/Pentecostals, tended to overemphasize negative experiences and even stress the irrelevance of the work of many NGOs and grassroots organizations of the recent past, in a deep desire to "get back to normal" as soon as possible. For non-Pentecostals this means primarily political apathy, whereas for Pentecostals it may mean a rediscovery of the desire for church growth. On the other hand there is also a more optimistic view on the prospects of the development of a less traditional kind of Pentecostalism. Ossa (1991, 28ff) rightly maintains that Chilean Pentecostals cannot be adequately described by an appeal to traditional stereotypes that present Pentecostals as a homogeneous and static group. The MIP and the work done by the church-related organization SEPADE are sufficient evidence to produce cracks in this image. Both the sharpest critics and the uncritical supporters, however, overlook the complexity and indeterminacy of these processes of cultural change. In this section, which precedes the final evaluation of prophetic Pentecostalism, I will limit myself to listing the main aspects of the phenomenon of Pentecostal politics, as I have termed SEPADE's activities during the last twenty years. Taken together with the MIP experience at the congregational level, this will also enable me to draw some conclusions as to the plausibility structure of prophetic Pentecostalism in the next chapter.

What started in 1974 with a loosely articulated set of ideas of a few MIP individuals, in the course of fifteen years, developed into a more or less smoothly running nongovernmental organization. The first written intentions consisted of fragmented ideas and goals, whereas later an ever more coherent discourse was produced that exuded self-confidence regarding the work that had to be done. The annual financial contributions (from the WCC and international development agencies) to SEPADE's endeavor increased steadily. The increasing scope for expenditure at ICCO from 1975 onward welcomed the opportunity to spend money on Latin America. Moreover, I showed—at least in the ICCO case—that belief in the correctness of the SEPADE efforts was strong and that expectations of success were equally high among Western donors. Among them, there was certainly a strong element of wishful thinking. For in the case of church-related organizations there was a firm belief in the effectiveness offered by the theology of liberation perspective. Organizing poor people in defense of their rights was considered something well worth sponsoring, and even more so if it involved changing the attitudes of Pentecostals, who in the early years of Pinochet had mainly attracted attention through their leaders' embrace of the regime. The emergence and growth of an NGO like SEPADE, then, can only be understood in the context of the existence of the military regime.

These circumstances, however, produced various reactions among Pentecostals, MIP members included, as we saw in the last chapter. Among the rank and file of the church there were few supporters of the regime, but there was clear opposition to the attempts to reformulate the traditional Pentecostal message. These attempts were strongly reinforced by the SEPADE leadership, which, particularly in the 1980s, tried to propagate a radical, socially committed gospel among its target groups. The fact that the bulk of the SEPADE projects consisted of technical assistance and community-building without direct religious connotations proves that the NGO had become markedly different from those ecclesiastical organizations that put faith and its propagation at the center of their activities. The comments I reproduced in earlier sections point to this fact, as the people uttering them charged SEPADE with having grown rapidly away from its original Pentecostal background.

The opinions about the organization can be roughly divided into three categories: those who were prepared and able to appropriate the radical, ecumenical, prophetic discourse, in other words, accept SEPADE's meaning-giving role; those who plainly rejected it; and third the majority who were not really affected by it but who were nonetheless prepared to reap the (material) fruits that came with the message. The latter group is the most difficult to get to grips with. Its Pentecostal habitus comprises both a sectarian closedness to new ideas and the element of the search for material benefits that is common to all forms of popular religion. SEPADE was therefore accepted by them insofar as it contributed to alleviating their material conditions, yet they instinctively withdrew when their (traditional) religious ideas and practices were in danger of being affected.

The SEPADE staff was very dedicated to ecumenism, participation, and community development, which had been the key concepts during the pre-Pinochet period of democracy. It saw the propagation of these principles among Pentecostals as a historical mission,[44] a conviction strongly confirmed by Western ecclesiastical donors like ICCO. Critics maintained that the reason for the emphasis on this mission was because it guaranteed SEPADE's power position (nationally and internationally) with respect to the allocation of funds; by these critics SEPADE was even accused of arrogance and pedantry. The more benevolent observers claimed to be impressed by the pivotal position SEPADE had managed to reach in the Protestant—ecumenical—world in Chile and Latin America and the important contributions made by some of its employees.[45]

My judgment of SEPADE is, however, in no way negative; I only
wish to emphasize that its prophetic stance, although partly given
shape during the democratic governments of Frei and Allende,
could only gain clear momentum, given the conditions of the military regime and the wide international support that could be mobi-
lized for defiance to it. On the other hand, this situation was
exceptional in the sense that an accelerated process of commitment
and concrete action was set in motion, which did not (and could
not) keep pace with the slow rhythm that processes of cultural
change generally tend to adopt. The claims of SEPADE—and the
MIP—to have spread a message of openness, ecumenism, and social
concern with substantial impact, therefore have to be evaluated critically.

Particularly now that donors' as well as recipient's (NGO) positions are subject to a process of professionalization and businesslike
transformation, the question of the impact of the prophetic message
becomes acute. How many people were eventually reached? What
was the real effect of all the popular education and teaching efforts?
SEPADE leaders claim to have affected the behavior of tens of thousands of people, but even if we accept this claim we are still left with
the question of what this coverage means, for instance in the
SEPADE-specific domain of changing religious attitudes. Downs and
Solimano give an impressive list of contributions the social policy
programs of Chilean NGOs are supposed to have provided for the
working-class sectors (1988, 72). Apart from the provision of material benefits (through the support of OEPs), people have been taught
to participate, they have been motivated to display a sense of democracy and community, which was considered a way of strengthening
Chilean civil society. SEPADE tried to do this for a specific working-
class sector: the Protestant/Pentecostal community. The difficulty
with most of the NGO work, including that of SEPADE, is that their
participatory, "popular education" methods are not easily subjected
to appraisal. As Salman, quoting Martinic (1991), remarks, participants in "popular education" NGO projects have done so for prag-
matic and concrete reasons (Salman 1993, 228–230). Or in the words
of another critical reviewer of development aid, "participation simply means different things to different people" (Oakley 1991, 269).
This kind of a critical assessment is certainly justified in the case of
a church-bound NGO like SEPADE, as I hope to have demonstrated in
the foregoing analysis.

At SEPADE, the outcomes of Pentecostal politics are said to be still mostly invisible. Even if one accepts that seeds have been "sown on a large scale," one could still object that it remains unclear whether "the seed has been sown on rocky or thorny ground, or instead on good soil." This biblical parable about the fruits of "the word of the kingdom" (Matthew 13:18–23) seems applicable to the SEPADE case. What I explicitly do not want to maintain is that all the sowing has been fruitless, but that the rocky ground—a good metaphor for the Pentecostal habitus—has proven to be more common than had been hoped.[46] If we look again at the recommendations of the external consultancy report and the changes that have been made in the SEP-ADE program, it looks as if insight into the problem of how to substantiate outcomes has grown. The plea for a more solid methodology of impact appraisal may have played a role in the termination of the "social participation of the churches" project and the neighborhood program; the growing discredit of "popular education" methods, both national and internationally, has also contributed to the abandonment of both projects.[47]

In this chapter we have moved far away from what most Chilean Pentecostals would regard as worth investigating. Assuming that Pentecostalism is to be studied at all, then research should at least concentrate on church life, believers often maintain. In the previous chapter I think I have partly met this common expectation. What I aimed for in this chapter is to provide a documented study of a Pentecostal development agency, which, if only for its rarity, deserves this attention. SEPADE's vicissitudes under the Pinochet regime and its continuous reflection on, and efforts to give shape to, a nontraditional Pentecostal code of social behavior proved illuminating for an understanding of meaning-making processes. Because the NGO SEPADE focused on social development, my study of it could well be considered the kind of development study Booth (1994) advances, because it tries to combine an actor-oriented and a structure-determined approach (of meaning-making), in an effort to contribute to the investigation and explanation of the diversity or heterogeneity of development processes. In this chapter, as well as in the previous, we have seen different categories of actors attributing different meanings to the same events. Their behavior varied according to context and over time. In a political time span in which democracy was succeeded by a long period of military rule, the memory of which most people are now rapidly trying to wipe out, the various actors we have distinguished constantly changed their behavior.

Within the MIP church we have seen that charity and indifference occurred alongside strong social commitment and the plain rejection of it, depending on whether one was looking at men, women, or youth. Another distinction must be made, namely between ordinary church members and the MIP leaders. I quoted Jorge who indicated that the former saw the latter as having a far higher cultural level. Translated into other terms, this interlocutor thought that a majority of the MIP people were still supporting traditional Pentecostal positions, when only a few had appropriated the liberation theological ideas that were offered to them by their leaders, and particularly through the SEPADE activities. During the last few years a tendency to turn away from the "progressive" religious discourse in favor of traditionalist spiritualism has become more tangible. At the SEPADE level this process has been accompanied by a similar shift of meaning. The strong liberation theological ideas, most clearly expressed in the NGO's participation discourse, gave way to a tendency toward professionalization, of which the previously quoted consultancy report was a telling example.[48] This tendency, however, had another close parallel in the world of international aid donors. For example, at SEPADE's main sponsor, ICCO, the same wind of professionalization and efficiency was beginning to blow at the end of the 1980s, when almost two decades of indestructible belief in the possibility of bringing about social, political, and cultural change through the NGO channel was severely undermined—a process that was only speeded up by similar changes at the Dutch Ministry of Development Cooperation. In the conclusion, I will raise the issue of development policy in a religious context again, because the implications of the complex development relations at the international, national, and local level do have important consequences for Pentecostal churches and their inhabitants.

Notes

1. The MIP's regulations from 1977 mention the existence and list the competence of a technical committee to be consulted by the church leadership over matters of education and social service (MIP 1977, 41). Moreover, this committee should coordinate the programs of the so-called regional centers and local churches. CTA (Comité Técnica Asesora) was from 1974—

before the church regulations even mentioned its feasibility—to assume this task. From the beginning there was discontent among the employees over the abbreviation CTA, which was believed to express very poorly the organization's objectives. The name SEPADE was used unofficially from 1978 onward, but only formally accepted by the MIP's general assembly in 1982. According to Marta Palma (1985, 227), this change of name was because of the fact that CTA work went far beyond the bounds of only the MIP denomination. SEPADE workers have always thought that CTA was a meaningless name, but the MIP pastors only reluctantly gave up this name, for CTA was a reminder of the MIP's control over the organization, whereas the use of SEPADE suggested a position independent from the church. This name-giving, thus, was not without meaning and may even be considered part of the Pentecostal politics I shall treat in this chapter. In 1983, SEPADE obtained greater autonomy from the MIP committee, when it was turned into a Centro de Educación y Servicio Social (CESS) with its own regulations. Yet this was only a difference in degree; the desire to obtain total independence from the church was kept alive by SEPADE workers. As we shall see later, it became an ever more important issue in the NGO-donor negotiations.

2. Among NGO staff, a disproportionly high number of sociologists and social workers were employed, which did not always correspond well to the NGO tasks to be performed.

3. Hojman's 1993 article only provides a general overview, to which other authors do not add very much in terms of case studies (e.g., Downs et al. 1989; Loveman 1991). This chapter aims to provide such a study, although it must be taken into account that SEPADE, because it was a church-owned institution, belongs to a special category.

4. All SEPADE founders had even been politically leftist activists, in the Socialist Party and especially the MAPU (a split off of the Christian-Democrats in 1969).

5. This same Narciso Sepúlveda claims that the first step toward the realization of social work came from the local church of Pedro Monnt, to which three of SEPADE's founders (Francisco, Marta Palma, and Gabriel Guerrero) belonged.

6. At that time the MIP still had the ambition of sending missionaries abroad, something that several MIP members regularly recall with nostalgia (see the story of camp leader Juan in Chapter 4).

7. I was told repeatedly that this split was a serious blow for the MIP, especially because Pavez's new church flourished while the MIP was left behind in agony. For my interlocutors the meaning of this was inscrutable. It was as if "God was blessing the erring" instead of those who chose the right path.

8. The ACE project has been a constant source of anxiety both within

Chile and among its foreign sponsors. ICCO, which was one of the main donors, has lengthy archive files on the case of this NGO. Examples of power struggle, mismanagement, and a veiled mix of church interests (particularly of the IPCH under Bishop Chávez) and NGO interests abound in these files. In the 1980s ICCO ordered a fact-finding mission, the results of which meant the end of a long-lasting relationship.

9. Erasmo Farfán was only persuaded to give up his job as accountant four years later, when he had been appointed director of CTA and the prospects of the NGO were promising.

10. I deliberately choose to present ICCO's work in Chile from the lips of desk officer Oskam (i.e., from his archive letters at the ICCO office). Of course his decisions were backed up by ICCO as an institution, but the responsibility for most decisions lay entirely with the regional desks, at any rate until the late 1980s.

11. CTA's first director Francisco was highly contentious. His work in Uruguay and Argentina had largely dissociated him from traditional Pentecostalism, and even from his own MIP. As someone told me, "he was the first MIP member to become depentecostalized." He drank, smoked, called his fellow pastors hypocrites, and even jumped on a Bible to show that the book in itself was just a bunch of paper and not a sacred object, a fetish. Thus he accused his fellow Pentecostals of clinging to the form rather than to the contents of the gospel. All other pioneers of CTA agree that under Francisco's leadership CTA was losing prestige rapidly, among MIP church members as well as among other churches and related NGOs. He was removed from his job in 1978 by the church committee. Besides, Francisco increasingly collided with the other staff people over political standpoints. Both sides accused each other of making NGO interests subservient to political interest, something that the church committee also feared.

12. At that time there were at least thirteen other organizations receiving funds from ICCO (ICCO 1981, 65–70).

13. Although SEPADE's church-directed activities have increased in the course of years, doubts about their usefulness continue to exist until the present day. As Juan Sepúlveda remarks, "the church program is still considered by many staff members as the NGO's stepchild." (personal letter, November 2, 1994).

14. From 1983 until 1989, another ICCO functionary was responsible for the Chile projects; thereafter the Chile desk was run by a range of cooperators, who rapidly succeeded each other after relatively short intervals in command. This last phase coincided with a thorough reorientation on the total ICCO exertion with Latin America and Chile in particular (after the return of democracy in 1989); a complex series of institutional reorganizations only further obfuscated ICCO's Chile policy.

15. In 1976, the WCC supported CTA with over $60,000, whereas in 1991

the SEPADE budget was well over 1,000,000 Dutch guilders. At one time, the SEPADE project was thereby the costliest among all Andean projects supported by ICCO.

16. Although in 1974 CTA started with only a handful of people, the 1986 internal evaluation named forty one paid employees and another forty temporary cooperators (SEPADE 1986, 55–58). At the time of my fieldwork the size of the SEPADE personnel was roughly the same. Imminent reductions of donor money had by then already set in motion a restrictive personnel management.

17. The label "community development" has been the denominator of SEPADE's triennial programs ever since 1977. The belief in the common interests of particular (poor) groups in Chilean society was never for the most part questioned. The 1994–1996 program, for example, sets out to help individuals and groups to "create the permanent capacity of organized communal answers . . . to achieve local community development" (SEPADE 1994, 4).

18. This was one of recommendations of the 1979 evaluation of the CTA project, which also recommended the permanent analysis of Chilean society (Carrasco et al. 1979, 97).

19. With respect to the contents of this ethic, reference is made to "the judgement of the nations," Matthew 25:31–46 (Canales et al., 143). In this text heaven (eternal life) is promised to those who give concrete form to their compassion for their suffering fellowmen. The Bible courses belonging to the CAP project treated this text and other texts of a similar tendency.

20. I do not mean that this type of criticism of distribution aspects lacks grounds; I rather want to emphasize that it did not primarily concern the— partly hidden—objective of affecting Pentecostal identity. Because the latter is my main concern in this chapter, I refrain from giving details on these other cases, although I realize that the two aspects cannot always be separated. I had, for example, extensive contacts with a man from La Victoria who seemed to me a strong supporter of the "enlightened" Pentecostalism of his pastor Erasmo Farfán. He received money for his job at the community center in the neighborhood, but as soon as he lost the job, as a result of a reshuffle in the SEPADE program, he not only began to scorn SEPADE's work, he and his family also withdrew from the church altogether (more details of this case will be given later).

21. Participation in this case means that I had a position very similar to the other participants in the workshops. Together with them, I tried to learn certain techniques, to give answers to pastoral problems, and reflect on the usefulness of the course. Interestingly enough, the roles of the counseling pastor and that of the investigating anthropologist appeared to have very much in common. During the seminar, I suggested that anthropological enquiries suffer from the same problems pastors are confronted with in

their daily work. For example, I explained that biased and suggestive interviewing was as much a danger for the researcher as pedantry was for the
pastoral agent. I even suggested that my fieldwork among Chilean Pentecostals was a lasting effort at active listening.

22. One of the leaflets used in the course reads that "to be open to such
an experience implies the possibility of being forced to reinterpret one's
own experiences. This can be alarming." It certainly was for the participating pastors.

23. As I shall make clear later in this chapter this tendency to refrain
from religious, Pentecostal, sources of motivation has a close relation to the
growing number of non-Pentecostals among the SEPADE staff. MIP members
had doubts about the Pentecostal identity of their church, yet SEPADE's Pentecostal character was questioned even more.

24. The SEPADE journal *Evangelio y Sociedad* regularly publishes interviews with feminist theologians, but these articles are not, or are only very
partially reaching, Protestant women (even most MIP pastors do not read
the journal, let alone ordinary church members).

25. In *Evangelio y Sociedad* no. 18 (1993) a hermeneutical interpretation
of Paul's famous passages on women (from Corinthians and Galatians) is
given by a well-known North American feminist theologian, Elsa Tamez.
Articles of the same tendency had already appeared in earlier numbers of
the magazine (1985, 1990). Again, there is no use in trying to establish
whether the interpretations given there are right or not; what puzzled me
during my research was why such interpretations were not employed in the
concrete activities of the SEPADE women's division.

26. The "Campaign for Life, Peace and Reconciliation in Chile," organized by the CCI in August 1986. During the entire month meetings of
prayer and reflection concerning the serious situation of the country were
held in many Santiago churches. At the end of the campaign—it was in a
way analogous to the classical Pentecostal rallies—an open letter of protest
was delivered to Pinochet (see also Chapter 3).

27. It is evident that particularly in this case the image provided is dis-
torted by frustration. Yet, a nucleus of truth must be in it, I conclude, when
reading the travel accounts by ICCO staff people in Chile; on several occasions the SEPADE management is asked to give advice on project proposals
by others. Eduardo's tirade was not unique in this respect. Others gave me
the image of SEPADE as a watchdog for Protestant development aid, too.

28. As the monthly magazine *Análisis* observes, this public manifestation
of political protest affected the public perception that Protestants were unconditional supporters of the Pinochet regime (*Análisis* 1986, 17), a viewpoint that was strongly advanced by the official, progovernment media. The
same article, for that matter, makes a passing reference to the SEPADE journal
Evangelio y Sociedad and its editor Juan Sepúlveda, noticing that "the

majority of the aspects mentioned [in the public letter] have received an in-depth treatment in that publication" (ibid., 18).

29. Vicaría lawyers, for example, were consulted over the final draft of the open letter to Pinochet, in order to avoid legal repercussions from the regime.

30. During the preparation of the open letter, one CCI meeting, recorded by Ossa (1992, 36), referred to a text from Ezekiel 33 (7–8): "So you, son of man, I have made a watchman for the house of Israel; [if] you do not speak to warn the wicked to turn from his way . . . his blood I will require at your hand." This text apparently expressed the common feeling that silence was not acceptable any longer.

31. I never spoke to any MIP believer who expressed his support of Pinochet. The CEP survey (Fontaine and Beyer 1991, 106) even shows that Protestants in general more strongly condemned Pinochet's military government than their fellow Chileans.

32. It would be interesting to know the list of subscribers especially of the first issues. The vast majority of magazine issues went to (foreign) institutional subscribers and within the churches even in the best case, only to the pastors. Significantly, from the seventh issue onward, a professional journalist was engaged to completely restyle the magazine.

33. The choice to concentrate on this particular issue was strongly motivated by the fact that the municipalities (*comunas*) remained under the government of the local politicians who were appointed by the military regime. It took until after the 1992 municipal elections for local democracy to be finally established.

34. In the elections, a former SEPADE officer, who had been appointed by president Aylwin in the new municipality of El Bosque, was reelected.

35. Ample references were made to the "founder" of the pedagogic method of "popular (adult) education," Paulo Freire, and his *Pedagogy of the Oppressed* (1970).

36. As I have already noted in Chapter 2, I had to handle constantly shifting loyalties. These were basically with regard to three actors: ordinary church people, SEPADE/MIP leaders, and ICCO officers.

37. It could indeed be typified as a case that shows the margins of power people have in popular religion. People may formally accept a particular discourse, but in practice they make use of their freedom of interpretation. Individuals' meaning-making happens to escape from the control of meaning-producing agencies (see for this "popular use of popular religions," Rostas and Droogers 1993).

38. Several other people from the MIP La Victoria church—especially youngsters—worked at the SEPADE office, although mostly in subordinate positions. My perception is that only a few MIP congregations have managed to have church members appointed at SEPADE (mainly La Victoria and

Ochagavía). This illustrates both the greater commitment of these congregations to the SEPADE work and the relatively easy access their leaders had to the NGO.

39. For Narciso Sepúlveda, it was characteristic of the present situation of SEPADE that he had been addressed once as "pastor S. from the Lutheran Church," although he had been MIP president for so many years and a loyal SEPADE supporter within living memory.

40. Sepúlveda tried to show me the logic of this process by referring to the unique figures of the Old Testament prophets: They also only raised their voices under fairly particular circumstances. When the latter changed, the prophetic voice died down again. The same can be said about the Chilean prophetic outcries. For Juan Sepúlveda this was also one of the main differences between the CCI and the Consejo de Pastores. The support the latter gave to Pinochet was strategic, serving to provide recognition and to thwart the Catholic Church. This sentiment did not disappear when democracy returned in Chile.

41. In the course of 1994 this same Gabriel Guerrero left SEPADE after almost twenty years of service to join the Ministry of Economy. Thus, the man who was one of strongest defenders of professionalization at SEPADE, made a significant professional step forward.

42. In 1990, Chile was therefore put on the list of countries the Netherlands maintained special relations of cooperation with. Discussions in parliament on the extreme fragmentation of Dutch Development Aid and a renewed priority list of the ministry itself meant that in 1993 Chile was removed from the list again (Minister van Ontwikkelingssamenwerking 1993, 168–169).

43. This observation, made by Juan Sepúlveda in a personal letter, and already referred to previously, seems correct to me. Yet I think an appeal to these particular historical conditions cannot neutralize the critique altogether.

44. The most recent project proposal by SEPADE speaks of "empowering the powerless through participation and constructing community ties among Protestants and non-Protestants." It also refers to Pentecostals' great sensitivity to community-building, which women and children especially reap the fruits of. The document does not allow contradiction: Pentecostals must rethink their relation to society and its sociocultural problems, which is supposed to bring them the insight that they share these problems with their non-Pentecostal fellow men (SEPADE 1994, 3–7).

45. Juan Sepúlveda, for example, has been involved in the preparation of several WCC meetings and commissions, and Marta Palma has been running the WCC Latin America desk from 1986 onward. Juan Sepúlveda is also one of the prominent members of CEPLA (Comisión Evangélica Pentecostal Latinoamericana, Latin American Pentecostal Committee), a group of ecumenical Pentecostal leaders from all over the continent.

46. Juan Sepúlveda refers to a lengthy article in *Evangelio y Sociedad* (1990, number 6), which summarizes the fifteen years of SEPADE's exertion with Pentecostal churches. In it, much effort is made to emphasize the NGO's accompanying role in the "awakening process" of these churches. SEPADE is explicitly not presented as a leading actor (*protagonista*) in this process.

47. Yet the consultancy report does not meddle with the Protestant character of SEPADE. To the contrary, it even urges SEPADE to reflect more profoundly on its position vis-à-vis the Protestant world and how to improve the quality of its participation in society (SEPADE 1992, 29, 30). There seems to be a common understanding of SEPADE's raison d'être as a Protestant agency. A follow-up of the church program is submitted to the WCC for financial support.

48. Juan Sepúlveda, the strongest defender of liberation theological ideas within SEPADE (see his *La liberación de la creación*, 1993, 24–28), prefers to mark this process as "professionalization of commitment," a characterization that allows him to "rescue" the liberating element from oblivion.

6

Conclusions and Perspectives

In the foregoing chapters much of the meaning of the events presented has been left implicit. I deliberately chose to apply a narrative approach, giving ample space to the interpretations, opinions, and comments of the characters appearing. In this final chapter I will try to pull together the strings that have been left untied so far and draw conclusions regarding the phenomenon of prophetic Pentecostalism. This means a shift from implicit description to explicitness, which boils down to an impact appraisal of the whole MIP project. This cannot be done without first presenting a major caveat: The impact of efforts at religious renewal is measurable only to a limited extent, since it belongs to processes of cultural change that are by nature indeterminate and stretch over a long time span. I have pointed out this basic aspect in Chapter 2, where I discussed the effort of cultural politics and the unconscious, but strongly determining, impact of habitus on human behavior. When I nevertheless come up with conclusions about the concrete conduct of people, my inferences are always made with reference to these notions. My concluding remarks concern two major fields: religious—Pentecostal—change, and the specific development policies linked to it. The variety of topics raised in the preceding chapters will be ranged under these main themes. The predicament of the scientific—anthropological—construction of knowledge on what is labeled prophetic Pentecostalism will be evaluated separately.

The Margins of Religious Change:
The Shifting Meanings of Pentecostalism

In Chapter 2 I paid close attention to the room people have for maneuvre within the structural conditions in which they are living.

They are actors who make sense out the wide range of events that daily life offers them. As a resource for this signification I called attention to the broad reservoir of meanings that are available in culture (including religion), on a conscious as well as an unconscious level. What I have emphasized is that Pentecostals unwittingly rely on a particular habitus to which their collective tradition has given shape. This affects their (physical) acting and thinking, the body and the mind. Although we are still far from understanding how this Pentecostal habitus exactly operates, what seems more easy to grasp is that it regulates the speed of change and the degree of uniformity to be found among the believers in the Pentecostal field. Therefore, habitus constitutes not so much the motor of change, but rather the flywheel of (church) life, which tends to reproduce traditional patterns of behavior and modes of thought.

The 1952 schism in the Iglesia Evangélica Pentecostal (IEP) that led to the formation of the Misión Iglesia Pentecostal (MIP) allowed a group of Chilean Pentecostals to rethink their Pentecostal identity. This did not mean that the young MIP church was radically different from the church from which it sprang. Meaning-making does not change overnight. What was an important difference is that the educational level of at least the MIP leaders was significantly higher than was the case in the IEP. The contacts that in the years following the schism were established with other Protestant churches and within the ecumenical circuit (notably the WCC), allowed for a gradual increase in the MIP proclivity for establishing equal relations with people in the surrounding world, that is, outside the church boundaries. In Chapter 3 I showed that the awakening interest of the Frei and Allende governments in working-class people and their possible social and political participation provided fertile soil for such a Pentecostal renewal. Pinochet's subsequent military dictatorship had an even stronger impact on the MIP church: It began to play a prominent role in the so-called prophetic response to this regime and to the group of church leaders—united in the Consejo de Pastores—that supported it. Within the MIP church itself the measure of involvement of members in practices pertaining to this response was diverse. Some became actively committed to neighborhood struggle and survival strategies, whereas others chose to fall back on purely religious participation or even to withdraw from the church altogether. The different MIP congregations all took their respective decisions in this matter, although the reactions were sometimes also very diverse within local churches. This I dealt with extensively in my treatment of the distinct reactions of men, women, and youth in the MIP La Victoria congregation.

I have argued that the remodeling of the individual conversion experience and redemption in classic Pentecostalism was largely the work of a particular layer of MIP church leaders, more precisely of those who had gained access to the ecumenical world and international donor agencies. Thus they happened to become familiar with the discourse of liberation theology that through them penetrated into local church communities. In the extensive case of the Pentecostal camp leader Juan, described in Chapter 4, I gave a detailed analysis of the ambiguity Pentecostals were prey to, when they became familiar with this—for them—new religious world. Juan describes himself as a person who is constantly in search of a balance between spirituality and commitment. The gospel of sharing, justice, and community he learned in his church led him to a leadership position in one of the biggest land seizures under Pinochet. When he rediscovered the "true Pentecostal spirit" during his exile in Argentina, he realized what prophetic Pentecostalism was missing: spiritual fervor and a proper identity. La Victoria's MIP pastor Erasmo Farfán once described this pull between two opinions—spirituality and commitment—as a "tidal swing," thus suggesting that it might be possible that "never the twain shall meet." Farfán realizes that this constant search for identity in his MIP is well expressed in the distinct types of leadership recognized. There is a conscious effort to produce professionally—theologically—trained pastors, but what people in the churches often prefer is a pastor who claims to have received a calling and whose pastoral work is conceived of as a vocation. The total availability of the latter is particularly highly appreciated. Within the MIP both types of pastorship, the ascribed and achieved, are present, but their coexistence is not always peaceful and smooth. Farfán noticed disappointedly that in his congregation members felt increasingly saturated by stories of liberation, participation, and community, which he himself had been preaching. People were apparently longing for something they found hard to describe, but was definitely conceived of as a revaluation of past experiences, something to which their pastor could not—and did not want—to return.

Was this, then, one of so many failed attempts at achieving sustained religious change in people? Does prophetic Pentecostalism suffer from the same disappointment or crisis the Catholic base communities (CEBs) are going through, where liberation theology has had a similarly limited impact on people? The answer cannot be affirmative nor negative. The limits of consciousness-raising by the "liberation project" were reached earlier than its supporters had hoped (see Burdick 1993, 194–195). Yet lasting outcomes have certainly been achieved, although not as many as had been thought possible. What part of the prophetic program has been realized then? My findings, particularly from the La Victoria case, suggest that at least some important changes have been accomplished. Although I noted the continuation of the traditional Pentecostal ideal and practice of "splendid isolation," I demonstrated that the focus on community was no longer simply narrowed down to the formal congregation. The plea to look over the church fence, which could be heard in MIP circles since the early days, has in fact found a clear response in La Victoria. The olla común the church sisters organized may have had limited impact outside the church, but it was by no means insignificant, as proven by the vehement reaction from (the male) part of the congregation.

More can be said about gender relations in the church. Despite the generally male-dominated character of church organization and the fact that female pastorship has, except occasionally, remained largely an illusion, women have gained access, for example to the church council, where they actively participate. Within the neighboring IMP congregation, by constrast, no women are even allowed to take part in this ruling church body. Although women's roles in church and in private life are within the MIP still to a large extent determined by traditional gender relations, women are noticeably less subservient to men than Pentecostal tradition would have it. At the MIP general assemblies, for example, they are entirely responsible for the domestic work, but they also raise their voices in the public sessions. I believe that the way the emphasis on the priesthood of *all* believers, men and women, has been applied within the MIP, has produced some cracks in the walls of gender relations, certainly when the situation is compared with other Pentecostal churches.

Young people, however, provide the clearest example of Pentecostal renewal, although here the outcomes are also revealing about the limited potential of the prophetic enterprise. In Chapter 4 I described how young people from La Victoria struggled with their desire to be and behave like others of their age group. In the 1983-

1985 protests the confrontation between the La Victoria youth and the police was a hard and bitterly fought one. The MIP youth, who had as a whole enjoyed the feeling of being of use to the neighborhood in various activities that pastor Farfán had encouraged them to join in, turned out to be divided over their role in what often resulted in a kind of guerrilla warfare with violent street battles. Many became involved, but others refused to take part. Although several people in retrospect maintained that they acted as a consequence of the Christian command to fight against injustice, the dominant reproach of the older church members was that this engagement was mainly politically inspired, and therefore illegitimate. Moreover, the youth were accused of not even having been inspired by the Pentecostal message of community and solidarity preached in the church and of having acted just like ordinary neighborhood people, entirely denying their Pentecostal identity.

The outcome of this episode was a serious setback to the congregation. It lost members who could not accept that such things were tolerated. Yet it also lost a considerable amount of youth who felt themselves hampered by the church and the church council in what they considered a legitimate struggle. Some of them returned later, but as I concluded from their testimonies, their experiences had alienated them from ordinary Pentecostal practices and from the prevailing code of conduct. They were, for example, reluctant to show common Pentecostal physical gestures, like raising their hands and praying aloud, and to use the traditionally preferred clothing. Some of them even had serious difficulty identifying themselves as Pentecostals. The mental gap between young and old was a serious problem in most other MIP churches too, although in some congregations the youth had stayed within the Pentecostal limits their church had drawn. In the post-Pinochet Sunday school sessions, for example, the spread of the outward-looking social gospel they had so much welcomed, continued, but could raise very little enthusiasm. In fact the youth hardly came to the classes anymore; they were no longer prepared to dedicate their entire free time to the church, which was the ideal cherished by many older Pentecostals, although they did not always put it into practice.

The MIP leaders, particularly pastor Farfán, had managed to convince people of the necessity of adopting a less classic Pentecostal worldview; there is no doubt about that. Nevertheless, for several reasons the effect has not been lasting. Because the "proof of the pudding is in the eating," an attempt must now be made to cast some light on the limited appeal of prophetic Pentecostalism, if only to counterbalance the unrealistically rosy image provided by some of its defenders. Ossa, for example, optimistically estimates that about 20 percent of Chile's Protestants are thinking differently; that is, they share a disposition to adopt open, nonauthoritarian tenets (1991, 33, 34). This may be correct, and it constitutes a political fact confirmed by other sources. However, it tells us little about religious openness (ecumenism) and social conduct. Although there can be little doubt that the heterogeneity among Chilean Pentecostals is greater than is usually assumed, I am less certain about the feasibility of the type of ecumenical Pentecostalism advanced by MIP leaders. I think Ossa's book contains too much wishful thinking. The very data he presents should have made him more cautious about the prospects of the tendency he suggests. He quotes, for example, a participant of a Sunday school class in La Victoria (ibid., 105) who explains very clearly how much time and effort it took before he could adopt a "revised Christian way of living," because "one is born and raised with that concept [avoidance of the world] and way of thinking." Ossa focuses primarily on the positive outcome of what he calls a process of transformation, while paying less attention to its lengthy and painstaking character, let alone to the possible obverse outcomes in other cases. My findings in the same La Victoria congregation suggest less glorious results. I realize that my "sample" also leaves little room for legitimate quantitative speculation, although I think the meager results are telling because the La Victoria congregation was considered one that had "advanced" most within the MIP.

Another telling piece of data on the social basis of prophetic Pentecostalism is the constantly dropping number of church members the MIP has faced over the last twenty years. This is a source of anxiety to the part of the membership who demands the restoration of classic proselytizing methods. They continue to uphold the classic view of a world that has to be conquered by converting its inhabitants. The prophetic Pentecostals try to establish a competing frame of reference that requires the fabrication of what Berger calls an alternative plausibility structure (1967, 48). Making predictions about the chances of the old Pentecostal paradigm is hard, and assessing the potential for enlarging the support of its prophetic rival is equally difficult. To put it in general terms, Chileans have returned to normality after almost twenty abnormal years, although not to the sort of normality that, as Salman puts it, holds high expectations of the state and political parties (1993, 376). Although this author questions the existence of a social movement of pobladores, he stresses the experiences of organizations at the neighborhood level and the effects the participation in them has had on people. Their opinions and ways of behavior have become more autonomous, although he also stresses that it only concerns a small minority. Most of the neighborhood dwellers are engaged in individual economic progress. Analogously to, and in accordance with, this conclusion, I would say that the individual route to success (both materially and spiritually) in Pentecostalism prevails right now also in its prophetic variant. Discourses of social participation and community are not very likely to gain adherence among people in the neighborhoods, and neither are they attractive to Pentecostals. The classic Pentecostal attention to the individual will probably be even more emphasized at the expense of the aspect of community-building and communal problem solving. The active social commitment of the prophetic type of Pentecostalism had some appeal among Pentecostals during the past period—first during the participation boom under Frei and Allende, and later in the struggle against the Pinochet dictatorship. In the preceding chapters I gave various examples of its success in manifesting itself publicly and in the private realm of motivating people. I do not mean, then, to conclude that the whole prophetic effort has been fruitless. It has transformed people and made them think differently. The context of the neighborhood mobilization, particularly during the 1980s, provided the appropriate conditions in which Pentecostals could make this religious switch, although as I demonstrated, it was highly contested by their coreligionists even in their own churches.

As I already made fleeting reference to in the previous chapter, my interpretation and evaluation of the heyday of prophetic Pentecostalism is influenced by the fact that I did my fieldwork during its aftermath. This is the central argument in the extensive comments on my writings by one of the principal actors in the events I describe, Juan Sepúlveda, former head of SEPADE's church program. In addition, he confirms that the political context has exercised a significant influence on the actors in this Pentecostal configuration. Yet, his principal observation is that projecting fieldwork findings into the past distorts my ex-post conclusions. For him, shaping

Pentecostal meaning-making has definitely not been the explicit aim of SEPADE from the start; he maintains that SEPADE's leading role was far more circumstantial than the explicit affirmative references by international aid donors like ICCO suggest. Moreover, Sepúlveda considers inaccurate the image of failure and obsolescence of the whole Pentecostal politics project as it emerges from the interviews I made in the post-Pinochet period. The image Sepúlveda defends is that SEPADE has definitely had a noticeable impact on Pentecostal thinking and acting, but that it was at the same time well aware of its limited capacity to produce the desired change. Indirectly, he suggests that donors have placed their expectations too high. I agree with that, but as far as the sustained effect of SEPADE's Pentecostal politics is concerned, it would be very useful to continue to dis-cuss—for example with people like Sepúlveda—the question of how many Pentecostals really have adopted the essentials of liberation theology. This discussion on impact has also relevance for the Cath-olic base communities.

Nowadays, the social and political context clearly differs from the Pinochet period. Pentecostal meaning-giving is therefore also likely to go in different directions, probably even more so if an important instrument of Pentecostal politics, like the NGO SEPADE, ceases to act as an influential provider of prophetic discourse in the churches. The various tendencies within Chilean Pentecostalism continue to exist, but without the sharp confrontations of the past. An ecumeni-cal brand will continue to exist, alongside the traditional "closed" churches, while incipient efforts are made to open up the middle classes as a resource for church growth, which will inevitably have consequences for the character of Pentecostalism. Just before my return from Chile in August 1992, I had an interview with the then president of the Consejo de Pastores, who estimated that the pros-pect for Pentecostal expansion was changing. In his view, the former target groups for evangelization—the lower classes—were gradually ceasing to be the pond to fish in. Therefore, a shift of attention toward the middle classes was obvious to him. He maintained that to have some appeal there, a completely different kind of discourse was needed than the one that had traditionally been applied to po-tential converts. He maintained that this project of "religious engi-neering" was still largely in its infancy, but he appeared to be very much convinced of its plausibility. Although it remains to be seen whether this prospect will take form in the near future, it shows that the Pentecostal world is no static entity. Nowadays, Pentecostal groups can already be found at all points of the sect-church scale I looked at in the introduction, and the various positions regarding worldly compromises can even be found in most churches and their local congregations. This diversity, or heterogeneity will only increase in the future.

If my study of the vicissitudes of the prophetic variant of Pentecostalism clarifies anything, it is that cultural processes to which its emergence pertains, belong to the *longue durée* of history. As practice approaches use to accentuate, outcomes are the result of the interplay between individual meaning-giving actors and what they perceive (partly subconsciously) as the structures that force them to act and think the way they do. Much of the reason for the limited results of prophetic Pentecostalism relates to the slowness of cultural processes. Getting results, that is, winning people for a cause, has been as much a preoccupation for the defenders of the prophetic stance as it is for traditional Pentecostalism with its sophisticated proselytizing methods. At times, although, the adage "small is beautiful" was defended, which served to ease the pain of disappointing results by reference to the biblical wisdom that says that "a prophet is not without honor except in his own country and in his own house" (Matthew 13:57). It is even conceivable for the MIP to return to traditional Pentecostal positions (its enemies would say "repent of its vices"). Some pastors did suggest that a countertendency was noticeable. I doubt whether such an initiative would have much chance of being successful at short notice, given the strong convictions the present leaders possess.

The MIP case shows a particular group of leaders becoming acquainted with, and supporters of, liberation theology and social movement ideals. Their horizon was much broader than that of the Pentecostal believers they tried to convince. The perspectives, from a neighborhood church and from the ecumenical movement on a world scale, respectively, produced a clash of two discourses. Leaders had to handle both alternately and often simultaneously. The experience of "shifting selves" this required (Ewing 1990), was by no means an easy one to cope with. The reconciliation of the highly individual religious experience and mode of conduct with which traditional Pentecostals were equipped, and an ecumenical and sociopolitical committed practice proved extremely difficult. On the one hand, the leaders promoting the prophetic "message" were viewed as having an interest in its success. There is no doubt they had, but the mix of power/interest and "genuine" meaning-production constitutes one of the most fascinating and intriguing aspects of the whole phenomenon. On the other hand, I think that the disappointment about the absence of more tangible and sustainable results was the fruit of an overrated belief in the practicability of such a project of cultural change. I think that most of the leading figures of prophetic Pentecostalism were well aware of its limited possibilities. Yet, in the special historical context of political tension and repression, they obviously sometimes promised more, and dressed up their projects more impressively than could be accounted for. That could only help to accelerate the process of decision making by outsiders, including foreign donor agencies, who were watching closely, prepared to support any initiative that could contribute to the return of normality (political democracy) in Chile. Thus, the dressing may occasionally have looked more tasty than the product itself.

One other important issue cannot be left out in an evaluation of the viability of this prophetic type of Pentecostalism: the effect of adopting an ecumenical position. It is at this point that the differences with the Iglesia Metodista Pentecostal (IMP) are most perceptible. In this church the absolute validity of its own doctrine is beyond all doubt, although individual members occasionally display more tolerant attitudes. Whether this will in the future continue to be a fruitful base for church growth remains to be seen, but it has certainly born fruit until now. The extent to which the respective MIP and IMP temples in La Victoria are filled during the Sunday services is sufficient proof of this. The very openness of the MIP has been a bone of contention from the beginning, but the accelerated pace of this process of opening up to the surrounding society and other churches produced increasing internal polarization. The enemies of openness and ecumenism clung to the old-time Pentecostalism, when street preaching could still achieve substantial numerical results. As they saw it, spending time (and money) on activities not directly related to the maintenance and expansion of the church was a waste, and even potentially counterproductive. When the value and primacy of proper church matters are given up, it was thought, the fences are down to all kinds of alien ideas and practices that may lead to the end of the original Pentecostal character. Ecumenism evidently supersedes two basic features of classic Pentecostalism, namely, anti-Catholicism and overt proselytism, and what is perhaps even more important, it introduces a far more rational discourse of community and solidarity, in which a full dedication to church matters is no longer required. "My soul has (still) a thirst for God, but drinking is not advisable all day," was how one interviewee poignantly summarized his position. Community and solidarity are of course not absent in, for example, IMP Pentecostalism, and total observance to the church is also very rare, but the church is generally viewed as the pivotal place where Pentecostals should practice and experience their faith. The best Pentecostal service is believed to be the one with the most weeping. It was the very absence of such noticeable religious fervor that made groups of MIP members complain and demand a return to the original church mission, a Pentecostal revival. Yet this is hardly to be expected under an ecumenical "regime."

The MIP has made some deliberate attempts to change Pentecostal identity. The four interrelated characteristics distinguished by Dayton (see introduction) are still present, but their contents have undergone a significant shift of meaning. Jesus' saving role is far less emphasized and principally understood as saving the world. Spiritual baptism becomes more of an inspiration than the reception of particular gifts. The healing is applied to social diseases as well as to individual illnesses. The eschatological element also remains, but the human role in preparing the way for Christ's return receives much attention. To this change in religious orientation a complete set of church and social practices corresponds, which have been given form under the specific historical circumstances. The support for these ecumenical, prophetic Pentecostal ideas and practices has been limited. The top-down strategy that the leaders followed has contributed to the fact the church has remained small and that part of its membership longs for the past, setting their hopes on a renewed quest for spiritual gifts. Those who are determined to continue the chosen path, care far less for possible quantitative growth than for the integration of their church in the Christian (world) community and the (spiritual) fruits emanating from social participation. Neglecting quantitative growth, which for many Pentecostals constitutes the core element of their identity, may turn out to lead to deadlock. In the next section I will present some consequences of all this in the field of development policy.

Development and Religion: On Pentecostal Politics

The present study discusses a religious phenomenon, Pentecostalism, but the brand of Pentecostalism I focus on is strongly related
to the realm of development politics. As I have shown in Chapter
5, prophetic Pentecostalism has been heavily sponsored by external
(foreign) donors. Solidarity with the Chilean people suffering from
the hardships of the Pinochet military dictatorship was widespread
in the Western world and provided the legitimation for Western
NGOs to invest in their Chilean counterparts. The SEPADE case I described makes clear that this will to contribute to the return of democracy was strong, both among Chilean NGOs and among its
sponsors. During my fieldwork I studied the impact of the SEPADE
work, and particularly its attempts to raise the social and political
consciousness of Pentecostals. It should be stressed that this last
aspect is only part of the SEPADE work, but was exactly the issue
through which it could distinguish itself from other NGOs. Moreover, it was precisely the effort to mobilize Pentecostals for social
development issues and to break their political indifference, that
caused aid donors like the Dutch ICCO to provide ample (financial)
support. The "Pentecostal politics," as I have labeled this part of the
SEPADE work, may have received disproportional attention by donor
agencies, as in fact it also does in my study, yet it is a clear illustration of the cultural change at which most development work explicitly or implicitly aims.

Yet even when such transformative goals figure prominently
among the startingpoints of development agencies, they seldom
form the subject of evaluation. Until recently, the field of development studies has also largely neglected the impact of the specific
role of NGOs. That is one reason why these development studies
have been provocatively called "irrelevant" (Edwards 1989). Another reason advanced for dismissing many development studies is
that they tend to exclude the participants in the development processes under study. I believe that my study can to an acceptable degree "pass the test" with regard to these two points. Yet it remains
extremely difficult to measure and evaluate the "real impact" of
NGO work, especially if that work directly aims at cultural—and in
this case religious—change. Prolonged—and ideally repeated—
periods of research (monitoring in development jargon) are indispensable. My research more or less meets this condition, although

it could be argued that a one-year period of fieldwork is still relatively short.

I would range my work under the kind of "post-impasse research" in development studies that takes into consideration heterogeneity, action and interaction, history, culture, and the social construction of reality, by that giving up the illusive certainties of the former grand development theories (Booth 1994, 10, 11). Practice theory, aiming at bridging the gulf between action-based and structuralist explanations (by stressing instead the interplay between structure and agency), seems to have also penetrated the field of development studies (ibid., 17, 27). These new insights in development studies are viewed as the intellectual counterpart of the growth of grassroots movements and the NGOs since the 1970s, which showed an immense variety of ways in which development problems could be approached. Yet even if some (Edwards 1989; Hulme 1994) make a strong plea for the participatory NGO road to development, there is no reason to exclude from the agenda research on precisely the role of these NGOs, and their development rhetoric. They can perfectly well be users as well as subjects of research (Hulme 1994).

If my study has any merits within this wide field of development studies, it is because it provides a detailed qualitative description of NGO cultural politics. It is the type of analysis rapid appraisals (through short missions, the most widespread evaluation technique of development agencies) cannot produce, and project monitoring even less so (see, e.g., IOV 1993). What these "research devices" normally do produce are quantitative results, but these prove difficult to obtain in the domain of "culture," which is nowadays becoming increasingly popular in (Dutch) development cooperation (Ministry of Foreign Affairs 1991, 190ff). My research has no quantitative pretensions, and I urge caution as to the extrapolation of the results I will list below.

SEPADE (in its initial phase called CTA) is a church-owned NGO, originating from the initiative of a group of MIP individuals with clear leftist political sympathies. In Pentecostal churches the ideal of helping other people materially alongside lifting them spiritually is not a strange one. Poor-relief boards are as old as Christianity, yet these generally do not operate outside the realm of the church community, let alone do they pursue political goals. The people in the MIP church that SEPADE sprang from could only with difficulty be warmed up for a discourse that plainly focused on such secular development issues. The world was none of their business, unless as a field in which converts could be harvested. A Christian discourse pursuing the same development goals was initially thought to be even harder to digest. Therefore SEPADE people presumed they could only work with churches at a rather practical level, providing food and shelter. The SEPADE initiators, who were definitely not average MIP members, if only for their high level of education, were less than satisfied by what they experienced as a welfare approach. They held clear political opinions and ideals, although they were far less unanimous about the feasibility of winning Pentecostal churches for these goals and about ways of getting them involved in what they viewed as the correct development path. The history of Pentecostal social behavior had made them pessimistic about the latter: was it not like carrying coals to Newcastle? And, on the other hand, they were not quite sure whether church projects would be considered positively by the sponsoring agencies, that is, whether sponsors would really view these as *development* projects.

SEPADE offered itself at a time, the mid-1970s, when in Holland—as in most other Western countries—funds for Chile were abundantly available through the private—nongovernmental—aid channel. ICCO was one of those allocating nongovernmental organizations that was trying to establish itself on the Latin American continent, where it had not really had a presence until then. It proved difficult, however, to find like-minded—Protestant—partners. The ICCO Latin America department was established almost overnight, largely by just one responsible officer. Whereas SEPADE gradually became a "families' affair," the ICCO part was more like a one-man show, at least during the early stage of the relationship.

My findings at the ICCO archives, based on written reports by this very officer, show that from the beginning expectations were high with regard to the MIP/SEPADE capacity to transform traditional Pentecostal attitudes, and the SEPADE desk officers thought that foreign agencies, including ICCO, had to be convinced of the value of a special focus on (Pentecostal) churches. The image arises then of an NGO that only reluctantly assumed its "prophetic task" for fear of antagonizing ordinary MIP church members, but also because SEPADE leaders thought that their development conceptions and those of the donors might drift apart, once the church work received more attention. Communication was evidently not the strongest point in the NGO-donor relation. The mutual positions only became more clearly defined toward the end of military rule in Chile.

This weakness, which is probably more common than this single case suggests, is part of the general precariousness of church-related development work. A major problem was the dependency on aid created among the beneficiaries of SEPADE projects. This is a problem most NGOs struggle with, but because SEPADE was a church-dependent organization, church people felt they were entitled to profit most from the (material) benefits resulting from the foreign aid contributions. Aid was considered a right belonging to church membership. This was particularly clear for the food help that was for long periods principally distributed through the (MIP) churches. Yet the spin-off in terms of payed work for church members was also viewed as a justified windfall. People from other churches felt excluded from these benefits, which they thought the MIP was monopolizing through SEPADE. Severe criticism of SEPADE's role as the route to the outside ecumenical world was often ventured. The tone of this kind of criticism was often quite scornful, because the MIP was considered an insignificant group, whose Pentecostal character was seriously questioned. Yet I wonder whether SEPADE was merely defending its pivotal (power) position and serving MIP interests, as the criticism goes. No other Pentecostal churches tried to assume responsibilities similar to those of SEPADE. Blaming SEPADE for nipping every attempt in the bud is too easy. Just as social scientists are sometimes accused of viewing reality, including religion, as merely a power game—as constantly shifting power balances—believers also regularly lose sight of the fact that signification is more than calculation. I mean to say that the MIP was open to accept ecumenical stances and engage in development activities that went beyond the familiar charity. I have little reason to doubt the genuine conviction of the SEPADE leaders, although their motivation cannot but have been strengthened by the power position external funding allowed them. Power to decide over money is, however, one thing; power to bring about shifts in the signification of people is of a different order. The new discourse has doubtless touched individual actors, but SEPADE's power to cause people to make these choices was remarkably limited: The supposedly powerless neighborhood Pentecostals could in fact exert substantial power by simply ignoring the offer made to them.

As my accounts in Chapters 4 and 5 clearly demonstrate, the gap between SEPADE (and part of the MIP) leaders and the church people has never been satisfactorily bridged, and has in some ways grown ever wider. SEPADE—like all other NGOs—has in its existence been exposed to the successive development discourses of foreign donors. In the case of ICCO, discourse has increasingly become secular, although without ever loosing sight of its ultimate Christian inspiration. *Justice, participation, communication,* and other key words from the development rhetoric have little by little been stripped of their religious connotations, because "gradually the insight grew that development is a task and a field of its own" (ICCO 1985, 28). The SEPADE staff, who in project proposals had smoothly adopted the current jargon, largely shared this view of their work. In a reaction to my original research plans, a SEPADE staff member once made the puzzling remark that I should realize that SEPADE was a predominantly secular institution. Whether ICCO's "insight" and SEPADE's self-understanding were totally correct or not, is not for scientists to decide; what I do want to establish is that the vast majority of Pentecostals can only partially agree with this position. If they consider development a task at all, then it is certainly not a separate one.

This continuous tension is a major obstacle to reconciling Pentecostalism and development ideas. My treatment of the pastoral feedback course on active listening clearly illustrates how extremely difficult, if not impossible, it is for Pentecostals to separate the application of "popular education" methods from their religious (Pentecostal) modes and codes of conduct. The absence of any religious references in training programs like the course I participated in was its Achilles' heel.

There is no denying, then, that in the case of SEPADE a continuous alienation of the (Pentecostal) NGO staff from ordinary Pentecostal practice has been taking place. Some church leaders have gained access to the field of development cooperation and to the ecumenical networks, where they became familiar with the successive "languages" spoken there, and the practice of distinguishing separate task fields. It can be maintained that this was to a certain extent a direct result of the donor exertion in the church and the NGO belonging to it. Donors seem to support initiatives they feel sympathy for, a sympathy that is not necessarily shared by the people belonging to the so-called target groups of these same donors. That biblical prophets did not have large multitudes of followers either, despite their intention to serve the people, must have been a comforting idea both for donors and recipients. The estrangement of leaders and ordinary church folk can be viewed as the unintended outcome of a development relation, which has, in addition, not been contributive to winning new "converts" to the prophetic stance either. It has even hampered other Protestant (Pentecostal) churches joining the effort, because what they viewed as preferential treatment of the MIP—through its NGO SEPADE—may well have inhibited further rapprochement. This part of SEPADE's work—in short, changing people's attitudes—has to a large extent been a "mission impossible."

It would, however, certainly go too far to put the blame entirely on thoughtless development policies. The Pentecostal renewal I deal with in this book took place under quite unfavorable political and socioeconomic conditions. Whether more Pentecostals would have tended to join under more favorable conditions remains an open question. Practicing social work in the direct neighborhood proved closely compatible with the Pentecostal religious experience of people, but adopting a wider political and ecumenical perspective was more than most of them could give a meaningful place to in their worldview.

In the present circumstances so-called professionalization is hitting hard in development circles. On the donor and the counterpart sides the emphasis on producing measurable results has become increasingly noticeable. The good intentions that dominated the Chile programs in the 1970s and 1980s have been replaced by a down-to-earth approach that has even been defended with the slogan "professionalization of commitment." The spirit of the 1990s has apparently no place for sponsoring cultural—religious—change, despite the increased awareness of the important role of culture in development processes. If because of this the donor support to SEPADE's work is cut down in the future, a long-lasting development relation will be ended, the results of which relation are largely unknown. The reason for stopping will certainly not be that a sufficient number of preestablished goals have been reached. It looks rather as if the belief in these very goals has withered. In any case they have rapidly lost priority with regard to (political, economic) development needs elsewhere. Chile has returned to democracy, its economy is doing well, and even the poorer sectors of the population are not complaining too much. What the vast amount of foreign aid through the NGO channel has contributed to that, is simply unknown (yet). It looks as if donor agencies prefer to leave it at that, now that their attention has shifted toward other places.

Research among Pentecostals: Afterthoughts

> We find ourselves entering a realm of fascination and paradox, all of
> which centers on the ambiguity of the "concrete." In particular, . . .
> as scientists, we are invited, indeed compelled, towards *an exploration
> of the concrete.* —Sacks 1985, 165

At the end of this book it is time to reflect on my journey among
Chilean Pentecostals. I have been an observer and unceasing inquirer, while simultaneously playing my part in the church meetings
and services. As a non-Pentecostal I have nevertheless been deeply
involved in church life, in particular in three local congregations,
one of which was La Victoria. In a way I have constantly been on
the threshold between inside and outside. Although I have never
been subject to direct proselytism, as others have—Pentecostals are
far less submissive to Western academic outsiders than other target
groups of research—my experience was that my role of a researcher
was never accepted as a self-explanatory one. Pentecostals simply
have great difficulty accepting people as neutral or detached observers, and even more so if the subject of research is Pentecostalism
itself. As for myself as a researcher, I have no trouble at all in accepting the truths Pentecostals advance in their testimonies and so on,
yet the present book does not try to assess or evaluate the miraculous events and claims believers often mention; I just took them
seriously. Yet the question remains—and I have repeated it throughout the book—of whether I have succeeded in giving a credible account of a part of Chilean Pentecostalism; in other words, did I
produce an acceptable piece of local knowledge? By credible, I mean
acceptable to the community I researched and to the scientific audience.

As I have mentioned in Chapters 2 and 3, most authors on Latin
American and Chilean Pentecostalism have to some extent been in-
fected by the Pentecostal tendency toward evaluation, moral judgment, and disputes about numbers, which can to a certain extent
be explained by their Christian commitment. Since I view people
primarily as meaning-givers, I am hardly surprised by this. My contribution to the debate has been to discuss the limits of this
meaning-making of "little people" and their daily life in a particular
historical case and context. I studied a socially committed, prophetic
type of Pentecostalism. It was a small group, but itself marked by

considerable internal differences. If only for this reason, this study barely allows for predictions on the Pentecostal future in Chile, let alone Latin America. Social scientists, for that matter, should abstain from prophesying anyhow, but researchers on Latin American Protestantism share a strong preference for growth figures and numbers. This quantitative preoccupation pervading most studies so far has pushed thinking actors into the background as mere puppets. One aim of my work is to make them reappear on the stage as meaning-makers, that is, as Pentecostal people trying to keep control over their own signification.

In the practice approach I chose for this study I tried to link daily Pentecostal practice to a wider social and political context. However, the way I have treated the vicissitudes of prophetic Pentecostalism has been largely narrative, that is, I closely reproduced and examined what some would call the actors' point of view. My treatment of people's religious experiences will, for some scholars, mean that I am crossing the fences of (social) science. For others it will simply mean that I chose one out of so many scientific alternatives. It all results from the desire to synthesize what people say about, and do with religion and the distinctive meanings they attribute to their practices.

In Chapter 2 I also pointed to the ethically delicate role I played in this field of actors. My constant moving between the various MIP church levels, the NGO SEPADE, and the international donors particularly confronted me with several ethical dilemmas. The role this book may play in development politics leaves me with ambivalent feelings. On the one hand, I feel that detailed accounts of projects, such as I give, are greatly needed for developers, wherever they operate; on the other hand, there is the risk that my uncalled-for information may be (ab)used as an argument for policy decisions, especially if only the concluding chapter is consulted. I have tried to give due attention to the many rival viewpoints I came across, but the respective assessments I made as a researcher inescapably reflect partiality. The ideal of presenting contested dialogic viewpoints (Hobart 1993) still largely remains an illusion. My book is an attempt to stick to the concrete, an approach defended in the theoretical Chapter 2. Confessing to such an approach is different from claiming to provide better knowledge, although I think that not a few theories are in need of "testing" by concrete studies like the present one. By being explicit about the research process and my role as an anthropologist among Pentecostals, I have tried to give the reader the tools to assess the credibility of the account I constructed.

As far as representativeness is concerned, I also have to show some modesty. The quantitative importance of the prophetic phenomenon is limited; I chose to study it for the very reason of the opportunity it offered to highlight a sort of Pentecostalism deviating from the general picture arising from most of the literature on the subject. The choice of this case study, however, entails that many other interesting subjects and actors are not dealt with, or are only barely mentioned. I could have chosen to study another—bigger—Pentecostal church, other NGOs working with churches, or within the MIP to concentrate on other congregations.

The increasing number of publications on the "culture and development" theme suggests that nowadays closer attention is paid to the culture of those people whom development projects are addressing. If that means that their opinion is taken seriously, that would mean real progress. Anthropological studies like the present one are a means to "bring culture into development," because they aim to elicit the meaning people give to development interventions.

Glossary and Acronyms

ACE	Ayuda Cristiana Evangélica. Protestant Aid, NGO created by the CEC in 1958 to distribute foreign aid
AIECH	Asociación de Iglesias Evangélicas de Chile. Association of Chilean Protestant Churches, founded in 1974/1975 by Protestant churches rejecting the military coup
Avivamiento	Revival. Spiritual, often Pentecostal, awakening within an institutionalized, often Protestant, church
Baptism with the Holy Spirit	Core Pentecostal characteristic referring to the events related in Acts 2; "baptized" believers may "speak in tongues," "prophesy," etc.
Bolsa de Cesantes	Unemployment Pool
Callampas	Squatter Settlements
Campamentos	Working-class encampments (similar to *callampas*)
Canutos	Traditional nickname for Pentecostals, from a famous Pentecostal preacher (a converted Spanish Jesuit) who preached in Chile during the first decades of this century
CAP	Centro de Abastecimiento Popular. Communal Purchase Center. A SEPADE project

CARITAS	Catholic Relief Services; mainly food donations
Catedral Evangélico	Principal IMP temple (see *Jotabeche*)
CCE	Comité de Coordinación Evangélica. Protestant Coordination Committee. Organism representing most Protestant and Pentecostal churches since 1991
CCI	Confraternidad Cristiana de Iglesias. Christian Fraternity of Churches; ecumenical, "prophetic" association of Protestant churches (since 1985)
CCPD	Commission of Churches' Participation in Development; WCC department
CEB	Christian Base Community; name of "progressive" Catholic lay discussion and action groups
CEC	Concilio Evangélico Cristiano. Protestant Council (1941; now dwindling)
CECH	Comisión Episcopal de Chile. Chilean Episcopal Commission (Catholic)
CESS	Centro de Educación y Servicio Social. Center for Education and Social Service; name for MIP departments with a specific field of action
CEMA	Centro de Madres. Mothers' Center. Government-directed organization for (poor) women
CEP	Centro de Estudios Públicos. Center for Civil Studies. Politically right-wing "think-tank"
CEPAL	Comisión Económica para América Latina. United Nations Economic Commission for Latin America
CEPLA	Comisión Evangélica Pentecostal Latinoamericana. Latin American Pentecostal Committee. Continental association of ecumenical Pentecostals

Charismata	Gifts of the Holy Spirit, e.g., speaking in tongues, prophesying, etc. See Baptism with the Holy Spirit
Christian Aid	British Protestant NGO
Church World Service	U.S.-based Christian Relief Agency
CICARWS	Commission on Inter-Church Aid, Refugees and World Service. WCC department
Ciclistas	Cyclists; traditionally a Pentecostal evangelizing group
CLAI	Consejo Latinoamericana de Iglesias. Latin American Council of Churches (1985). Ecumenical
Clase	In IMP language "annex." Also used for a particular group within the church, e.g., clase de jóvenes, youth group
CMI	Consejo Mundial de Iglesias. World Council of Churches (WCC)
Colonias urbanas	Summer camps. SEPADE activity for working-class children
Comedor (popular)	Communal Kitchen (see *Olla común*)
Comprando juntos	Communal purchasing (food products, to reduce costs)
Comuna	Municipality
Consejo de Pastores	Council of Pastors; group of Pentecostal pastors supporting Pinochet. Organizers of the Pentecostal *Te Deum*
Corporación	Chilean legal term for Pentecostal denomination
CORVI	Corporación de Vivienda. Housing Department
CRI	Centro de Recreación Infantil. Recreation Center for Children; SEPADE project

CTA	Comisión Técnica Asesora. Technical Advisory Commission; predecessor of SEPADE (1975)
CTE	Comunidad Teológica Evangélica. Protestant Theological Community of Chile; Protestant High School (1966)
Culto	Church service
Diego de Medellín	Ecumenical NGO in Santiago, spreading the message of liberation theology
Dorcas	Pentecostal Women's Group (after a Bible verse, Acts 6:36ff)
ECLOF	WCC Ecumenical Loan Fund; financing church building
Educación popular	"Popular Education." Widely applied technique of informal education (by NGOs, churches) for consciousness-raising of working-class people
Encargado	Deputy pastor
Escuela dominical	Sunday school; weekly teaching session in Protestant churches
Evangélico	General term indicating Latin American Protestants (non-Catholics)
Evangelio y Sociedad	Gospel and Society; SEPADE journal
Evangelista	Evangelist. Nickname for Pentecostals, because of their strong proselytism
FASIC	Fundación de Ayuda Social de Iglesias Cristianas. Protestant Foundation for Social Action; ecumenical NGO focusing on human rights (1975)
FOSIS	Fondo de Solidaridad e Inversión Social. Solidarity and Social Inversion Fund; State organism channeling foreign and national aid since the return of democracy (1990)
Fuego de Pentecostés	"Pentecostal Fire," IEP journal

Guía de clase	Deputy pastor (IMP); also group leader within the church
Hacendado	Large landowner
Hermano/ hermana	Brother/sister. They way Pentecostals address each other
Hogar de Cristo	Catholic Housing Organization
ICCO	Interkerkelijke Coördinatie Commissie Ontwikkelingssamenwerking. Dutch Interchurch Organization for Development Cooperation. Cofinancing agency
IEP	Iglesia Evangélica Pentecostal. Evangelical Pentecostal Church; second largest, most traditional Pentecostal church; "mother church" of the MIP
Iglesia Reformada	Reformed Church; an ecumenical Pentecostal Church in Chile
Iglesia Wesleyana	Wesleyan Church (officially Misión Evangélica Wesleyana Nacional, 1928); belonging to the prophetic wing of Pentecostalism
IMP	Iglesia Metodista Pentecostal. Pentecostal Methodist Church; biggest Pentecostal church in Chile; supporter of the Pinochet regime; organizer of the *Te Deum*
INE	Instituto Nacional de Estadística. National Institute of Statistics; State organism
Institucionalistas	Supporters of a transition to democracy that give priority to (political) institutions
IPCH	Iglesia Pentecostal de Chile; third biggest Pentecostal church (1947, ecumenical)
Jotabeche	Main church of the IMP, also called *catedral evangélico*. Opened in 1974 in the presence of general Pinochet
Junta de oficiales	Church council (in Protestant churches)
Junta de vecinos	Neighborhood council

La Victoria	Famous working-class neighborhood in Santiago; location of the principal MIP congregation appearing in this book
Latifundio	Large estate ownership (contrast *minifundio*-smallholders)
Lutheran World Relief	Lutheran relief agency
Machismo	Cult of manhood; contrast to *marianismo*
MAPU	Movimiento de Acción Popular Unitario. Movement for Unitarian Action of the People; Leftist split-off (1969) from the Christian-Democrats
Marianismo	Cult of femininity (to Mary); contrast to *machismo*
MIP	Misión Iglesia Pentecostal. Pentecostal Mission Church; small, but influential ecumenical church of the prophetic wing
Movimentistas	Supporters of the idea of a social movement of working-class people
Mundo	"World" For Pentecostals, the outside, sinful place they live in; also synonym for sin
NGDO	Nongovernmental Development Organization
NGO	Nongovernmental Organization
OEP	Organización Económica Popular. Working-class economic organization; often selfhelp group
Olla común	Communal kitchen; for the preparation of meals in common (see *comedor*)
PC	Partido Comunista. Communist Party
PDC	Partido Demócrata Cristiano. Christian-Democratic Party
Pentecostalismo criollo	Indigenous Pentecostalism; to distinguish from Pentecostal churches founded as a result of foreign mission

Población	Working-class neighborhood
Poblador	*Población* dweller
PROAL	Programa de Promoción Alimentaria. Food Program SEPADE
Protestas	Series of violent protests against the regime, especially in the period 1983–1984
PS	Partido Socialista. Socialist Party; formerly heavily divided
PUEC	Proyecto Unido de Educación Cristiana. United Project of Christian Education, preparing materials for Sunday school teaching (until 1993)
Sembrando	Periodical of the MIP
SEPADE	Servicio Evangélico Para El Desarrollo. Protestant Development Service; leading ecumenical NGO
SOH	Stichting Oecumenische Hulp. Dutch Interchurch Aid; Dutch food donor
Te Deum	Protestant/Pentecostal Thanksgiving service, held from 1975 onward in the *Jotabeche* cathedral in the presence of general Pinochet
SUR	NGO, mainly doing research among working-class sectors
Toma	Land seizure
Vicaría de la Solidaridad	Catholic Vicariate of Solidarity. Main human rights organization since 1973
WCC	World Council of Churches; Large association of more than 300 ecumenical mainly Protestant churches (1948)

Bibliography

Alexander, Jeffrey C. 1990. Analytic Debates: Understanding the Relative Autonomy of Culture. In *Culture and Society: Contemporary Debates*, ed. Jeffrey C. Alexander and Steven Seidman, 1–27. Cambridge: Cambridge University Press.

Alvarez, Carmelo. 1987. Latin American Pentecostals: Ecumenical and Evangelical. *Pneuma*. 9 (1): 91–95.

———. 1992. Lo popular: clave hermenéutica del movimiento pentecostal. In *Pentecostalismo y liberación: Una experiencia latinoamericana*, ed. Carmelo Alvarez, 89–100. San José: DEI.

Análisis. 1986. Separando aguas con Pinochet. *Análisis*. September 17–19.

Angell, Alan. 1993. Chile since 1958. In *Chile since Independence*, ed. Leslie Bethell, 129–202. Cambridge: Cambridge University Press.

Annis, Sheldon. 1988. *God and Production in a Guatemalan Town*. Austin: University of Texas Press.

Archer, Margaret S. 1988. *Culture and Agency: The Place of Culture in Social Theory*. Cambridge: Cambridge University Press.

———. 1990. Human Agency and Social Structure: A Critique of Giddens. In *Anthony Giddens. Consensus and Controversy*, ed. Jon Clark, Celia Modgil, and Sohan Modgil, 73–84. London, New York, Philadelphia: The Falmer Press.

Asad, Talal. 1983. Anthropological Conceptions of Religion: Reflections on Geertz. *Man, n.s.*, 18: 237–259.

Aylwin, Mariana, et al. 1985. *Chile en el siglo XX*. Santiago: Emisión.

Barrett, David B. 1982. Chile. In *World Christian Encyclopedia*, ed. David B. Barrett, 226–230. Nairobi: Oxford University Press.

Bauman, Zygmunt. 1973. *Culture as Praxis*. London and Boston: Routledge and Kegan Paul.

Beijaard, Frans. 1983. *Huisvestingsbeleid en zelfbouwwijken in Chili: gezichtspunten op de rol van de overheid*. Amsterdam: VU.

Bent, Ans J. van der, ed. 1982. *Handbook of Member Churches*. Geneva: World Council of Churches.

Berger, Peter L. 1967. *The Sacred Canopy: Elements of a Sociological Theory of Religion*. Garden City, New York: Doubleday and Company.

Berger, Peter L. and Thomas Luckmann. 1991 [1966]. *The Social Construction of Reality: A Treatise in the Sociology of Knowledge*. London: Penguin Books.

Blakemore, Harold. 1993. From the War of the Pacific to 1930. In *Chile since Independence*, ed. Leslie Bethell, 33–85. Cambridge: Cambridge University Press.

Booth, David, ed. 1994. *Rethinking Social Development: Theory, Research and Practice*. Burnt Mill, and Harlow, Essex, England: Longman House.

Boudewijnse, Barbara, André Droogers and Frans Kamsteeg, eds. 1991. *Algo más que opio: Una lectura antropológica del pentecostalismo latinoamericano y caribeño*. San José: DEI.

———. 1998. *More Than Opium. An Anthropological Approach to Latin American and Caribbean Pentecostal Praxis*. Lanham, Md., & London: The Scarecrow Press, Inc.

Bourdieu, Pierre. 1971. Genèse et structure du champ religieux. *Revue française de sociologie*. 12: 295–334.

———. 1977. *Outline of a Theory of Practice*. Cambridge: Cambridge University Press.

———. 1986. *Distinction: A Social Critique of the Judgement of Taste*. London: Routledge and Kegan Paul.

———. 1988a. *Homo Academicus*. Cambridge: Polity Press.

———. 1988b. Vive la crise! For Heterodoxy in Social Science. *Theory and Society*. 17: 773–788.

———. 1989. *Opstellen over smaak, habitus en het veldbegrip*. Amsterdam: Van Gennip.

———. 1990. *The Logic of Practice*. Cambridge: Polity Press.

———. 1992a. Habitus, illusio en rationaliteit. In *Argumenten voor een reflexieve maatschappijwetenschap*, Pierre Bourdieu, 73–92. Amsterdam: SUA.

———. 1992b. Sociologie als socioanalyse. In *Argumenten voor een reflexieve maatschappijwetenschap*, Pierre Bourdieu, Pierre, 38–56. Amsterdam: SUA.

———. 1992c. *Language and Symbolic Power*. Cambridge: Polity Press.

Brunner, José Joaquín, Alicia Barrios and Carlos Catalán. 1989. *Chile: transformaciones culturales y modernidad*. Santiago: FLACSO.

Brusco, Elizabeth E. 1986a. Colombian Evangelicalism as a Strategic Form of Women's Collective Action. *Feminist Issues*. 6 (2): 3–13.

———. 1986b. *The Household Basis of Evangelical Religion and the Reformation of Machismo in Colombia*. Ann Arbor: UMI.

Burdick, John. 1993. *Looking for God in Brazil*. Berkeley: University of California Press.

Butler Flora, Cornelia. 1975. Pentecostal Women in Colombia: Religious Change and the Status of Working-Class Women. *Journal of Interamerican Studies and World Affairs*. 17 (4): 411–425.

———. 1978. *Pentecostalism in Colombia: Baptism by Fire and Spirit*. Cranbury, N.J.: Associated University Presses.

Canales, Manuel, Samuel Palma, Juan Sepúlveda and Hugo Villela. 1987. *La subjetividad popular, la religión de los sectores populares: el campo pentecostal*. Santiago: SEPADE.

Canales, Manuel, Samuel Palma and Hugo Villela. 1991. *En tierra extraña II. Para una sociología de la religiosidad popular protestante*. Santiago: Amerinda.

Carrasco, Carlos, Juan Flores and Robinson Coz. 1979. *Evaluación de las instituciones Ayuda Cristiana Evangélica y Comisión Técnica Asesora de Chile*. Santiago: CTA.

CCI (Confraternidad Cristiana de Iglesias). 1987a. *Separata, primera y segunda parte*. Santiago: CCI.

———. 1987b. Carta Abierta al general Pinochet, 29 August 1986. *Evangelio y Sociedad*, 4 (appendix).

CCPD/CICARWS. 1979. *Project Overview 1979*. Geneva: WCC.

CEPAL (Comisión Económica Para América Latina). 1972. De stedelijke situatie. In *Sociologie en sociale verandering in Latijns Amerika I*, ed. A. E. Niekerk, 43–68. Rotterdam: UPR/SWU.

Chateau, Jorge, et al. 1987. *Espacio y poder: Los pobladores*. Santiago: FLACSO.

Clifford, James. 1988. *The Predicament of Culture: Twentieth-Century Ethnography, Literature and Art*. Cambridge, Mass., London: Harvard University Press.

Cohen, Anthony P. 1985. *The Symbolic Construction of Community*. Chichester, London, and New York: Ellis Horwood Limited, Tavistock Publications.

ColinsBible. 1952. *The Holy Bible (Revised Standard Version)*. New York, Glasgow, and Toronto: HarperCollins Publishers.

Comisión Episcopal de Chile. 1989. *Pentecostalismo, sectas y pastoral*. Santiago: Comisión Episcopal de Chile.

Connerton, Paul. 1992. *How Societies Remember*. Cambridge: Cambridge University Press.

Corporación (Iglesia Evangélica Pentecostal). 1977. *Historia del avivamiento. Origen y desarrollo de la Iglesia Evangélica Pentecostal*. Santiago: Eben-Ezer.

Correa, Enrique and José Antonio Viera-Gallo. (n.d). *Iglesia y dictadura*. Santiago: CESOC.

260 *Bibliography*

Crick, Malcolm. 1976. *Explorations in Language and Meaning. Towards a Semantic Anthropology.* London: Malaby Press.

Cucchiari, Salvatore. 1990. Between Shame and Sanctification: Patriarchy and its transformation in Sicilian Pentecostalism. *American Ethnologist.* 17 (4): 687–707.

Dayton, Donald W. 1987. *Theological Roots of Pentecostalism.* Grand Rapids, Mich.: Francis Asbury Press.

———. 1991. *Raíces teológicas del pentecostalismo.* Buenos Aires and Grand Rapids, Mich.: Nueva Creación, William B. Eerdmans Publishing.

Dolgin, Janet L., David S. Kemnitzer and David M. Schneider, eds. 1977. *Symbolic Anthropology. A Reader in the Study of Symbols and Meanings.* New York: Columbia University Press.

Downs, Charles and Giorgio Solimano. 1988. Alternative Social Policies from the Grassroots: Implications of Recent NGO Experience in Chile. *Community Development Journal: An International Forum.* 23 (2): 62–73.

Downs, Charles, Giorgio Solimano, C. Vergara and L. Zúñiga, eds. 1989. *Social Development from the Grassroots: Non-Governmental Organizations in Chile.* Boulder: Westview Press.

Drake, Paul. 1993. Chile, 1930–1958. In *Chile since Independence*, ed. Leslie Bethell, 87–128. Cambridge: Cambridge University Press.

Droogers, André F. 1991. Visiones paradójicas sobre una religión paradójica. Modelos explicativos del crecimiento del pentecostalismo en Brasil y Chile. In *Algo más que opio. Una lectura antropológica del pentecostalismo latinoamericano y caribeño*, ed. Barbara Boudewijnse, André Droogers, and Frans Kamsteeg, 17–42. San José: DEI.

———. 1992. Pentecostalisme: een lopend vuurtje. *Wereld en Zending.* 21: 3–11.

Droogers, André F. and Hans Siebers. 1991. Popular Religion and Power in Latin America: An Introduction. In *Popular Power in Latin American Religions*, ed. André Droogers, Gerrit Huizer and Hans Siebers, 1–25. Saarbrücken/Fort Lauderdale: Verlag Breitenbach Publishers.

Edwards, Michael. 1989. The Irrelevance of Development Studies. *Third World Quarterly.* 11 (1): 116–135.

Equipo Evangelio y Sociedad. 1985. Dios quiere que todos vivamos en condiciones dignas. *Evangelio y Sociedad.* 1: 40–46.

———. 1990a. Debemos pasar de una sociedad egoista a una sociedad fraterna. *Evangelio y Sociedad.* 5: 6–7.

———. 1990b. Sepade: 15 años acompañando el despertar solidario de la iglesias pentecostales. *Evangelio y Sociedad.* 6: 22–29.

Espinoza, Vicente. 1988. *Para una historia de los pobres de la ciudad.* Santiago: SUR.

Ewing, Katherine P. 1990. The Illusion of Wholeness: Culture, Self, and the Experience of Inconsistency. *Ethos.* 18: 251–278.

Falk Moore, Sally. 1975. Epilogue: Uncertainties in Situations, Indeterminacies in Culture. In *Symbol and Politics in Communal Ideology. Cases and Questions*, ed. Sally Falk Moore and Barbara G. Myerhoff, 210–239. Ithaca and London: Cornell University Press.

Falk Moore, Sally and Barbara Myerhoff. 1977. Introduction: Secular Ritual: Forms and Meanings. In *Secular Ritual*, ed. Sally Falk Moore and Barbara G. Myerhoff, 3–24. Assen/Amsterdam: Van Gorcum.

Fernandez, James W. 1986. *Persuasions and Performances: The Play of Tropes in Culture*. Bloomington: Indiana University Press.

Fontaine T., Arturo, and Harald Beyer. 1991. Retrato del movimiento evangélico a la luz de las encuestas de opinión pública. *Estudios Públicos*. 44: 63–125.

Freire, Paulo. 1970. *Pedagogy of the Oppressed*. New York: Herder and Herder.

Frerks, Georg E. 1991. *Participation in Development: Activities at the Local Level: Case Studies from a Sri Lankan Village*. Islamabad: Barqsons (Pvt.) Ltd.

Galilea W., Carmen. 1987. *Lugares de culto religioso en Santiago: Distribución, población y perspectivas*. Santiago: Centro Bellarmino, CISOC.

———. 1991. *El predicador pentecostal*. Santiago: Centro Bellarmino, CISOC.

Garfinkel, H. 1967. *Studies in Ethnomethodology*. Englewood Cliffs, N.J.: Prentice-Hall.

Garrard-Burnett, Virginia and David Stoll, eds. 1993. *Rethinking Pentecostalism in Latin America*. Philadelphia: Temple University Press.

Geertz, Clifford. 1973. *The Interpretation of Cultures*. New York: Basic-Books.

———. 1993 [1983]. *Local Knowledge*. Hammersmith, London: Fontana Press.

Geuijen, Karin. 1992. Postmodernisme in de Antropologie. *Antropologische Verkenningen*. 11 (1): 17–36.

Giddens, Anthony. 1981. Agency, Institution, and Time-Space Analysis. In *Advances in Social Theory and Methodology: Toward an Integration of Micro- and Macro-Sociologies,* ed. K. Knorr-Cetina and A. V. Cicourel, 161–174. Boston, London: Routledge and Kegan Paul.

———. 1985. *The Constitution of Society: Outline of a Theory of Structuration*. Cambridge: Polity Press.

Glaser, B. G. and A. L. Strauss. 1967. *The Discovery of Grounded Theory*. Chicago: Aldine.

Glazier, Stephen D., ed. 1980. *Perspectives on Pentecostalism: Case Studies from the Caribbean and Latin America*. Washington, D.C.: University Press of America.

Godoy, Daniel. 1993. Algo no está bien. . . . *Pastoral Popular*. 44 (233): 40.

Gros, Jeffrey. 1987. Confessing the Apostolic Faith from the Perspective of the Pentecostal Churches. *Pneuma.* 9 (1): 5–16.

Guba, Egon C. 1990. The Alternative Paradigm Dialogue. In *The Paradigm Dialogue*, ed. Egon C. Guba, 17–27. Newbury Park, London, New Delhi: Sage.

Guerra Vicencio, Ernesto. 1984. *La ética social en la Misión Wesleyana Nacional.* Santiago: CTE.

Hannerz, Ulf. 1992. *Cultural Complexity: Studies in the Social Organization of Meaning.* New York: Columbia University Press.

Hanson, F. Allan. 1975. *Meaning in Culture.* London and Boston: Routledge and Kegan Paul.

Hardy, Clarisa. 1989. *La ciudad escindida.* Santiago: PET.

Harris, Marvin. 1968. *The Rise of Anthropological Theory: A History of Theories of Culture.* New York: Thomas Y. Crowell.

Headland, Thomas N., Kenneth L. Pike and Marvin Harris, eds. 1990. *Emics and Etics. The Insider/Outsider Debate.* Newbury Park, London, New Delhi: Sage.

Hobart, Mark. 1993. Introduction: The Growth of Ignorance? In *An Anthropological Critique of Development: The Growth of Ignorance*, ed. Mark Hobart, 1–30. London, New York: Routledge.

Hoebink, Paul. 1988. *Geven is nemen: de Nederlandse ontwikkelingshulp aan Tanzania en Sri Lanka.* Nijmegen: KUN.

Hoffnagel, Judith Chambliss. 1979. *The Believers: Pentecostalism in a Brazilian City.* Berkeley: University of California.

Hojman, David E. 1993. Nongovernmental Organizations (NGOs) and the Chilean Transition to Democracy. *European Review of Latin American and Caribbean Studies.* 54: 7–24.

Hollenweger, Walter J. 1982. Methodism's Past in Pentecostalism's Present A Case Study of Cultural Clash in Chile. *Methodist History.* 20 (4): 169–182.

———. 1992. Belofte en noodlot van de pinksterbeweging. *Wereld en Zending.* 21: 12–33.

Hulme, David. 1994. Social Development Research and the Third Sector NGOs as Users and Subjects of Social Inquiry. In *Rethinking Social Development: Theory, Research & Practice*, ed. David Booth, 251–275 Burnt Mill, Harlow: Longman Scientific and Technical.

ICCO (Interkerkelijke Coördinatie Commissie Ontwikkelingssamenwerking). 1979. *Jaarverslag ICCO 1977–1979.* Zeist: ICCO.

———. 1980. *Jaarverslag ICCO 1980.* Zeist: ICCO.

———. 1985. *Development and Participation: ICCO from 1980 to 1985, Five Year Report.* Zeist: ICCO.

———. (n.d.). *Correspondence Chile Projects.* Zeist: ICCO.

INE (Instituto Nacional de Estadística). 1970. *Censo oficial.* Santiago: INE

————. 1993. *Resultados generales 1992.* Santiago: INE.

IOV (Inspectie Ontwikkelingssamenwerking te Velde). 1993. *Evaluatie en monitoring: De rol van projectevaluaties en monitoring in de bilaterale hulp.* Den Haag: Ministerie van Buitenlandse Zaken.

Jenkins, Richard. 1992. *Pierre Bourdieu.* London: Routledge.

Kamsteeg, Frans H. 1991. Pentecostal Healing and Power: a Peruvian Case. In *Popular Power in Latin American Religions,* ed. André Droogers, Gerrit Huizer and Hans Siebers, 196–218. Saarbrücken/Fort Lauderdale: Verlag Breitenbach Publishers.

————. 1993. The Message and the People—The Different Meanings of a Pentecostal Evangelistic Campaign. A Case from Southern Peru. In *The Popular Use of Popular Religion in Latin America,* ed. Susanna Rostas and André Droogers, 127–144. Amsterdam: CEDLA.

Kessler, Jean Baptiste. August. 1967. *A Study of the Older Protestant Missions and Churches in Peru and Chile, with Special Reference to Problems of Division, Nationalism and Native Ministry.* Goes, The Netherlands: Oosterbaan and Le Cointre.

Kievid, Jan de. 1993. *Brood, werk, gerechtigheid en vrijheid. Chili tussen dictatuur en democratie.* Amsterdam: Uitgeverij Ravijn.

Kiernan, J. P. 1976. Prophet and Preacher: An Essential Partnership in the Work of Zion. *Man,* n.s., 2: 356–366.

Kloos, Peter. 1988. No Knowledge without a Knowing Subject. *Studies in Qualitative Methodology.* 1: 221–241.

————. 1993. Ontwikkeling is een cultuurverschijnsel. In *Cultuur en Ontwikkeling: RAWOO lunchlezingen 1992,* ed. Marijke Veldhuis, 65–75. Den Haag: RAWOO.

Kruijt, Dirk and Menno Vellinga, eds. 1983. *Ontwikkelingshulp gestest: resultaten onder de loep.* Muiderberg, The Netherlands: Countinho.

Lagos Schuffeneger, Humberto. 1988. *Crisis de la Esperanza: Religión y Autoritarismo en Chile.* Santiago: PRESOR/LAR.

Lalive d'Epinay, Christian. 1969. *Haven of the Masses: A Study of the Pentecostal Movement in Chile.* London: Lutterworth Press.

————. 1975. *Religion, dynamique sociale et dépendance: Le mouvements protestants en Argentine et au Chili.* Paris/La Haye: Mouton.

————. 1978. Conformisme passif, conformisme actif et solidarité de classe. Commentaire à l'article de J. Tennekes. *Social Compass.* 25 (1): 81–84.

Lawless, Elaine J. 1988. *God's Peculiar People. Women's Voices & Folk Tradition in a Pentecostal Church.* Lexington: University Press of Kentucky.

Layder, Derek. 1981. *Structure, Interaction and Social Theory.* London, Boston and Henley: Routledge and Kegan Paul.

Lechner, Frank J. 1991. Fundamentalism and Modernity: a Sociological Interpretation. In *Naar de letter. Beschouwingen over fundamentalisme,* ed. Pieter Boele van Hensbroek, Sjaak Koenis and Pauline Westerman, 103–125. Utrecht: Stichting Grafiet.

Lehmann, David. 1990. *Democracy and Development in Latin America: Economics, Politics and Religion in The Post-War Period*. Cambridge: Polity Press.

Lemuñir E., Juan. 1990. *Crónicas de La Victoria*. Santiago: Ediciones documentas, CEMPROS.

Lett, James. 1990. Emics and Ethics: Notes on the Epistemology of Anthropology. In *Emics and Ethics. The Insider/Outsider Debate*, ed. Thomas N. Headland, Kenneth L. Pike, and Marvin Harris, 127–142. Newbury Park, London, New Delhi: Sage.

Long, Theodore E. 1986. Prophecy, Charisma, and Politics: Reinterpreting the Weberian Thesis. In *The Politics of Religion and Social Change. Religion and the Political Order*, Jeffrey K. Hadden and Anson Shupe, 3–17. New York: Paragon House.

———. 1988. A Theory of Prophetic Religion and Politics. In *The Politics of Religion and Social Change. Religion and the Political Order. Volume II*, ed. Anson Shupe and Jeffrey K. Hadden, 3–16. New York: Paragon House.

Loveman, B. 1991. NGOs and the Transition to Democracy in Chile. *Grassroots Development*. 15 (2): 8–19.

Lowden, Pamela. 1993. The Ecumenical Committee for Peace in Chile (1973–1975): The Foundation of Moral Opposition to Authoritarian Rule in Chile. *Bulletin of Latin American Research*. 12 (2): 189–203.

Maduro, Otto. 1982. *Religion and Social Conflict*. Maryknoll, New York: Orbis.

Maldonado, Jorge E.. 1993. Building "Fundamentalism" from the Family in Latin America. In *Fundamentalisms and Society. Reclaiming the Sciences, the Family and Education*, ed. M. E. Marty and R.S. Appleby, 214–239. Chicago/London: University of Chicago Press.

Marcus, George E., and Michael M. J. Fischer. 1986. *Anthropology as Cultural Critique. An Experimental Moment in the Human Sciences*. Chicago, London: University of Chicago Press.

Mariz, Cecília. 1994. *Coping with Poverty: Pentecostals and Christian Base Communities in Brazil*. Philadelphia: Temple University Press.

Martin, David. 1990. *Tongues of Fire: The Explosion of Protestantism in Latin America*. Oxford: Basil Blackwell.

Martinic, Sergio. 1991. Popular Education; the Viewpoint of the Participants. In *Popular Culture in Chile. Resistance and Survival*, ed. Kenneth Aman and Cristián Parker, 155–172. Boulder/Oxford: Westview Press.

Marty, M. E. and R. S. Appleby, eds. 1993. *Fundamentalisms and Society: Reclaiming the Sciences, the Family and Education*. Chicago/London: University of Chicago Press.

McGuire, Meredith B. 1992. *Religion: The Social Context*. Belmont, Calif.: Wadsworth Publishing Company.

Merton, R. K. 1949. *Social Theory and Social Structure*. Glencoe, Ill.: The Free Press.

Minister van Ontwikkelingssamenwerking. 1993. *Een wereld in geschil: De grenzen van de ontwikkelingssamenwerking verkend*. Den Haag: SDU.

Ministry of Foreign Affairs (DVL/OS). 1991. *A World of Difference: A New Framework for Development Cooperation in the 1990s*. The Hague: SDU Publishers.

MIP (Misión Iglesia Pentecostal). 1977. *Estatutos y reglamentos Misión 'Iglesia Pentecostal.'* Santiago: MIP.

———. 1984. *Breve reseña histórica sobre la Misión 'Iglesia Pentecostal.'* Santiago: SEPADE.

———. (n.d.). *Libro de Actos MIP, tomo II*. Santiago: MIP.

Misión Evangélica Wesleyana Nacional. 1990. *Himnos Escogidos*. Concepción: Misión Evangélica Wesleyana Nacional.

Moser, Caroline O. N. 1989. Gender Planning in the Third World: Meeting Practical and Strategic Gender Needs. *World Development*. 17 (11): 1799–1825.

———. 1993. *Gender Planning and Development: Theory, Practice & Training*. London: Routledge.

Muñoz R., Humberto. 1989. Los Pentecostales. In *Sectas en América Latina*, ed. Osvaldo Santagada D. et al., 139–155. Lima: Ediciones Paulinas/CELAM.

Muratorio, Blanca. 1980. Protestantism and Capitalism Revisited in the Rural Highlands of Ecuador. *The Journal of Peasant Studies*. 8(1), 37–61.

Oakley, Peter, ed. 1991. *Projects with People: The Practice of Participation in Rural Development*. Geneva: ILO.

Orellana U., Luis. 1989. *Breve historia del movimiento pentecostal chileno en su primer estadio (1909–1932)*. Santiago: CTE.

Ortiz, Juan. 1993. Presencia de las iglesias evangélicas en Chile en el siglo XIX. *Evangelio y Sociedad*. 18: I–VIII.

Ortner, Sherry B. 1984. Theory in Anthropology since the Sixties. *Comparative Studies in Society and History*. 26 (1): 126–166.

———. 1989a. *High Religion: A Cultural and Political History of Sherpa Buddhism*. Princeton, N.J.: Princeton University Press.

———. 1989b. Cultural Politics: Religious Activism and Ideological Transformation among 20th Century Sherpas. *Dialectical Anthropology*. 14: 197–211.

Ossa, Manuel. 1989. *Espiritualidad popular y acción política: El pastor Víctor Mora y la Misión Wesleyana Nacional. 40 años de historia religiosa y social (1928–1969)*. Santiago: REHUE.

———. 1991. *Lo ajeno y lo propio: Identidad pentecostal y trabajo*. Santiago: REHUE.

———. 1992. *Crónica de la Confraternidad Cristiana de Iglesias (CCI)*. Santiago: unpublished draft.

Palma, Irma, ed. 1988. *En tierra extraña: Itinerario del pueblo pentecostal chileno*. Santiago: Amerinda.

Palma, Marta. 1985. A Pentecostal Church in the Ecumenical Movement. *Ecumenical Review*. 37: 223–229.

Pastor, Anibal, Susana Mena, Sandra Rojas, and Walter Parraquez, eds. 1993. *De Lonquén a Los Andes: 20 años de Iglesia Católica chilena*. Santiago: REHUE.

Pinto, Aníbal. 1974. Chili: Sociale structuur en politieke implicaties. In *Sociologie en sociale verandering in latijns amerika II*, ed. A. E. van Niekerk, 1–31. Rotterdam: UPR/SWU.

Pool, Robert. 1991. Postmodern Ethnography? *Critique of Anthropology*. 11: 309–331.

Pottier, Johan, ed. 1993. *Practising Development: Social Science Perspectives*. London, New York: Routledge.

PRESOR, INPRODE, FLACSO. 1988. *Concepción 88, Una encuesta regional*. Concepción, Chile: PRESOR, INPRODE, FLACSO.

PUEC. 1991. *Semilla de nuevos tiempos*. Santiago: PUEC.

Quarles van Ufford, Philip and Matthew Schoffeleers. 1988. Towards a Rapprochement of Anthropology and Development Studies. In *Religion & Development. Towards an Integrated Approach*, ed. Philip Quarles van Ufford and Matthew Schoffeleers, 1–30. Amsterdam: Free University Press.

Razeto, Luis, Arno Klenner, Apolonia Ramirez, and Roberto Urmeneta. 1990. *Las organizaciones económicas populares 1973–1990*. Santiago: PET.

Robertson, Roland. 1986. Liberation Theology in Latin America: Sociological Problems of Interpretation and Explanation. In *Prophetic Religions and Politics. Religion and the Political Order*, ed. Jeffrey Hadden and Anson Shupe, 73–102. New York: Paragon House Publishers.

Rolim, F. C. 1985. *Pentecostais no Brasil, uma interpretaçao socio-religiosa*. Petrópolis: Vozes.

Rostas, Susanna and André Droogers. 1993. The Popular Use of Popular Religion in Latin America: Introduction. In *The Popular Use of Popular Religion in Latin America*, ed. Susanna Rostas and André Droogers, 1–16. Amsterdam: CEDLA.

Russell Bernard, H. 1989. *Research Methods in Cultural Anthropology*. Newbury Park, London, New Delhi: Sage Publications.

Sacks, Oliver. 1985. *The Man Who Mistook his Wife for a Hat*. London: Picador.

Salazar V., Gabriel. 1986 *Religiosidad popular en Chile: Algunas problemas históricos del movimiento pentecostal (notas para una investigación) II*. Santiago: unpublished paper.

Salman, Ton. 1993. *De verlegen beweging. Desintegratie, inventiviteit en verzet van de Chileense pobladores, 1973–1990*. Amsterdam: CEDLA.

————. 1994. Challenging the City, Joining the City: the Chilean Pobladores between Social Movement and Social Integration. *Bulletin of Latin American Research*. 13: 79–90.

Santagada D., Osvaldo. 1989. Caracterización y contenido de las sectas en América Latina. In: *Sectas en América Latina*, ed. Oswaldo Santagada D. et al., Lima: 9–38. Ediciones Paulinas/CELAM.

Schäfer, Heinrich. 1994. Fundamentalism: Power and the Absolute. *Exchange*. 23: 1–24.

Schoffeleers, J. M. 1985. *Pentecostalism and Neo-traditionalism: The Religious Polarization of a Rural District in Southern Malawi.* Amsterdam: Free University Press.

————. 1988. *Gebedsgenezing en politiek: De medicalisering van het christendom in Zuid-Afrika.* Amsterdam: VU.

Schuurman, Frans J. 1991. *Niet-gouvernementele organisaties in Chili: NGO landenstudie Chili, Impactstudie Medefinancieringsprogramma.* Oegstgeest, The Netherlands: GOM.

Seibert, Ute and Pedro Correa. 1989. *Historia del protestantismo en Chile.* Santiago: REHUE.

Sembrando. 1985. 1era convención de escuelas dominicales, Santiago, 15 al 17 de agosto de 1985. Relato e informe de acuerdos. *Sembrando.* 1–16.

SEPADE. 1984. *Desarrollo comunitario integral, 1984–1986.* Santiago: SEPADE.

————. 1985. Editorial. Para una ética social evangélica. *Evangelio y Sociedad.* 1: 1–2.

————. 1986. *Informe de evaluación interna.* Santiago: SEPADE.

————. 1987. *Proyecto 1987.* Santiago: SEPADE.

————. 1988. *Desarrollo comunitario 1988–1990.* Santiago: SEPADE.

————. 1991. *Plan trienal 1991–1993.* Santiago: SEPADE.

————. 1992. *Informe de consultoría organizacional.* Santiago: SEPADE.

————. 1994. *Programa de desarrollo comunitario, periodo 1994–1996.* Santiago: SEPADE.

Sepúlveda, Juan. 1987. El nacimiento y desarrollo de las iglesias evangélicas. In *Historia del pueblo de Dios en Chile: La evolución del cristianismo desde la perspectiva de los pobres*, ed. Maximiliano Salinas C., 247–289. Santiago: CEHILA, Ediciones REHUE.

————. 1988. Pentecostalismo y democracia: Una interpretación de sus relaciones. In *Democracia y Evangelio*, ed. Arturo Chacón H., 229–250. Santiago: REHUE.

————. 1989. Pentecostalism as Popular Religiosity. *International Review of Mission.* 78 (309): 80–88.

————. 1991a. *Pentecostalismo y teología de la liberación: Dos manifestaciones del trabajo del Espíritu Santo por la renovación de la iglesia.* Santiago: unpublished paper.

————. 1991b. *Crisis y dinámica del protestantismo actual: El caso chileno.* Santiago: unpublished paper.

————. 1992a. El crecimiento del movimiento pentecostal en América Latina. In *Pentecostalismo y Liberación: Una experiencia latinoamericana,* ed. Carmelo Alvarez, 77–88. San José: DEI.

————. 1993. La liberación de la creación. *Evangelio y Sociedad.* 16: 24–28.

————. 1994. The Perspective of Chilean Pentecostalism. *Journal of Pentecostal Theology.* 4: 41–49.

Sepúlveda, Juan, ed. 1992b. *I Encuentro Nacional de Diálogo Pentecostal: 'Identidad y Diversidad del Pentecostalismo Chileno.' Concepción, 4 y 5 de diciembre de 1991.* Santiago: SEPADE.

Sepúlveda, Narciso. 1992. Breve síntesis histórica del movimiento pentecostal en Chile. In *Pentecostalismo y liberación. Una experiencia latinoamericano,* ed. Carmelo Alvarez, 37–45. San José: DEI.

Smith, Brian H. 1982. *The Church and Politics in Chile.* Princeton: Princeton University Press.

————. 1990. The Catholic Church and Politics in Chile. In *Church and Politics in Latin America,* ed. Dermott Keogh, 321–343. London: Macmillan.

Spradley, J.P. 1979. *The Ethnographic Interview.* New York: Holt Rinehart Winston.

————. 1980. *Participant Observation.* New York: Holt Rinehart Winston.

Stoll, David. 1990a. *Is Latin America Turning Protestant? The Politics of Evangelical Growth.* Berkeley, Los Angeles, Oxford: University of California Press.

————. 1990b. A Protestant Reformation in Latin America? *The Christian Century.* January 17: 44–48.

Stuurgroep. 1991. *Betekenis van het medefinancieringsprogramma: Een verkenning.* Oegstgeest, The Netherlands: GOM.

Tamez, Elsa. 1993. Pautas hermenéuticas para comprender G . 3.28 y 1 Co. 14.34–35. *Evangelio y Sociedad.* 18: 28–32.

Ten Have, Paul. 1977. *Sociologisch veldonderzoek.* Meppel, Amsterdam: Boom.

Tennekes, Johannes. 1978. Le mouvement pentecôtiste chilien en la politique. *Social Compass.* 25 (1): 55–80.

————. 1985. *El movimiento pentecostal en la sociedad chilena.* Amsterdam/Iquique: CIREN/Subfacultad de antropología cultural de la universidad libre de Amsterdam.

————. 1990. *De onbekende dimensie: Over cultuur, cultuurverschillen en macht.* Leuven/Apeldoorn: Garant.

Turner, Frederick C. 1970. Protestantism and Politics in Chile and Brazil. *Comparative Studies in Society and History.* 12: 2.

Tweede Kamer, Vergaderjaar 1989–1990. *Samenvatting van het verslag van een ambtelijke missie naar Chili (21 300 V, nr. 125).* Den Haag: SDU.

Urrea, Juan Carlos. 1992. *Los nuevos movimientos religiosos en América Latina*. Santiago: Ediciones Paulinas.

Vergara, Ignacio. 1962. *El protestantismo en Chile*. Santiago: Editorial del Pacífico.

Vicaría (de la Solidaridad). 1978. *La libertad religiosa en Chile, los evangélicos y el gobierno militar. Tomo 3, anexos*. Santiago: Vicaría de la Solidaridad.

Wacquant, Loïc J. D. 1992. Inleiding. In *Argumenten voor een reflexieve maatschappijwetenschap*, Pierre Bourdieu, 11–34. Amsterdam: SUA.

Weber, Max. 1963. *The Sociology of Religion*. Boston: Beacon.

———. 1978. *Economy and Society: An Outline of Interpretive Sociology*. Berkeley: University of California Press.

Wester, Fred. 1987. *Strategieën voor kwalitatief onderzoek*. Muiderberg: Coutinho.

Willems, Emilio. 1967. *Followers of the New Faith: Culture Change and the Rise of Protestantism in Brazil and Chile*. Nashville, Tenn.: Vanderbilt University Press.

Wils, Frits. 1991. *NGOs and Development in Brazil: An Overview and Analysis. Impactstudie Medefinancieringsprogramma*. Oegstgeest, The Netherlands: GOM.

Wilson, Bryan R. 1978. A Typology of Sects. In *Sociology of Religion*, ed. Roland Robertson, 361–383. Hammondsworth: Penguin Books.

———. 1990. *The Social Dimensions of Sectarianism: Sects and New Religious Movements in Contemporary Society*. Oxford: Clarendon Press.

Wit, J. H. de. 1991. *Leerlingen van de armen*. Amsterdam: VU Uitgeverij.

Yinger, J. Milton. 1970. *The Scientific Study of Religion*. London: MacMillan.

Zenteno C., Edmundo, ed. 1990. 1909–1989: 80 años de la Iglesia Metodista Pentecostal en Chile. *La Voz Pentecostal*. 24: 1–80.

Index

Pentecostal cathedrals, 83; catedral evangélico, 80, 250; church of La Victoria, 113–20; IMP, 83–84; Jotabeche, 84, 105n17, 148, 154–57, 160, 167n45

Pentecostal Church of Chile. *See* Iglesia Pentecostal de Chile

Pentecostal habitus, 91, 158–59, 193–94

Pentecostalism, 1–9, 11, 132, 216; characteristics of worship, 47; Chilean, 8, 19–23, 63–108; classic, 94–103; conversion to, 66; description of, 96; ecumenical, 234; enlightened, 223n20; growth (1909–1973), 67–79; IMP, 239; indigenous, 68; Latin American, 17–62; La Victoria, 157–61; meaning of, 146, 229–39; Methodist, 70; MIP, 117, 158; new, 213; open, 158; practice approach to, 26–37; prophetic, 11–14, 146, 158–59, 214, 231, 234; recent perspectives, 22–26; show, 23; socially committed, 182; studies, 17–62; takeoff, 67–71; vicissitudes of, 63–108, 237

pentecostalismo criollo, 68, 254

Pentecostal Methodist Church. *See* Iglesia Metodista Pentecostal

Pentecostal Mission Church. *See* Misión Iglesia Pentecostal

Pentecostal politics, 186–87, 240–45

Pentecostals, 1–2, 9–10, 57n1, 105n12, 142–43; *canutos*, 15n7, 249; characterization of, 156; *evangelistas*, 15n7; fieldwork among, 45–47; MIP congregations, 103, 109–67; Pinochet and, 79–94; progressive, 157; research among, 246–48

Pentecostal Te Deum, 85, 149

Pentecostal Women's Group. *See* Dorcas

people's economic organizations. *See* organizaciones económicas populares (OEPs)

Pinochet, 1, 26–27, 36, 43, 46, 61n33, 95, 106n21, 114, 120, 131, 148, 230; open letter to, 200–201, 224n26, 225n29; and Pentecostals, 79–94

poblaciones (populations or working-class neighborhoods), 72, 104n8, 109–67

pobladores (working-class neighborhood dwellers), 78, 111, 204

political mobilization: attempts, 196–215; critical voices, 203–8

politicization, 49

politics, 71–79, 105n16; Pentecostal, 186–87, 216–20, 240–45

popular Catholicism, 74, 78

popular culture, 104n10

popular education, 177, 181, 186, 203, 214, 218–19, 244; founder of, 225n35

popular religion, 104n10

population, 161nn1–2; IEP membership, 106n22, 108n33; IMP membership, 106nn22–23; MIP membership, 102–3, 108n33; Protestant, 72, 80, 104n9, 106nn22–23, 161n2

postmillenialists, 4–5

postmodernism, 39

practice, 32; approach, 26–37, definition of, 59n16; playing, 52–55

prayer campaign, 198

preaching, 150–57, 166n40; in Jotabeche, 155–56

premillenialists, 4, 21

Presbyterians, 107n27, 165n36

PROAL. *See* Programa de Promoción Alimentaria

professionalization, 245; of commitment, 227n48, 245

About the Author

Frans Kamsteeg (1958) read cultural anthropology and is lecturer at the Culture, Organization and Management Department at the *Vrije Universiteit* of Amsterdam. He did fieldwork in Peru in 1987 and 1989, where he studied the growth of Pentecostalism in the southern city of Arequipa. Together with Barbara Boudewijnse and André Droogers, in 1991 he published *Algo más que opio: Una lectura antropológica del pentecostalismo latinoamericano y caribeño* (San José: DEI) and *More Than Opium: An Anthropological Approach to Latin American and Caribbean Pentecostal Practice* (Scarecrow Press, 1998). In 1991 and 1992 he spent a year in Chile, studying the vicissitudes of a prophetic type of Pentecostalism. His research, the results of which are presented in this book, includes an evaluation of the impact of development policies at the local level.

About the Author